Doing a Literature Review

Doing a Literature Review

Releasing the Social Science Research Imagination

Chris Hart

Los Angeles • London • New Delhi • Singapore

SAGE Publications Ltd
1 Oliver's Yard
55 City Road
London EC1Y 1SP

SAGE Publications Inc
2455 Teller Road
Thousand Oaks
California 91320

SAGE Publications India Pvt. Ltd
B1/11 Mohan Cooperative Industrial Area
Mathura Road, New Delhi 110 044
India

SAGE Publications Asia-Pacific Pte Ltd
33 Pekin Street #02-01
Far East Square
Singapore 048763

British Library Cataloguing in Publication data
A catalogue record for this book is available from the British Library

Library of Congress Control Number: 9861375

Printed on paper from sustainable sources

ISBN-978-0-7619-5974-8
ISBN-978-0-7619-5975-5 (pbk)

Typeset by Mayhew Typesetting, Rhayader, Powys
Printed and bound in Great Britain by
Cromwell Press Limited, Trowbridge, Wiltshire

Contents

List of figures and tables

FIGURES

TABLES

Preface

Undertaking research for a thesis or dissertation is an experience that most people never forget. Worries about what topic to investigate, how to go about doing the research and writing at length are common concerns raised by research students. No one can do the research for you; the responsibility is yours and yours alone. This often leads to feelings of isolation and sometimes to a loss of confidence. But, with a little planning, careful thought and the adoption of the right attitude, you will be able to set realistic objectives and find that the stress and anxiety of doing the research can be managed and even enjoyable! Few experiences match the sense of achievement and exhilaration that result from finishing your thesis or dissertation.

This book has been written for postgraduate research students at both master's and doctoral level. It came about from my personal experience of doing research, first for a master's dissertation and then for a doctoral thesis, and subsequently from teaching postgraduate students over number of years. In both my dissertation and thesis, a search of the literature was necessary along with a critical analysis of what was found. I did not find books or articles on either searching or reviewing. Advice from supervisors was to read other people's reviews to see how they had gone about the task. This was good advice and I saved a great deal of effort using other people's summaries of research – time I would otherwise have spent searching the literature, reading what was obtained and writing an analysis. But it did not a provide proper solution to the main problems that I and other research students faced at the time. We needed guides to show us how to search for materials on our topics and how to analyse what we were reading.

Luckily, at the time, I began teaching sociology on an *Information Studies* degree and was exposed to the systems and procedures by which knowledge and information was organized for storage and retrieval. I quickly came to realize that an entire discipline had the knowledge sought by other disciplines on how to search for literature relevant to a research topic. The range of methods by which information was arranged in the different libraries around the world and the technologies for accessing information were all new to me; words like OPAC, Dialog, DataStar and JANET all meant nothing to those of us with a social science background. This was the early 1980s, a time when computers had yet to make an impact on higher education.

Knowledge of how information was organized contributed immeasurably to the success of my dissertation and subsequent thesis. In the intervening time period I have developed practical and conceptual knowledge about searching for relevant literature and have taught this to successive postgraduate students. At the same time I have collected and developed ideas and practical methods for analysing and synthesizing ideas found in the literature. Meanwhile, along with my students, I awaited books that could be used by most people undertaking postgraduate research. As none have appeared, this book is the result. It attempts to provide an introduction to one of the most difficult of tasks, that of literature reviewing.

This book is not a manual nor is it prescriptive. It is an introduction, aimed at postgraduates, on what it means and what is involved in reviewing a research literature. It therefore looks at explaining as well as describing the ideas on which the methods and techniques for analysing a literature are based – those ideas and methods that research students have found to be useful when doing their literature reviews.

There are examples, at the end of each chapter, which can be used as a guide to the literature review, but the main purpose is to help you, as the reader, to understand what it means to be a research student. This is based on the assumption that if you can work out how the ideas, techniques and methods found in the literature can be adapted and used in your own research, then you will have taught yourself some very useful skills that no manual can provide. One of these skills is to learn *how* to learn. In reading this book you will be forced, in some places, to think seriously about the meaning of literature reviewing, the implications of methodology and the role of argument in research. You will therefore be encouraged to avoid copying what others have done and, instead, teach yourself how to analyse, evaluate and synthesize ideas and so produce work that is distinctively yours.

On a practical level, a number of references are provided that might be useful sources to more information on a particular topic or issue. The examples are chosen to illustrate particular methods and techniques, rather than for their content, and hence the citations in the examples and quotations have not been given, for these refer to the original source.

Acknowledgements

I would like to thank my colleagues in the School of Information Studies, at the University of Central England in Birmingham, for their contributions, both indirect and direct, to this book. I would especially like to thank Denis Readon for long and enjoyable talks on and about research and for his comradeship; the book has benefited greatly from the outcome of these conversations. To postgraduate students past and present I express thanks for their honest feedback on the usefulness of materials for literature reviewing. In particular, I thank Mo Bains and Katheryn Jones who were subjected to drafts of this book when undertaking their own doctoral research. Thanks go to the Open University course team D820 *The Challenge of the Social Sciences*, who were all supportive of this project at the early stage when encouragement was needed. I give special thanks to Mark Smith for his phone calls checking on progress and giving feedback from the course team, to Keith Stribley for detailed ideas on grammar and style, and to Jonathan Hunt, from the OU Copublishing Department, for his help in bringing this book to print. Thanks go to Lynne Slocombe and Gareth Williams for copyediting the manuscript and for advice on style and structure. Thanks also go to Karen Phillips and the editorial team at Sage who had the foresight to see the need for this kind of book. Finally, I wish to thank Beverley, who with an extremely busy schedule, found the time and effort to help and who allowed precious holiday time to be used for work on the text.

The author gratefully acknowledges permission to reproduce the following: Geoff Payne (1993), 'The community revisited: some reflections on the community study as a method', British Sociological Association Annual Conference, University of Essex, 5–8 April, a version of this paper is also published in E.S. Lyon and J. Bushfield (eds) (1996), *Methodological Imaginations*, Basingstoke, Macmillan; Kathryn Jones (1997) for the table 'An etymological summary of the concept "community" 1880–1990', reproduced in Chapter 5, from her doctoral thesis, 'Community as a documentary reality', UCE, Birmingham, and Darren Bolton, (1997) 'A retrospective case study of convergence within a higher education institution', MA dissertation, School of Information Studies, UCE, Birmingham; and the Oxford University Press for the extract from the *Shorter Oxford English Dictionary of Historical Principles* (3rd edn, 1944).

Chris Hart
Kingswinford 1998

1

The literature review in research

It has become an annual ritual for graduate researchers embarking on their projects to ask about the literature review. They usually want to know what a review of the literature looks like and how they should do one. Students and tutors find that there is no single text that can be used to guide them on how to conduct the literature review; hence the purpose of this book. It is a guide to reviewing literature for research.

The book, however, is not about reviewing or critical evaluation of the kinds of articles found in the review sections of newspapers such as *The Times Educational Supplement* or *Guardian*. It is about reviewing a research literature. It introduces and provides examples of a range of techniques that can be used to analyse ideas, find relationships between different ideas and understand the nature and use of argument in research. What you can expect, therefore, is explanation, discussion and examples on how to analyse other people's ideas, those ideas that constitute the body of knowledge on the topic of your research.

Initially we can say that a review of the literature is important because without it you will not acquire an understanding of your topic, of what has already been done on it, how it has been researched, and what the key issues are. In your written project you will be expected to show that you understand previous research on your topic. This amounts to showing that you have understood the main theories in the subject area and how they have been applied and developed, as well as the main criticisms that have been made of work on the topic. The review is therefore a part of your academic development – of becoming an expert in the field.

However, the importance of the literature review is not matched by a common understanding of how a review of related literature can be done, how it can be used in the research, or why it needs to be done in the first place.

Undertaking a review of a body of literature is often seen as something obvious and as a task easily done. In practice, although research students do produce what are called reviews of the literature, the quality of these varies considerably. Many reviews, in fact, are only thinly disguised annotated bibliographies. Quality means appropriate breadth and depth, rigour and consistency, clarity and brevity, and effective analysis and synthesis; in other words, the use of the ideas in the literature to justify the particular approach to the topic, the selection of methods, and demonstration that this research contributes something new. Poor reviews of a topic literature cannot always be blamed on the student researcher. It is not necessarily their fault or a failing in their ability: poor literature reviews can often be the fault of those who provide the education and training in research.

This book has been written primarily for student researchers, although it may also be of use to those who provide education and training in research. It is intended to be an introduction to those elements of the research process that need to be appreciated in order to understand the how and why of reviewing a topic-specific literature. As such, an attempt has been made to provide an introduction to a range of generic techniques that can be used to read analytically and to synthesize ideas in new and exciting ways that might help improve the quality of the research.

This book is aimed at people working within the social sciences, which includes the disciplines listed below. This list is not exhaustive; archaeology, for instance, might have been included in this list.

built environment and town planning	economics	psychology
business studies	educational studies	religious studies
communication and media studies	environmental studies	social and political theory
community studies	gender studies	social anthropology
cultural studies	human geography	social policy and administration
economic and social history	literature	social research
	organizational studies	sociology
	policy analysis	
	political studies	

The main aim of this book is therefore to provide researchers with a set of ground rules, assumptions and techniques that are applicable for understanding work produced in the whole range of disciplines that make up the social sciences. The assumptions outlined in the book form a basis for the understanding and cross-fertilization of ideas across disciplines. The various techniques aim to provide the tools for a systematic and rigorous analysis of subject literature. Suggestions are also made on writing up the analysis of ideas in ways that can give clarity, coherence and intelligibility to the work.

This chapter will introduce you to the skills needed for research, the place of the literature review in research and the importance of the review to master's and doctoral study. In Chapter 2 we look at the purpose of the review in research and what is meant by the research imagination. Chapter 3 examines the types of research to be found in the literature, together with examples of reviews undertaken in a range of subject areas. It also shows examples of good practices that you should be able to adapt and utilize in your own work, especially in reading to review. Chapter 4 is about understanding arguments. To analyse a literature on a topic necessarily involves understanding the standpoint (moral and ethical) and perspective (political and ideological) an author has used. Chapters 5 and 6 are about the tools and techniques of analysis and synthesis. Essential techniques such as analysing an argument, thinking critically and mapping ideas are explained. A thread running through these chapters is guidance on how to manage information. This is because, without strict management of materials and ideas, any thesis will lack the technical standards required of the postgraduate student. The final chapter is about writing up your review of the literature. Guidance is given on how your review can be used to justify your topic as well as on what structures and formats might be used.

SKILLS FOR RESEARCH IN THE SOCIAL SCIENCES

The breadth and depth of the various subject disciplines that make up the social sciences, some of which have been listed above, are not easily classified. There are also the increasing opportunities for students to study a range of modules which cut across different areas of knowledge. Combined with these is the pace of development of the electronic systems being used increasingly in all types of research.

Adapting to change

The expansion of education has been accompanied by a massive and growing expansion of information available to research students. In printed and electronic form the pace of information generation continues to increase, resulting in libraries acquiring only a very small proportion of that available. As a consequence, many academic libraries have become gateways to information rather than storehouses of knowledge. You will find that nearly all university libraries and public libraries are able to serve your needs as a researcher.

The move of university libraries away from storehouses of knowledge towards information resource centres has been accompanied by an increase in the use of information technology (IT). Many libraries manage the expansion of information with the aid of computer systems able to communicate around the globe – a development which has opened up a range of new possibilities to researchers. It is now possible for you to access information that would previously have been difficult and expensive to find. A single day searching a CD-ROM database or the internet can throw up many more sources than might have been found from weeks of searching through printed abstracts and indexes. However, there are two problems you may encounter in this area. One is the lack of understanding of technology and how it can be used in research. The other is a lack of understanding about how knowledge is generated and organized through the use of tools, such as abstracts and indexes, in order to make it accessible.

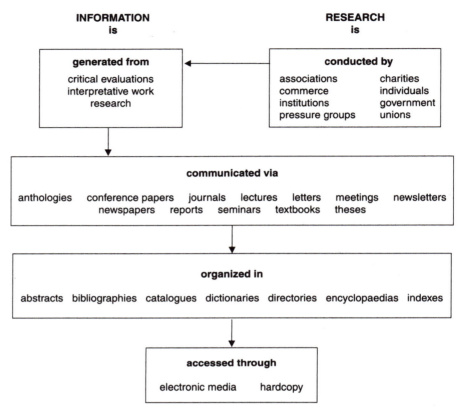

Figure 1.1 *The generation and communication of research knowledge and information*

Figure 1.1 provides an overview showing the main sources of knowledge and the tools by which most of it is organized for retrieval.

More recently there has been a move in higher education and research to learn from other disciplines, to be cross-disciplinary. Students on social studies and humanities courses are expected to undertake training in computing and to become competent in the use of statistical techniques, employing computers for data analysis and presentation. Added to this is the trend towards combined degrees. A consequence is that researchers need to be more flexible in their attitude to knowledge. To do this they need much broader skills and knowledge bases to take full advantage of higher education.

The changing requirements placed on the student have begun to manifest themselves in a terminology of skills, competencies and professional capabilities. Alongside a traditional education, students are expected to acquire a set of personal transferable skills. The basic elements of communication, such as writing reports, making presentations and negotiating, might be included in these skills. The emphasis on skills is not something unique to a social sciences education – skills are becoming important to the careers of graduates and to quality research in general.

Undergraduate and postgraduate research is an ideal opportunity for such personal transferable skills to be acquired and developed. Although searching and reviewing a literature do not cover the whole spectrum of skills, they do cover some key ones. These include: time management, organization of materials, computer use, information handling, on-line searching and writing.

The research apprenticeship

It is not an easy matter to demonstrate the kinds of skills and abilities expected of a competent researcher in the report of the research. The skills required are considerable and are increasingly subject to detailed evaluation. As the opportunities to undertake research have expanded, so too has the demand for better and improved education and training for researchers. In its response to these demands the Economic and Social Research Council (ESRC) in the UK produced a set of guidelines which include a number of basic proposals for research training which are intended to promote quality research. The following list indicates the two basic types of skills required from researchers.

- Core skills and abilities: while the differences make subject disciplines distinctive, there exists a common core of skills and attitudes which all researchers should possess and should be able to apply in different situations with different topics and problems.

- Ability to integrate theory and method: research for all disciplines involves an understanding of the interrelationship between theory, method and research design, practical skills and particular methods, the knowledge base of the subject and methodological foundations.

Both of these proposals call for a research training that exposes the apprentice to the range of general academic research skills and expertise expected of a professional researcher. The academic skills and expertise common to all subject fields within the social sciences can be grouped as shown in Table 1.1 (overleaf).

In addition to the common academic skills the ESRC guidelines also identify subject-specific skills, abilities and knowledge to be expected of postgraduate students. Examples of these for two subject areas, linguistics and sociology, can be seen in Table 1.2 (p. 7).

Table 1.1 *Research areas for the application of skills and abilities*

Literature search and evaluation	For example: library searching and use of abstracts and indexes; bibliographic construction; record keeping; use of IT for word-processing, databases, on-line searching and electronic mail; and techniques for the evaluation of research, including refereeing, reviewing and attribution of ideas.
Research design and strategy	For example: formulation of researchable problems and translation into practicable research designs; identifying related work to rationalize the topic and identify a focus; organize timetables; organize data and materials; understand and appreciate the implications of different methodological foundations; and how to deal with ethical and moral considerations which may arise.
Writing and presenting	For example: planning writing; skills for preparing and submitting papers for publication, conferences and journals; use of references, citation practices and knowledge of copyright; construction and defence of arguments; logical, clear and coherent expression; and understanding of the distinction between conclusions and recommendations.

It is important that research education and training does produce researchers who are competent and confident in a range of skills and capabilities and who have an appropriate knowledge base. An element common to the core areas is a thorough understanding of information. This means that as a researcher you need to become familiar with: accessing and using the vast resources of academic, public and commercial libraries in the world, through, for example, JANET (Joint Academic Network), OPAC (On-line Public Access Catalogues) and the British Library; keeping accurate records and establishing reliable procedures to manage materials; applying techniques to analyse bodies of literature and synthesize key ideas; and writing explicit reviews which display depth and breadth and which are intellectually rigorous. All these are part of the essential transferable skills of the researcher.

Most disciplines introduce their students to the theoretical and historical traditions that give shape and distinctiveness to the subject knowledge. But in so doing the methodological bias, disciplinary boundaries and mis-understanding about other subjects is perpetuated. This often creates barriers to cross-disciplinary studies and a lack of appreciation of alternative ways of researching and understanding the world. This book aims to show ways in which these kinds of barriers can be overcome and we begin by considering what we mean by scholarship.

Scholarship

Most people are capable of doing a piece of research but that capability has to be acquired – for instance, you cannot simply write a questionnaire as if you are writing a shopping list. A sound knowledge of the whole research

Table 1.2 ESRC guidelines on subject knowledge and skills: linguistics and sociology

	Core training	Descriptions of skills and abilities expected from the research student
LINGUISTICS	Philosophy of linguistics	Issues of theory construction, problem formulation, and explanation; basic themes e.g., realism, mentalism, nominalism, empiricism, behaviourism and logicism; ontological and epistemological issues; status of data and use of informant judgements; role of formalism; argumentation and status of examples; relationship between theory and data; search for universals; ideological implications of idealization; cultural partiality; Kuhnian paradigms.
	Research methods in linguistics	*Qualitative methods* use of informants; audio and video recording; phonetic and orthographic transcription; descriptive linguistics (diachronic and conversation analysis). *Computational methods* use of linguistic corpora grammar systems; speech workstation; phonological and morphological analysis; basic programming in high-level language, e.g., Prolog. *Formal methods* mathematical linguistics (set, string, tree, grammar, equivalence, hierarchy, lambda calculus); theory of inferences and semantics of first-order logic; feature structures and unification. *Quantitative methods* experimental design; validity and conduct of experiments; questionnaires; interviewing; sampling and survey design; statistics software; descriptive and inferential statistics.
SOCIOLOGY	Philosophy of the social sciences	Understanding of the major alternative philosophical positions for theory construction, appraisal and testing, for explanatory goals of theories and for the use of models. Understanding of how various positions affect research design, research choices, data-collection and analysis techniques. Understanding of the theoretical context of research; theoretical issues and debates for those engaged in empirical work; and evaluation of research.
	Research design	Stages and processes in formulating researchable problems and translating them into practical research designs. Making informed judgements about ethical and moral issues. Understanding of the uses and implications of: experimental study; survey research; comparative studies; longitudinal research; ethnography; case studies; replication studies; evaluation research; prediction and action research.
	Data collection and analysis	Awareness of range of sources, e.g., archival and historical data; agency records; official statistics; pictorial materials; and textual data. Knowledgeable of data-collection techniques by participant and non-participant observation, ethnographic field work, group discussion, various types of interviews and questionnaires, and through unobtrusive measures. Methods of recording data such as note taking, audio and video; data coding and identifying relationships between concepts/variables; the principles of descriptive and inferential statistics and bi- and multivariate analysis; the systematic analysis of textual data and other qualitative materials; and use of computer packages for data management.

process is required and you need to understand where data collection fits into the global picture of what you are doing. This means knowing how to state the aims and objectives of your research, define your major concepts and methodological assumptions, operationalize (put into practice) those concepts and assumptions by choosing an appropriate technique to collect data, know how you are going to collate results, and so on. Competent research therefore requires technical knowledge. There is, however, a difference between producing a piece of competent research and a piece of research that demonstrates scholarship.

Scholarship is often thought to be something academic high-brow types do. We are all familiar with the popular image of the scholar as one of an ageing bespectacled man with unkempt hair, dressed shabbily in corduroy with a thick old leather-bound book in hand. Many of you may be aware of places of scholarship epitomized in television programmes such as *Morse* and in novels such as *Brideshead Revisited*. The surreal surroundings of the Oxbridge colleges, with their high towers, the oak-clad library full of books and manuscripts, and with the smell of dust and leather, are common images of scholarly places. Many universities do have traditional oak-clad libraries, but many others today do not. It is more common for universities to have modern well equipped learning resource centres brimming with technology, than to have rows of books on shelves. Scholarship is an activity: it is something a person can do. You do not have to be of a certain social class, gender, ethnic origin or to have successfully jumped over formal educational hurdles. We can say that scholarly activity encompasses all of these and more. Scholarly activity is about knowing how to: do competent research; read, interpret and analyse arguments; synthesize ideas and make connections across disciplines; write and present ideas clearly and systematically; and use your imagination. Underpinning all of these are a number of basic ground rules, which we look at in more detail in the next section. But what they amount to is an attitude of mind that is open to ideas and to different styles and types of research, and is free of prejudices about what counts as useful research and what type of person should be allowed to do research.

A key element that makes for good scholarship is integration. Integration is about making connections between ideas, theories and experience. It is about applying a method or methodology from one area to another: about placing some episode into a larger theoretical framework, thereby providing a new way of looking at that phenomenon. This might mean drawing elements from different theories to form a new synthesis or to provide a new insight. It might also mean re-examining an existing body of knowledge in the light of a new development. The activity of scholarship is, therefore, about thinking systematically. It might mean forcing new typologies onto the structure of knowledge or onto a taken-for-granted perspective. Either way, the scholar endeavours to interpret and understand. The intent is to make others think about and possibly re-evaluate what they have hitherto taken to be unquestionable knowledge. Therefore, systematic questioning, inquiring and a scrutinizing attitude are features of scholarly activity.

At master's level, this might mean looking at applying a methodology in ways not tried before. At doctoral level, it might mean attempting to refigure or respecify the way in which some puzzle or problem has traditionally been defined. The anthropologist Clifford Geertz (1980: 165–6) suggests that refiguration is more than merely tampering with the details of how we go about understanding the world around us. He says refiguration is not about redrawing the cultural map or changing some of the disputed borders, it is about altering the very principles by which we map the social world. From the history of science, for example, Nicolas Copernicus (1473–1543) re-examined theories about the cosmos and the place of the earth within it. Traditional theory held the view that the earth was motionless and stood at the centre of the universe: the sun, other stars and planets were believed to revolve around the earth. Copernicus asked himself if there was another way of interpreting this belief. What if, he asked, the sun was motionless and the earth, planets and stars revolved around it? In 1541 he outlined his ideas and there began a refiguration of how the cosmos was mapped. We can see a classic example of refiguration in the work of Harold Garfinkel. Garfinkel respecified the phenomena of the social sciences, especially sociology (see Button, 1991). He undertook a thorough scrutiny of traditional sociological theory and found that social science ignored what real people do in real situations; the result was that he originated the technique of ethnomethodology. So radical was this respecification that traditional social science has marginalized the work of Garfinkel and others who undertake ethnomethodological studies of social life.

SKILLS AND THE LITERATURE REVIEW

The researcher, at whatever level of experience, is expected to undertake a review of the literature in their field. Undergraduates researching for a thesis or dissertation are expected to show familiarity with their topic. Usually this takes the form of a summary of the literature which demonstrates the skills to search on a subject, compile accurate and consistent bibliographies and summarize key ideas showing a critical awareness. They are expected to weigh up the contribution that particular ideas, positions or approaches have made to their topic. In short, they are required to demonstrate, on the one hand, library and information skills, and on the other, the intellectual capability to justify decisions on the choice of relevant ideas and the ability to assess the value of those ideas in context.

Undergraduates who move on to postgraduate research find that expectations change. The scope, breadth and depth of the literature search increases. The research student is expected to search more widely, across disciplines, and in greater detail than at undergraduate level. The amount of material identified increases the amount of reading the researcher has to do. In addition, reading materials across several disciplines can be difficult because of the different styles in which various disciplines present ideas. Also, the vocabularies of different subjects and what are taken to be the core, researchable problems for a particular discipline constitute further difficulties. For example, the student of management may be totally unfamiliar with the verbose and seemingly commonsense style of, say, sociology. Conversely, they may find the going less difficult if faced with advanced social statistics. The result may be the dismissal of the verbose style and admiration of the numerical formulae. The acceptance of one style over another is often due to disciplinary compartmentalization. Management students might be expected to be more familiar with statistics than with social theories. They might also have a more pragmatic attitude, influencing them to favour clarity and succinctness. As a consequence, potentially interesting and relevant ideas might be missed.

Our discussion so far has been about the kinds of assumptions that might help overcome disciplinary compartmentalization and so encourage cross-disciplinary understanding. In practice, this addresses two main features of academic research: one is the central place argument has in academic work, and the other is the need to be open-minded when reading the work of other people. We look more closely now at each of these in turn.

Communicating your argument

Most authors attempt to make their writing clear, consistent and coherent – something very difficult to achieve in any work, whatever its length or topic. Nevertheless, clarity, consistency and coherence are essential, because without them a work can be unintelligible. As a consequence the work might be misunderstood, dismissed or used in ways not intended by the author. Most important, the main idea, no matter how interesting, might be lost. Conversely, what seems clear and coherent to the writer can be utterly incomprehensible to the reader. Unfamiliarity with the style, presentation or language use is nearly always a cause of frustration to the reader.

We need to acknowledge that effort is required and to accept that clarity, consistency and coherence are not mysterious qualities able to be practiced only by the few. These can be achieved through explicit expression in writing and explicit commitment in reading. A problem for the academic author, however, is the time that readers allocate to their reading and the level of effort they are willing to invest in order to grasp the ideas in a text. At the same time, some authors seem to neglect the needs of their potential readers and manage to make relatively simple ideas confusing.

In terms of reviewing a body of literature – made up of dozens of articles, conference papers and monographs – one problem is diversity. Texts which originate from several disciplines and which have been written in different styles engender the need for a flexible and open-minded attitude from the reviewer. Added to this, there is often a lack of explicitness: it is rare to find an account of a piece of research that systematically lays out what was done, why it was done and discusses the various implications of those choices. The reviewer needs to appreciate some of the reasons for the lack of explicitness. First, it takes considerable effort and time to express ideas in writing. Secondly, limitations placed on space or word counts often result in editing not deemed ideal by the author. Also, being explicit exposes the research (and researcher) to critical inspection. Presumably, many able researchers do not publish widely so as to avoid such criticism.

The need for open-mindedness

As we saw earlier, competence in reading research is not easily acquired. It is a part of the process of research training and education. It takes time and a willingness to face challenges, acquire new understandings and have sufficient openness of mind to appreciate that there are other views of the world. This begins by recognizing that the reviewer undertakes a review for a purpose – and an author writes for a purpose. While an author may not always make their ideas clear, consistent and coherent, the reviewer is required to exercise patience when reading. The reviewer needs to assume (no matter how difficult the reading) that the author has something to contribute. It is therefore important to make the effort to tease out the main ideas from the text under consideration. It also means making the effort to understand why you are having difficulty in comprehending the text. This means not categorizing the text using prejudicial perceptions of the subject discipline, but instead placing the research in the context of the norms of the discipline and not judging it by the practices of the discipline with which you are most familiar.

As a part of this attitude the researcher needs to exercise a willingness to understand philosophical (or methodological) traditions. The choice of a particular topic, together with the decision to research it using one specific strategy rather than another and to present it in a certain style, are design decisions often based on prior commitments to a view of research. An individual piece of research can therefore be placed, in general terms, in an intellectual tradition such as positivism or phenomenology. But the reviewer needs to take care not to criticize that research purely on general terms and especially from different standpoints. The different intellectual traditions need to be appreciated for what they are and not for what they are assumed to lack from another standpoint.

This can be illustrated with a brief example. Many social science students will have come across ethnomethodology, but apart from a few notable exceptions, ethnomethodology is quickly passed over in most programmes of study. We have found, from experience, that this is often due to the extreme difficulty of understanding what ethnomethodology is about and how to do an ethnomethodological study. An example from the work of the founder of ethnomethodology, Harold Garfinkel, illustrates this point. This is the title from a recent article by him: 'Respecification: evidence for locally produced, naturally accountable phenomena of order, logic, reason, meaning, method, etc. in and as of the essential haecceity of immortal ordinary society (I) – an announcement of studies' (Garfinkel, 1991: 10).

Those unfamiliar with ethnomethodology might now appreciate the difficulties in merely understanding what Garfinkel is trying to say. But there are two very relevant points here. The first is that tenacity is required to understand an approach such as ethnomethodology. Simply because Garfinkel's work is not instantly recognizable as sociology is not sufficient reason to dismiss it. Secondly, Garfinkel's ideas might be important – if they are dismissed because the reader is not willing to invest time and effort, then an important opportunity for learning might be missed. The only way to become competent enough to comment on complex ideas, such as those proposed by Garfinkel, is to read the works of the theorist and follow through what is said.

The assumptions discussed in this section are the basis for later chapters. Collectively what they amount to is an operationalization of scholarship and good manners in research. They also signpost the need for reviewers of research to be informed about, and to be able to demonstrate awareness of, the different styles and traditions in research.

THE ROLE OF THE LITERATURE REVIEW

The product of most research is some form of written account, for example, an article, report, dissertation or conference paper. The dissemination of such findings is important because the purpose of research is to contribute in some way to our understanding of the world. This cannot be done if research findings are not shared. The public availability of research findings means that accounts of research are reconstructed 'stories' – those serendipitous, often chaotic, fragmented and contingent aspects of most research (the very things that make research challenging!) which do not find their way into the formal account. We therefore need to get an initial understanding of what the role of the literature review is and where it fits into the thesis or dissertation.

The structure of the formal report for most research is standardized and many of the sections found in a report are also found in a proposal for research (see Table 1.3 overleaf). The full arrangement for the research proposal is shown in Appendix 1. Within this arrangement the author of the account usually employs a range of stylistic conventions to demonstrate the authority and legitimacy of their research and that the project has been undertaken in a way that is rigorous and competent.

Table 1.3   *Some sections commonly found in both a research proposal and report*

Section	Aim
Introduction	To show the aims, objectives, scope, rationale and design features of the research. The rationale is usually supported by references to other works which have already identified the broad nature of the problem.
Literature review	To demonstrate skills in library searching; to show command of the subject area and understanding of the problem; to justify the research topic, design and methodology.
Methodology	To show the appropriateness of the techniques used to gather data and the methodological approaches employed. Relevant references from the literature are often used to show an understanding of data-collection techniques and methodological implications, and to justify their use over alternative techniques.

From Table 1.3 you can see that the review of related literature is an essential part of the research process and the research report – it is more than a just stage to be undertaken or a hurdle to be overcome. Figure 1.2 (p. 14) shows some of the questions that you will be able to answer from undertaking a literature review on your topic.

The literature review is integral to the success of academic research. A major benefit of the review is that it ensures the researchability of your topic before 'proper' research commences. All too often students new to research equate the breadth of their research with its value. Initial enthusiasm, combined with this common misconception, often results in broad, generalized and ambitious proposals. It is the progressive *narrowing* of the topic, through the literature review, that makes most research a practical consideration.

Narrowing down a topic can be difficult and can take several weeks or even months, but it does mean that the research is more likely to be completed. It also contributes to the development of your intellectual capacity and practical skills, because it engenders a research attitude and will encourage you to think rigorously about your topic and what research you can do on it in the time you have available. Time and effort carefully expended at this early stage can save a great deal of effort and vague searching later.

Definition: Literature review

The selection of available documents (both published and unpublished) on the topic, which contain information, ideas, data and evidence written from a particular standpoint to fulfil certain aims or express certain views on the nature of the topic and how it is to be investigated, and the effective evaluation of these documents in relation to the research being proposed.

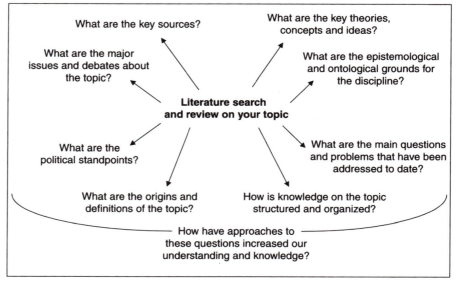

What are the key sources?

What are the key theories, concepts and ideas?

What are the major issues and debates about the topic?

What are the epistemological and ontological grounds for the discipline?

Literature search and review on your topic

What are the political standpoints?

What are the main questions and problems that have been addressed to date?

What are the origins and definitions of the topic?

How is knowledge on the topic structured and organized?

How have approaches to these questions increased our understanding and knowledge?

Figure 1.2   *Some of the questions the review of the literature can answer*

REVIEWING SKILLS AND THE POSTGRADUATE THESIS

A major product of academic programmes in postgraduate education is the thesis. This section will look at the place of the literature review in relation to the thesis. It will attempt to outline some of the dimensions and elements that provide evidence for assessing the worthiness of a thesis. Whereas undergraduate projects are often assessed according to pro forma marking schedules, a postgraduate thesis is assessed for its worthiness and the literature review plays a major role in the assessment. A problem, however, is saying just what constitutes an undergraduate dissertation or project and how this differs from, say, a master's thesis, although this is not the place to look closely at this question. Table 1.4 (p. 15) provides a summary of the function and format of the literature review at these different levels.

Note that the main concern is not only to satisfy assessors but to produce a competent review of a body of literature. The two descriptions that follow are not intended to be read as separate criteria for a master's and for a doctorate. Rather, they are intended to be read as guides to what might be expected from postgraduate research. We begin with the master's, which also gives the necessary prerequisite skills for a doctorate.

The master's

What we will focus on here is the skills element necessary for the master's thesis. If we take research for a master's thesis as being a significant piece

Table 1.4 *Degrees and the nature of the literature review*

Degree and research product	Function and format of the literature review in research at these levels
BA, BSc, BEd *Project*	Essentially descriptive, topic focused; mostly indicative of main, current sources on the topic. Analysis is of the topic in terms of justification.
MA, MSc, MPh *Dissertation or thesis*	Analytical and summative, covering methodological issues, research techniques and topics. Possibly two literature-based chapters, one on methodological issues, which demonstrates knowledge of the advantages and disadvantages, and another on theoretical issues relevant to the topic/problem.
PhD, DPhil, DLitt *Thesis*	Analytical synthesis, covering all known literature on the problem, including that in other languages. High level of conceptual linking within and across theories. Summative and formative evaluation of previous work on the problem. Depth and breadth of discussion on relevant philosophical traditions and ways in which they relate to the problem.

of investigative work, then the following opportunities (or educational aims) are embodied in that investigation.

1 An opportunity is provided for the student to design and carry out a substantial piece of investigative work in a subject-specific discipline. The review of related and relevant literature will be very important to the research whether in the field or from a desk.
2 An opportunity is provided to take a topic and, through a search and analysis of the literature, focus it to a researchable topic. This puts to the test the student's ability to search for and manage relevant texts and materials and to interpret analytically ideas and data.
3 An opportunity is provided for the student to recognize the structure of various arguments and to provide cogent, reasoned and objective evaluative analysis. This puts to the test the ability to integrate and evaluate ideas.

As the product of your time and research the master's thesis (which at master's level may also be called the *dissertation*) is a learning activity. The intent of the activity is that you acquire a range of skills at an appropriate level that are related to doing capable and competent research. The thesis is the evidence that you have acquired the necessary skills and can therefore be accredited as a competent researcher. The kinds of skills needed are those associated with research design, data collection, information management, analysis of data, synthesis of data with existing knowledge and evaluation of existing ideas along with a critical evaluation of your own work. We will look at these important points in more detail in a moment. Remember that your thesis is the only opportunity you will have to demonstrate your ability to apply these skills to a particular topic: this demonstration *is* the thesis. So, the thesis should be coherent and logical, and not a series of separate and inadequately related elements. There should be clear links between the aims of your research and the literature review, the choice of research design and means used to collect data, your discussion of the issues, and your conclusions and recommendations. To summarize, we can say that the research should:

1 focus on a specific problem, issue or debate;
2 relate to that problem, issue or debate in terms that show a balance between the theoretical, methodological and practical aspects of the topic;
3 include a clearly stated research methodology based on the existing literature;
4 provide an analytical and critically evaluative stance to the existing literature on the topic.

A master's thesis is therefore a demonstration in research thinking and doing. It is intended to show that the student has been capable of reasoning over which methodological approach to employ. It is also a demonstration on how to operationalize key concepts of methodology through the use of a range of data-collection techniques.

There are, then, a range of skills that often form the basis for the criteria on which a master's thesis is assessed. Table 1.5 (overleaf) provides an overview of the criteria normally used for assessing the worthiness of a master's thesis and it also shows how an excellent piece of work can be distinguished from a poor one. It may be useful, at this stage, to say a little more about some of the general skills and capabilities. Here we have picked out four that are very important and which require special attention by the research student.

Prior understanding   You will be expected to demonstrate a sufficient level of prior understanding of the topic and methodology. The focus for these is usually in the literature review and chapter on methodology. The latter, is, of course, often heavily dependent on the use of the literature dealing with methodology. Therefore, if your main methodology was survey based you would be expected to show familiarity with the literature on surveys. This might involve critical appraisal of key works that advocate a positivistic approach to research, identifying core authors and relevant studies as exemplars to justify your choice of approach. This involves the construction of an argument. The literature will help you to provide evidence and substance for justifying your choice. At the same time you will become familiar with the literature on the methodology and be able to show this in your thesis.

Perseverance and diligence   You will not normally find all the information you require in a few weeks. You will therefore need to be persistent in

Table 1.5   *Criteria for assessing a master's dissertation*

	Excellent and distinctive work	Competent work	Significantly deficient work
Aims, objectives and justification	Clear aims able to be operationalized. Explanation of the topic with succinct justification using the literature. Shows full awareness of the need to focus on what is able to be done.	Clear aims and objectives. Acceptable justification with identification of the topic.	Aims and objectives unclear due to no logical connections between them. Insufficient attempt to justify the topic. Actual topic not clear due to lack of focus.
Methodology and data collection	Choice of methodology explained in comparative terms showing considerable evidence of reading and understanding. Overall research design abundantly clear and logical for the student to apply. Strengths and weaknesses in previously used methodologies/data-collection techniques are recognized and dealt with.	Methodology described but not in comparative terms; so no explanation given for choices; nevertheless, an appropriate methodology employed. Research techniques clear and suitable for the topic. May have replicated weaknesses or bias inherent in previous work on the topic.	No explanation of the methodology, its choice or appropriateness for the research. No indication of reading on methodology or data-collection techniques, so no demonstration of ability to collect data in a systematic way. No overall research design.
Literature review and evaluation	Thorough review of the relevant literature; systematically analysed and all main variables and arguments identified. Critical evaluation firmly linked to justification and methodology.	Review of the main literature with main variables and arguments identified. Some links made to methodology and justification.	No review of the literature; annotations of some items but no attempt at a critical evaluation, therefore no arguments or key variables identified relevant to the topic. No bibliography or too large a bibliography to have been used.

continued overleaf

Table 1.5 (continued)

	Excellent and distinctive work	Competent work	Significantly deficient work
Style and presentation, including the use of graphic materials	Clear and cohesive structure. Very well presented with accurate citations and bibliography. Impressive use of visual and graphic devices, and effective arrangement of materials. Accurate and proper use of English, employing scholarly conventions.	Clear structure and arrangement of materials with accurate citations, appropriate use of visual and graphic devices.	Structured presentation but very thin on substantive content. Citations mostly correct but not consistent. Little evidence of thought about the use of visual or graphic devices. Sloppy use of language.
Overall coherence and academic rigour	Systematic and considered approach; critically reflexive; clarity and logic in the structuring of argument; proper use of language; assumptions stated; charity of interpretation; identification of gaps and possibility for further research. Of a publishable standard.	Considered approach; clarity in the structure of presentation; satisfactory use of language; assumptions mostly stated, though some implicit; conclusions and ideas for further research identified.	Not a considered approach therefore no planning evident. Poor use of technical terms and overuse of cliché. No argumentative structure evident. Some attempt at interpretation, but not based on the data.

your work. This is especially the case with the search of the literature. Initial search strategies may not reveal what you might have wanted; you therefore need to be flexible and search more widely or use more complex combinations of words and phrases. Persistence also means being thorough in your search; by making detailed records of how you managed the administration of the activity. This is because a comprehensive search for the literature on a topic is very much a matter of managing the administration of search sheets, records, databases, references located, items obtained and those ordered from the library, and so on. The use of all relevant sources and resources is therefore required to be shown in your thesis. This can be written up in the methodology chapter or the review of the literature.

Justification   A major requirement is that you provide sufficient argument to justify the topic for your research which means showing that what you propose to research is worthy of research. This involves the use of existing literature to focus on a particular context. The context might be, for example, methodological, in that you propose to employ a methodology on a topic in an area in which it has not previously been used. This might involve constructing an argument to show how a methodology relates to the topic and thereby suggest what its potential might be. Alternatively, you might provide a summative or integrative review. This would involve summarizing past research and making recommendations on how your research will be an addition to the existing stock of evidence. In this case you would be proposing to apply a tried approach to your topic. Whatever you use as the focus for your justification one thing must always be seen: evidence from the literature. You are therefore expected to avoid using personal opinions and views and never submit a statement without sufficient backing.

Scholarly conventions   You are required to use the literature in a way that is proper. At the most basic level this means citing references in a standard format recognized by the academic community. You will find guidance on this in Appendix 2. It also means using the literature in a way that is considered and considerate. You might not be able to cite all the references that you locate in your search. You will therefore need to exercise judgement as to which references are the most important, that is, the most relevant to your purpose. An attitude of critical appraisal will be necessary to avoid simplistic summative description of the contents of articles and books. This involves being charitable to the ideas of others while at the same time evaluating the usefulness of those ideas to your own work.

The master's is a limited piece of research. Taking approximately 10,000 to 15,000 words, the thesis or dissertation is a relatively modest piece of writing equivalent to, say, three or four extended essays. Its key elements are: the research; design of the research; application of data-collection techniques; management of the project and data; and interpretation of the findings in the context of previous work. To do these things in a way that is scholarly demands effective management of the research. A summary of the standards required is given in Appendix 3.

The doctorate

There appear to be seven main requirements, generally agreed across the academic profession, covering the content, process and product of a doctoral thesis. These are:

1 specialization in scholarship;
2 making a new contribution to an area of knowledge;
3 demonstrating a high level of scholarship;
4 demonstrating originality;
5 the ability to write a coherent volume of intellectually demanding work of a significant length;
6 the ability to develop the capacity and personal character to intellectually manage the research, including the writing of the thesis;
7 showing in-depth understanding of the topic area and work related to the research.

We might also add an eighth criterion; one more specific to the doctoral viva:

8 defending orally what was produced in terms of the reason for doing the research and choices over the way it was done.

These statements do not capture the scope and depth of all doctoral research. They do, however, provide a set of requirements which show the crucial importance of the literature review in the research process and in the content of the thesis itself. The first three show the input that can be made by a thorough search and reading of related literature. It is these, together with demonstrating originality, that will now be discussed.

Specialization   Although some universities allow candidates to enroll for higher degrees without a first degree the model used here assumes an academic career in which scholarship is developmental and not conveyed through a title. That career normally consists of a first degree followed by postgraduate work, both of which can be full-time or part-time study. Through an academic career a student gradually acquires a cumulative range of skills and abilities, and focuses their learning on a subject-specific knowledge. The availability of choice of degree and options within degrees means that subject specialization of some form is inevitable. In terms of skills and ability most undergraduates are expected to acquire and develop a wide range of personal transferable skills. Figure A4.1 in Appendix 4 gives an indication of the information management task involved in reviewing a literature; Appendix 4 also includes guidance on how to manage the technical elements of the review.

The raw materials, for undergraduate work, commonly in the form of articles from journals, periodicals, anthologies and monographs, are the ideas of other people, usually the 'founding theorists' and 'current notables' of the discipline. In order to understand the specifics of the subject, it is essential that the undergraduate comes to terms with the ideas of the founding theorists and current notables. Only when they have done this will they have sufficient subject knowledge to be able to talk coherently about and begin to analyse critically the ideas of the subject. This means demonstrating comprehension of the topic and the alternative methodologies that can be used for its investigation.

While it might be possible to reach a level of advanced standing without an appropriate intellectual apprenticeship, the academic career is likely to be a more reliable method of acquiring the in-depth knowledge demanded of a doctoral student. There are sound academic reasons for the academic career as preparation for higher degrees research. The ability and capacity to manage cognitively massive amounts of information, play with abstract ideas and theories and have insights is usually gained through intensive academic work and not short-term, drop-in programmes, or the production of occasional publications.

Making a new contribution The section on originality which follows relates to what is said here, that the requirement for postgraduate research to advance understanding through making a new contribution, is directly dependent upon knowledge of the subject. That knowledge can only be obtained through the work and effort of reading and seeking out ways in which general ideas have been developed through theory and application. This process requires from the researcher the kinds of skills already mentioned in relation to using libraries. But it also requires a spirit of adventure (a willingness to explore new areas), an open attitude that avoids prejudging an idea and tenacity to invest the time and effort even when the going gets tough.

What we are talking about here is resisting the temptation to make prior assumptions about any idea or theory until one is knowledgeable about that idea. This involves the spirit of research: looking for leads to other works cited by the author which have influenced their thinking. Garfinkel's ethnomethodology, for example, like many other new and interesting developments in all subject fields, did not emerge from nothing. It was a development from an existing set of theories and ideas. Garfinkel systematically worked through a range of existing theories in order to see where some ideas would lead if applied. Through his reading and thinking he was able to explore, in the true spirit of adventure, the foundations and boundaries of social science.

What enabled Garfinkel to make a new contribution, even though the amount of work he has produced is relatively small, was his ability to see possibilities in existing ideas. Making new insights is not merely about being able to synthesize difficult and large amounts of materials, it also involves knowing how to be creative and, perhaps, original. It cannot be overemphasized, however, that to make a new contribution to knowledge you do not have to be a genius. The size of the contribution is not what matters, it is the quality of work that produces the insight. As you will see shortly, originality can be defined and is often systematic rather than *ad hoc*.

Demonstrating a high level of scholarship   As we have noted earlier, the thesis is the only tangible evidence of the work and effort that has gone into the research. For this reason it needs to provide enough evidence, of the right type and in an appropriate form, to demonstrate that the desired level of scholarship has been achieved. A key part of the thesis which illustrates scholarship is the review of the literature. It is in this section that the balance and level of intellectual skills and abilities can be fully displayed for scrutiny and assessment.

The review chapter might comprise only 30 to 40 pages, as in a doctoral thesis, or 15 to 20 in a master's thesis, although the actual length often depends on the nature of the research. Theory-based work tends to require a longer review than empirical work. Either way this is a very short space to cover all that is required and expected. Typically, the review chapter is an edited down version of the massive amount of notes taken from extensive reading. The material of all reviews consists of what has been searched, located, obtained and read, but is much more than separate items or a bibliography. The reader of the thesis is being asked to see this literature as representing the sum total of current knowledge on the topic. It must also demonstrate the ability to think critically in terms of evaluating ideas, methodologies and techniques to collect data, and reflect on implications and possibilities for certain ideas. Scholarship therefore demands a wide range of skills and intellectual capabilities.

If we take the methodological aspect of the thesis we can see that underpinning all research is the ability to demonstrate complete familiarity with the respective strengths and weaknesses of a range of research methodologies and techniques for collecting data. It is therefore important to read widely around the literature on the major intellectual traditions such as positivism and phenomenology. This is because it is these traditions that support and have shaped the ways in which we tend to view the nature of the world and how it is possible to go about developing knowledge and understanding of our world. Knowledge of historical ideas and theories, or philosophy and social theory, is essential. In a similar way to skills, knowledge of, say, Marx or the postmodernists might be seen as essential personal transferable knowledge.

As a researcher you must also demonstrate the ability to assess methodologies used in the discipline or in the study of the topic in order to show clear and critical understanding of the limitations of the approach.

This will show your ability to employ a range of theories and ideas common to the discipline and to subject them to critical evaluation in order to advance understanding. It involves demonstrating the capacity to argue rationally and present that argument in a coherent structure. So, you need to know how to analyse the arguments of others – the reader of your thesis (an external examiner) will be looking to see how you have analysed such theories and how you have developed independent conclusions from your reading. In particular, your reader will be interested to see how you develop a case (argument) for the research you intend to undertake.

Demonstrating originality   The notion of originality is very closely related to the function of the search and analysis of the literature. We have already indicated that through a rigorous analysis of a research literature one can give focus to a topic. It is through this focusing process that an original treatment of an established topic can be developed. Placing aside until later chapters how this has and can be done, we need to turn our attention here to the concept of originality. In Figure 1.3 (p. 24) we show some of the associations that can be made from the different definitions of originality. Use these to grasp the meaning of the term. This is important because in academic research the aim is not to replicate what has already been done, but to add in some way, no matter how small, something that helps further our understanding of the world in which we live.

All research is in its own way unique. Even research that replicates work done by another person is unique. But it is not original. Being original might be taken to mean doing something no one has done before, or even thought about doing before. Sometimes this kind of approach to thinking about originality equates originality with special qualities assumed to be possessed by only a few individuals. The thing to remember is that originality is not a mysterious quality: it is something all researchers are capable of if they know how to think about, manage and play with ideas.

There is an imaginary element to research. This is the ability to create and play with images in your mind or on paper, reawakening the child in the adult. This amounts to thinking using visual pictures, without any inhibitions or preconceived ideas and involves giving free rein to the imagination.

Theorists such as Einstein attribute their ideas to being able to play with mental images and to make up imaginary experiments. This technique is used to make connections among things that you would not normally see as connectable. Einstein, for example, described how he came to think about the relativity of time and space in the way he did by saying it all began with an imaginary journey. Einstein was able to follow his fantasy through to produce his famous equation $e = mc^2$.

The point to note is that Einstein's journey was a small episode; something most of us are capable of experiencing. Einstein's achievement was in following through his ideas to their theoretical conclusions. He stopped short his work when he realized that his ideas could have a dark side: the

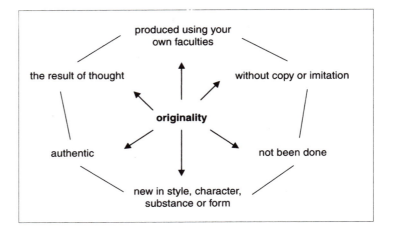

Figure 1.3   *Map of associations in definitions of originality*

development of a nuclear weapon (it is reassuring to know that very few people will find themselves in a similar situation to that of Einstein). It is sufficient to say that such episodes are an essential part of the research imagination. You will often find yourself having such episodes as a part of the thinking process. You will often find yourself understanding things that just a few days or weeks previously seemed difficult or incomprehensible because, as you apply more energy to your topic, you will increase your capacity for understanding. Therefore, notions and beliefs about having to be some kind of genius in order to be original can be placed to one side. Once this is done we might be able to see and learn how to be original in research.

Phillips and Pugh (1994), in their study of doctoral research, identified nine definitions of what it means to be original. These are:

1   doing empirically based work that has not been done before;
2   using already known ideas, practices or approaches but with a new interpretation;
3   bringing new evidence to bear on an old issue or problem;
4   creating a new synthesis that has not been done before;
5   applying something done in another country to one's own country;
6   applying a technique usually associated with one area to another;
7   being cross-disciplinary by using different methodologies;
8   looking at areas that people in the discipline have not looked at before;
9   adding to knowledge in a way that has not previously been done before.

The list presented by Phillips and Pugh is close to what might be expected from doctoral students, since it is oriented towards methodology and scholarship. It assumes the student already has an understanding of a subject knowledge.

CONCLUSION

There is no such thing as the perfect review. All reviews, irrespective of the topic, are written from a particular perspective or standpoint of the reviewer. This perspective often originates from the school of thought, vocation or ideological standpoint in which the reviewer is located. As a consequence, the particularity of the reviewer implies a particular reader. Reviewers usually write with a particular kind of reader in mind: a reader that they might want to influence. It is factors such as these that make all reviews partial in some way or other. But this is not reason or excuse for a poor review, although they can make a review interesting, challenging or provocative. Partiality in terms of value judgements, opinions, moralizing and ideologues can often be found to have invaded or formed the starting point of a review. When reading a review written by someone else or undertaking a review, you should be aware of your own value judgements and try to avoid a lack of scholarly respect for the ideas of others.

Producing a good review need not be too difficult. It can be far more rewarding than knocking something up quickly and without too much intellectual effort. A large degree of satisfaction can be had from working at the review over a period of time. For a master's or doctoral candidate this might be up to a year or more. A large measure of that satisfaction comes from the awareness that you have developed skills and acquired intellectual abilities you did not have before you began your research.

2

Reviewing and the research imagination

The originality of a research topic often depends on a critical reading of a wide-ranging literature. The nature of this concerns, on the one hand, immersing oneself in the topic to avoid the shallowness of quick and 'dirty' research and, on the other, there is the need to identify the key ideas and methodologies from which some contribution to knowledge might be made. Without a systematic search and critical reading of the literature it would be very difficult to see how academic research could make a new application of a methodology or contribute in some way, no matter how small, to knowledge. In other words, knowledge generation and understanding is an emergent process and not a universal product. In order to know the nature and character of the implications of a development you need to know the intellectual context of that development. This chapter therefore looks at the purpose of the literature review and what is meant by the research imagination.

THE PURPOSE OF THE REVIEW IN RESEARCH

The review of a literature differs significantly from the review of a book on a topic. Whereas the review of, say, a novel by Virginia Woolf might aim to make the public aware of the novel and contribute to contemporary literary debate, the review of a topic literature has a personal dimension that aims to develop the skills and abilities of the researcher as well as having a public dimension. This latter dimension embodies the design features of the research, for example, the plan for the research. It also embodies the educational purposes of carrying out a piece of independent research.

Reviewing the literature on a topic can therefore provide an academically enriching experience, but only if it is done properly. To achieve this the review should be regarded as a process fundamental to any worthwhile research or development work in any subject irrespective of the discipline. The research student has the responsibility to find out what already exists in the area in which they propose to do research before doing the research itself. The review forms the foundation for the research proper. The researcher needs to know about the contributions others have made to the knowledge pool relevant to their topic. It is the ideas and work of others that will provide the researcher with the framework for their own work; this includes methodological assumptions, data-collection techniques, key concepts and structuring the research into a conventional academic thesis.

A basic requirement for the research student is that they should understand the history of the subject they intend to study. This means acquiring sufficient knowledge of the subject area along with comprehending the significance of work already done in the field. This knowledge serves the purpose of providing a perspective on how the subject has developed and become established, and assists in the development and acquisition of the appropriate vocabulary.

By becoming familiar with the history of the subject the researcher will also become acquainted with the current research and debate on their topic. This will make it possible to identify the general areas of concern that might give pointers to specific matters worth studying. Areas of concentrated, current interest and, possibly, areas of relative neglect will become apparent. The review will also help the researcher to gain an understanding of the interrelationships between the subject being considered and other subject areas. Thus, they will be better placed to recognize or establish a context in which the subject for study exists. The overall result is that the researcher will become thoroughly knowledgeable about a topic and they will be ready to do research that advances knowledge on that topic. We can therefore say that the review serves at least the following purposes in research:

1   distinguishing what has been done from what needs to be done;
2   discovering important variables relevant to the topic;
3   synthesizing and gaining a new perspective;
4   identifying relationships between ideas and practice;
5   establishing the context of the topic or problem;
6   rationalizing the significance of the problem;
7   enhancing and acquiring the subject vocabulary;
8   understanding the structure of the subject;
9   relating ideas and theory to applications;
10 identifying the main methodologies and research techniques that have been used;
11 placing the research in a historical context to show familiarity with state-of-the-art developments.

These purposes should not be seen as ranked in order of importance. No one purpose is of greater significance than any other. They are all equally important in a review of relevant literature. In many cases the individual purposes merge into one another and manifest themselves in numerous places and in various ways in a review. There are some good reasons therefore to take time on a search of the literature. At a very basic level, a thesis that duplicates what has already been done is of very little use and is a waste of resources. It might even be invalidated and rejected by the university concerned. The search of the literature can help to avoid this. Getting to know who is doing what and where they are doing it enables the researcher to evaluate its relevance. Other researchers in the field are therefore worth noting because they can be very good sources for ideas or even to use in further search strategies. It may also prove possible to identify people and organizations with whom, or with which, some degree of co-operation may be fruitful and who may be able to suggest sources and ideas that will help in the research.

Your methodological starting point

One of the most important outcomes of the search and review will be the identification of methodological traditions which, in turn, will help to identify data-collection techniques that can be considered for use in the work.

Definition: Methodology

A system of methods and rules to facilitate the collection and analysis of data. It provides the starting point for choosing an approach made up of theories, ideas, concepts and definitions of the topic; therefore the basis of a critical activity consisting of making choices about the nature and character of the social world (assumptions). This should not to be confused with techniques of research, the application of methodology.

When reviewing the work of others you will be able to identify the methodological assumptions and research strategies that they have employed. In evaluating the relative merits of current methodologies you will soon become acquainted with thinking about the importance of methodology. This will assist you in deciding on the methodological assumptions for your own work while helping you to make decisions on the design features of your research strategy. In Example A at the end of this chapter we can begin to see how a group of cognitive psychologists, Oakes and colleagues, developed an argument for their own work through the process of reviewing the literature on their topic.

Oakes et al. (1994), in the study of stereotyping, dedicate two chapters of their book (based on their research) to outlining the nature and scope of the literature on stereotyping. In the first chapter they provide a detailed description of the origins of academic interest in the topic and explicate the main points from the landmark studies. In the second chapter they critically analyse previous approaches to stereotyping to show how their work differs from previous work, while at the same time aiming to show how it forms a development in our understanding of stereotyping. In the example we can see many of the things that we have just been discussing. Read the example and see if you can identify the ways in which the authors:

1　place the topic in a historical perspective;
2　identify key landmark studies selecting what they consider to be the key sources and authors;
3　establish a context for their own interest;
4　distinguish what has been done in order to identify a space for their own work.

Turn to Example A now on p. 32.

In Example A we see the social psychological approach and explication of a key area which is of concern to social psychologists. Different subject disciplines tend to have differing ways of framing their approach to a given problem. Some disciplines have specific issues and debates that are particular to that discipline. The researcher can only become sufficiently familiar with disciplinary debates and perspectives through an investigative search and analytical reading of the literature. Knowledge of the perspectives distinct to the discipline or topic will be required in order to establish the significance of the topic. This needs to be done in order to be able to justify a research topic from within the conventions and intellectual tradition of the most relevant discipline.

As a consequence, familiarity with subject knowledge will enable gaps and anomalies in previous research to be identified. Questions can then be asked that have significance and which can be turned into a viable research topic. The literature is therefore an essential resource: it can help to find an appropriate and valid topic. The same materials are nearly always useful in defining the parameters, dimensions and scope of what is to be investigated.

THE RESEARCH IMAGINATION

In his short and useful book, *The Sociological Imagination* (1978), C. Wright Mills provides the would-be researcher with some guides on how to think, how to manage large amounts of information and how to generate an attitude conducive to a research imagination. In his definition of the sociological imagination, Mills provides us with a starting point for understanding the need for a research imagination:

> The sociological imagination, I remind you, in considerable part consists of the capacity to shift from one perspective to another, and in the process to build up an adequate view of a total society and of its components. It is this imagination, of course, that sets off the social scientist from the mere technician. (1978: 232)

A researcher therefore needs to have the basic skills to do competent research. Some of these have already been mentioned, such as being able to use a library. However, what Mills is saying is that the effective use of these skills involves the development of an *imaginative* approach to research. It is something not easily acquired. A research imagination takes time to develop: something that is part of the research apprenticeship. For Mills, the research imagination is about: having a broad view of a topic; being open to ideas regardless of how or where they originated; questioning and scrutinizing ideas, methods and arguments regardless of who proposed them; playing with different ideas in order to see if links can be made; following ideas to see where they might lead; and it is about being scholarly in your work. What better examples of the research imagination, claims Mills, than the work of some of the founding theorists. It is thinkers like Marx, Weber, Spencer, Mannheim and Durkheim, according to Mills, who can provide illustrations of what a research imagination can promise:

> The sociological imagination enables us to grasp history and biography and the relations between the two within society. That is its task and its promise. To recognize the task and its promise is the mark of the classical social analyst. It is characteristic of Herbert Spencer – turgid, polysyllabic, comprehensive; of E.A. Ros – graceful, muckraking, upright; of August Comte and Émile Durkheim; of the intricate and subtle Karl Mannheim. It is the quality of all that is intellectually excellent in Karl Marx; it is the clue to Thorstein Veblen's brilliant and ironic insight; to Joseph Schumpeter's many-sided constructions of reality; it is the basis of the psychological sweep of W.E. Lecky no less than of the profundity and clarity of Max Weber. (1978: 12)

These and other social theorists (including many women) may be dead and some long forgotten, but Mills emphasizes the usefulness of reading their work. This is because contemporary society is dominated by information rather than knowledge. Many academic libraries have embraced the concept of *just in time* rather than *just in case*. They have become access points to information. It is for these reasons that the researcher faced with this confusing mass of information needs to acquire the searching skills to exploit the technology and develop an intellect that enables them to think their way through it; to be able to construct summations of what is going on in the world. But where and how do you begin? Mills suggests that the researcher should adopt a questioning and critical attitude. The following, adapted from his book (1978: 13) are some of the sorts of questions which can be useful when beginning a journey into the literature of a topic: they can lead back to those social theorists whose names and works are forgotten or have become vague, but which laid the foundations on which contemporary ideas, views and standpoints have been built.

The first set of questions relates to the structure of the knowledge on a topic.

- What is the structure of the knowledge on this topic?
- What and who are the key works and theorists?
- What methodological and moral assumptions have been deemed necessary in order to study this topic?

- How are different studies related together?
- What are the consequences of the general approach in the literature for the topic itself?

The second set of questions relates to the history of the topic.

- How are assumptions about the topic rooted in historical assumptions about social change?
- What components have been singled out for special treatment and why?
- What is the role of these components in the development of knowledge on the topic?
- How has the original definition of the topic been developed and changed?

Constructing parameters for your topic

But how do you use such a diverse and seemingly ambiguous set of questions? This is where an example might help. Example B at the end of this chapter is a case study which considers the issues we have looked at so far. It illustrates how it is possible to use a search of the literature to construct the parameters that make up the paradigm of a topic. It shows how the kinds of questions suggested by C. Wright Mills can be used to bring about a shift from a traditional perspective on a topic to a more imaginative and contentious one. Do not get concerned about any of the terms or references to technology, the main thing to grasp is the use of the literature to provide the following:

- the construction of a map of the literature;
- a demonstration of familiarity with the subject area;
- the acquisition of a knowledge base from which previous research can be analysed critically;
- a justification for a new approach to a well worn topic area;
- the development of various skills, such as information handling and classification;
- the operation of a non-partisan stance (methodological indifference).

The case study in example B is a partial reconstruction of a comprehensive and time-consuming search and evaluation of the literature about advertising, undertaken as part of a doctorate (Hart, 1993a). The case study begins with a description of a research situation and reports on the process by which the research problem was identified, defined and alternative approaches to the topic generated. An essential part of the process was the classification and categorization of information which can be demonstrated in a subject relevance tree (such as the one in Figure 6.5, which we discuss fully later). Mills may not have used the phrase 'subject relevance tree', but he certainly had something like it in mind when he said:

Table 2.1   *Planning a literature search*

Define the topic   Start with some general reading to familiarize yourself with the topic. Consult subject-specific dictionaries and encyclopaedias. Take notes on the concepts used and note which authors are cited. Prepare a list of terms for further searching, for example, of the library catalogue. Begin to think about the shape of the topic so that you can map it out at a later stage.

Think about the scope of the topic   Ask questions about which language or languages it might be necessary to search; what time frame, i.e. how far back you might need to search; and what subject areas might be relevant. Make a list of terms and phrases you will use to search: this is known as the search vocabulary.

Think about outcomes   Your proposal for your research will have stated an aim pertinent to the search and review of the literature. Think therefore about what it is you want to get out of the search and why you are undertaking a search in the first place.

Think about the housekeeping   Design a means by which you will record what you find and how you will cross-reference materials. It is important to keep consistent records not only of what you have searched but how you searched. This is because you may need to go back to undertake further searches of the same source using different terms. Your search might also be required to be written up as part of the methods by which you did your research.

Plan the sources to be searched   Prepare a list of likely relevant sources of information such as encyclopaedias, OPAC and indexes. An interview with the subject librarian can be very useful at this stage. Also use guides to the literature which are discussed below to identify relevant sources to be searched. They will guide you to the most relevant material and possibly show you how to use some of the technology available.

Search the sources listed   Work through the list of sources you have made. Start with the general sources, for example, encyclopaedias, moving on to abstracts and indexes. Be systematic and thorough, making consistent references as you go along. Make notes on possible further leads and ideas to be followed up. As each source is searched cross it off the list.

> Many of the general notions you come upon, as you think about them, will be cast into types. A new classification is the usual beginning of fruitful developments. The skill to make up types and then search for the conditions and consequences of each type will . . . become an automatic procedure. . . . Rather than rest content with existing classifications . . . search for their common denominators and for differentiating factors within and between them. . . . To make them so you must develop the habit of cross-classification. (1978: 234)

The research problem in the case study in Example B was the common one faced by postgraduate students: identifying the specific aspects of the topic to study and defining in clear terms the problem to be investigated. The topic chosen was advertising. The starting point for the research was a re-search and analysis of what had already been done. There were a number of reasons for this. Without a comprehensive, painstaking and critical analysis of the literature the topic and problem definition would not have had the clarity it had, nor would it have had the purposeful justifi-cation and rationale as a topic for serious sociological study. The review of the literature provided a focus for the research which was specific and fully justified in terms of meeting the criteria of uniqueness and creativity. **Turn now to Example B and see just how the research and evaluation into advertising was carried out.**

Having read Example B we can briefly review the items and stages typical to a literature search. Table 2.1 describes the kinds of things that need to be considered when planning to do a search while Figures 2.1 (p. 34) and 2.2 (p. 35) provide an overview of the stages in a typical search and what tools can be used to locate relevant items on a topic. It is worth noting here that one of the techniques, citation analysis, mentioned in the example needs to be treated with some care; the most cited work is not necessarily the most important. A frequently cited work merely stands for reference to that work by other authors in the field and nothing more. A citation is not a judgement of quality or importance. It is a nominal count of use by others.

EXAMPLE A   STEREOTYPING

Extracts from Oakes et al. (1994).

The extracts analysed in this example show the use of the chronological arrangement for the presentation of a literature review.

Extract from Oakes et al. (1994: 2–3)	Comments
Lipmann (1922) initiated formal enquiry into stereo-typing with the publication of his book *Public Opinion*. The attraction of this work has been enduring, primarily because it identifies a number of features of stereotypes and stereotyping that were to form the basis of subsequent understanding.	*Key landmark study.* *Indication of Lipmann's influ-ence on stereotyping research.*
In *Public Opinion* stereotypes were characterized as being selective, self-fulfilling and ethnocentric, ideas summed up in the claim that they 'constitute a very partial and inadequate way of representing the world', the word 'partial' here conveying the double sense of incomplete and biased (1922: 72). Other apparent shortcomings were noted. Stereotypes were under-stood as defences that justify individuals' own positions and blind spots that preclude objective, balanced reasoning. They were seen to be rigid in the sense of being both 'obdurate to education or criticism' and insensitive to changes in reality (1922: 65). They presented overgeneralized, exaggerated images which overlooked variability and denied individuality.	*Summary of* Public Opinion. *Some key concepts and phrases.* *Quote to show core proposi-tions.* *Page number verification.* *Summary of Lipmann's view of the stereotype.*

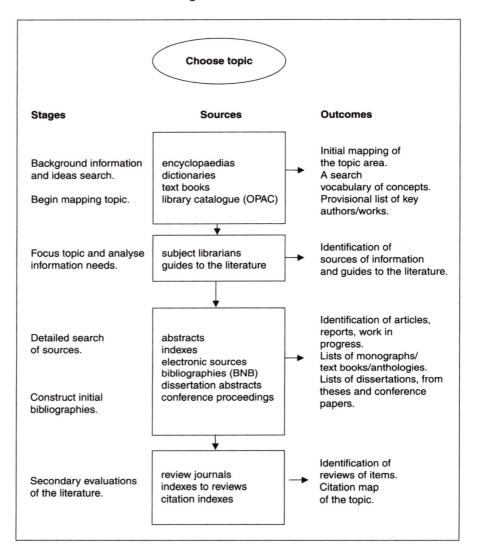

Figure 2.1   *Flow chart of the literature search*

In any study of stereotyping, reference to Lipmann (1922) is essential because it was his initial work that set a foundation for the study of the topic. Oakes et al. (1994) show the relevance of Lipmann by describing some of the main points he made. In later sections of their review they pick up many of these briefly stated points and show how they were used by different authors to develop a broader understanding of the topic. This next extract shows how a watershed was reached in the research on stereotyping.

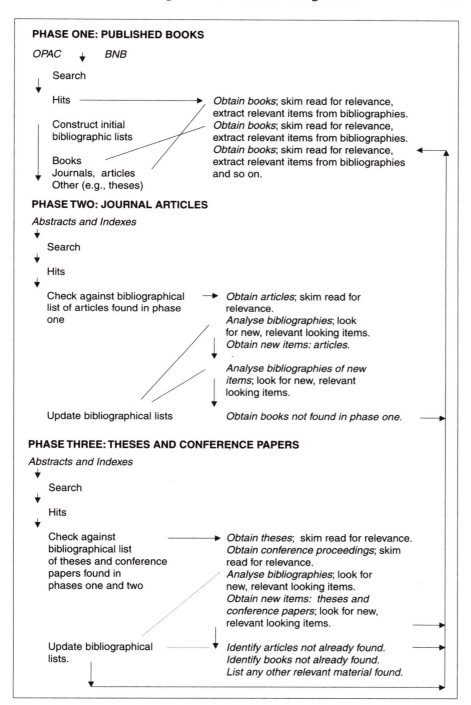

Figure 2.2   *Identifying relevant items through bibliographical analysis*

Extract	Comments
In the 1950s two distinct trends are discernible in stereotyping research, each elaborating one aspect of the Kernel of Truth Debate [already mentioned by the authors in a section preceding this extract]. The majority of researchers continued to concentrate on the deficiencies of stereotyping (e.g. Bogardus, 1950; Hayakawa, 1950; Klineberg, 1950, 1951) while others began to question the assumptions which underpinned this traditional position (e.g. Laviolette and Silvert, 1951).	*Chronological development of research shown with a framework for making distinctions between perspectives. Reference to a major debate among social psychologists.* *Key references to be followed up indicates a critical position is to be developed towards traditional assumptions.*
Related ideas were presented by Fisherman (1956) and Vinacke (1956, 1957). Fisherman argued that stereotypes were valid to the extent that they served to reflect the nature of interaction between stereotyped and stereotyping groups (1956: 60), while Vinacke suggested that stereotypes were representations of authentic high-level conceptual relationships between individuals (i.e. social groupings; 1957: 329). The radical implication of all of this work was that stereotypes were by nature neither irrational nor 'bad'.	*Shows a shift in understanding of the rationality of stereotypes. Inversion of Lipmann's original view of stereotypes points out implications of the inversion.*

What the reader is given here are some directions for categorizing the literature of stereotyping. Two trends are identified with indicative but key references that could be followed up and work on ideas related to these two trends is indicated, for example, in the work of Fisherman that Oakes et al. cite. Again, what can be seen here is a setting of the context of the topic through a chronological presentation of landmark and related studies. In this extract the use of related works is noted, an example of the convention to cite relevant references. This is in the last few sentences above which conclude with the implications of Vinacke's work. In the extract that follows later in the review, we see how exceptions to conventional approaches to stereotyping are shown. These are mentioned, not merely to provide a full coverage of the literature, but to introduce key developments and research insights which can be picked up and developed at a later stage of the review, especially in justifying the study by Oakes and colleagues.

Extract pages 5–6	Comments
Not all research which approached stereotyping as an aspect of prejudice followed this line. Notably . . . Allport (1954) discussed the extent to which the *categorization process* (i.e. cognitive grouping of	*Introduces exceptions to the norm.* *Provides an initial claim to the psychological basis of stereotyping. Continuity from previous work.*

Extract pages 5–6	Comments
individual objects as identical, interchangeable) was involved in prejudice. Whilst he emphasized that categorization was essential to 'orderly living' (in particular, its general flexibility and responsiveness to the changing definition of ingroups and outgroups), he continued to regard stereotypes as deficient because they exaggerated the properties of the categories with which they were associated and stood in the way of differentiated thinking. Moreover, in his discussion of these issues Allport maintained a clear distinction between the rational and irrational use of categories as associated with the behaviour of tolerant and prejudiced people respectively. Allport took a crucial theoretical step forward in suggesting that prejudice might be a product of normal processes, but his analysis contained an inherent contradiction. It suggested that the processes of categorization implicated in stereotyping were essentially rational (cf. Asch, 1952; Vinacke, 1957) but that their rationality was nonetheless contingent upon the character of the individual stereotype (cf. Adorno et al., 1950; see Billing, 1985).	*Shows how even the exception maintained the distinction between rational and irrational. Major claim that is the basis of the study.* *Shows how this major claim has not hitherto been explored.* *Traditional focus on the individual and character in traditional work.*

In the final extract below the authors, having established the context and history of the topic from the perspective of social psychology, provide a summary of the main points of their initial review of the literature. This is usefully done in a table which is not reproduced in the extract. Their reason for doing this is to make their claim for the relevance of their study and for their approach being different from what has been done before.

Extract page 9	Comments
Table 1.1 [not included here] summarizes what we see as the major milestones in the study of social stereotyping up to Tajfel (1981). While personality theories of the type advanced by Adorno et al. have now more or less disappeared from the stereotyping scene, research into both intergroup relations (following Sherif and Tajfel) and individual cognition (following Allport and Tajfel) is still active and crucial. In the 1981 paper Tajfel tried to begin a process of rapprochement between the hitherto rather disparate cognitive (individual) and intergroup (social) traditions in the area, having himself been closely involved in	*The scope of the study is narrowed down by the exclusion of early personality theories (Adono, etc.).* *Re-emphasis of what they consider relevant to the topic.* *Mentions previous attempts at what they are attempting to do.* *Emphasizes the focus they intend to take and claim it is different from, but related*

Extract page 9	Comments
both. In some ways this book can be seen as a continuation of that effort.	to, what others have looked at, that is, justification is provided.
Broadly speaking, we aim to elaborate the argument that in order to understand the psychology of group phenomena (such as stereotyping) it is necessary to examine the ways in which cognition both mediates and is mediated by individuals' group memberships and social relations (see Tajfel, 1979, 1981; Turner and Oakes, 1986). In these terms, processes of perception and cognition are social psychological, not merely because they involve the processing of information about people, but because they are the psychological products of an interaction between mind and society. In this . . . we focus these ideas on the issue of stereotyping, and in so doing aim to achieve a better understanding of the role of this fascinating process in the individual's adaptation to the social environment.	Focus on cognition between social groups based in information processing. Initial warrant for their claim to have a different research focus than previous studies based on individuals', that is, the social psychological in the context of the broader social environment.

EXAMPLE B   SOCIAL SCIENCE AND ADVERTISING

Based on Hart (1993a).

The research began by planning a search of the literature. Information on previous and current works on the topic of advertising were located using hard copy and electronic databases, such as Sociofile, British National Bibliography (BNB), ABI/Inform, Dissertation Abstracts and the Social Science Citation Index. These are all tools that enable relevant items on topics within the social sciences to be identified. They were selected in the search strategy stage according to general criteria. For example, Sociofile provided information on articles in sociology, BNB and other book bibliographies provided a current and retrospective account of what had been published in book form; specialist bibliographies located bibliographies on advertising and sociology; ABI/Inform provided articles on advertising from a management and business perspective; the library OPAC (catalogue) provided information on books in the local academic library; and JANET gave access to the catalogues of most academic libraries in the UK and some in the USA and Australia. Journals covering and including articles on advertising were identified, as were journals that provided abstracts of articles about advertising. Other materials, such as conference papers, reports and theses, were identified using various other sources available from the reference section of the university library.

The general sweep of the databases produced thousands of records or 'hits'. The problem was one of too much data, too many records to be looked at in terms of the time available and cost of ordering through inter-library loans. The advice from C. Wright Mills was, 'to know when you ought to read, and when you ought not to' (1978: 236). The requirement was to identify the books and articles considered by the sociological community to be key works and sources on the study of advertising. Narrowing the search was therefore important. The problem was: how could the search be narrowed? The answer to this problem emerged from the records already located. By singling out BNB and Sociofile items specifically categorized as 'sociological studies' of advertising, meant that those items aimed at practitioners in advertising were not selected and therefore did not appear in the list.

There were still hundreds of potentially relevant items on the list. Various tactics could have been employed at this point to reduce the list even further. All records could have been looked at in their full version, but this would have been too time-consuming. Alternatively, looking at abstracts of all the records was possible. This would have given a good idea of the contents of the articles. A particular issue in the records – for example, advertising and children – might have been specified. This would have prohibited drawing a full map of the topic to be drawn. Finally, a language or data limit could have been used to narrow down the number of records. Some of these tactics were, in fact, chosen. The search was narrowed by specifying that items be in English, but the main tactic employed consisted of using citation indexes, JANET and Sociofile.

Using JANET, the library catalogues of academic libraries from around the world were searched to find out what items they had in their collections (the internet can now be used to access library catalogues). A simple comparison of the lists showed which items were stocked by most libraries. The result, after a relatively short time, was a list of monographs in the sociology of advertising held by most academic libraries in the UK, North America and Australia. It was a straightforward job to subject the list (bibliography) to what is called *citation analysis*. This amounted to looking in special indexes (citation indexes) to find out which authors and works were most frequently cited by other authors. The procedure employed for this was chronologically based. The frequency of citation for each work was obtained starting with the oldest book in the list and working through to the most recent. The individual frequencies of citation were then plotted onto a chart showing the increase and decrease of citations of a work over time. The starting point for the chart was the earliest published reference.

Citation frequencies provide a useful picture of current knowledge in the field and what techniques had been used to collect evidence. Citation frequencies allow for the construction of a 'relevance tree' extending forwards in time. These trees show which books, and subsequently which articles, embody and disseminate the core ideas of the literature. Core works are those which have had a major influence methodologically and morally and which have fostered cross-disciplinary work. The following list gives the criteria which helped in identifying core works.

- An item, published or unpublished, which had an important effect on subsequent work on the topic as a whole and on the development of sub-areas within the main topic.

  An example here was the work of Raymond Williams (1980). His short essay 'Advertising: the magic system' was the most frequently cited reference in most works published from 1980 across all social science disciplines. The methodological assumptions he stated about advertising, including the moral stance he took against advertising, was explicated through a large part of the literature.

- An application of a technique or methodology which others had replicated and which was consistent with the methodological assumptions of how the topic had been traditionally defined.

  An example here was the *Elements of Semiology* by Roland Barthes (1967). This was found to have been a technique of analysis commonly employed across disciplines to reveal hidden structures of coded messages in advertisements.

- An item that had been used across several disciplines and movements so that the topic became a research topic in those disciplines and movements.

  An example here was *Decoding Advertisements* by Judith Williamson (1979). She brought semiological and psychoanalytical analysis to bear on advertising from a feminist standpoint.

Knowing which works were most cited also identified articles and books in which they were cited focusing the search towards more relevant materials. The resulting tree showed how different ideas and studies had contributed to different lines of inquiry and, particularly, the way in which advertising had been approached as a research topic by sociologists. The identification of key authors and works was an important step. It provided the basic materials for the construction of a subject relevance tree. This consisted of mapping out on a piece of paper the relevances in the literature on advertising.

Articles and books tended to fall into one of three main categories: those items concerned with the role and reason for advertising; those concerned with how advertising worked; and those concerned with the effects of advertising. Within each main category individual works were placed and listed according to their major concerns. This allowed for the extended development of this tree in combination with the citation tree. Naturally, these trees do get a little messy due to cross-referencing but their value is incalculable for the analysis of a topic.

The map of the concerns of the literature produced the parameters around the methodological foundations of studies about advertising. It also made visible the interrelationships between differing concerns and the use of common views. In short, the sociological paradigm of advertising was mapped out. This showed a number of interesting and problematic findings. First, advertising was generally regarded as something 'bad'. A variety of moral and ethical judgements were being used as starting points for research into advertising. Secondly, advertising was seen as a modern phenomenon that was essential to the maintenance of capitalist social relations and social structures. Thirdly, advertising was seen to use various psychological or referent methods to influence people, such as subliminal messages. Fourthly, various analytical methods, such as semiological analysis and content analysis, were assumed appropriate to study an advertisement and for revealing the real meaning of an advertisement. Fifthly, the effects of advertising were often cast in terms of 'bad' things in everyday life in a deductivistic application of certain concepts. For example, advertising was blamed for creating and maintaining sexism, racism, ageism and alienation. At this stage it might have been logical to undertake a study of advertising using these assumptions. One could have looked at a batch of advertisements aimed at children to show sex-role stereotyping; in other words, do much of what had already been done. However, this strategy was not followed.

The subject relevance tree demonstrated the circular feedback analysis in current approaches to the topic of advertising. It showed how initial assumptions about the role, place and effects of advertising were often the starting point for studies of advertising. It also showed the need for a sound knowledge of the history of sociological thought: 'Some knowledge of world history is indispensable to the sociologist; without such knowledge, no matter what else he [*sic*] knows, he is simply crippled' (Wright Mills, 1978: 237).

These assumptions about the dysfunctional nature of advertising provided a general methodological framework and common research problem. The methodological framework was characterized by holism and contrast. The holistic approach of conflict structuralism (see Cuff and Payne, 1984, for a description of the sociological development of this approach) was used to relate advertising to capitalism and to locate advertising as a product of the great transformation (see Francis, 1987, for a description of the great transformation debate). Advertising was seen as a product of industrial society. Therefore, a contrast was made between pre-industrial and industrial society. Contrast and holism provided grounds on which other concepts could be used. For example, rationality was a common concept in the literature. It was used to make a contrast between the irrationality or non-rationality of advertising and what might be if advertising did not exist in association with capitalism. Advertising was generally seen as an irrational phenomenon of modern society. Consequently, the effects it had on people were regarded as generally irrational.

In the traditional literature the research problem of advertising was almost wholly conceived of how might the real character of advertising be revealed? The puzzle for the bulk of the sociological literature about advertising was: how does advertising work? Why don't people see it for what it is? What are the effects of advertising? How can these effects be shown? The literature on advertising is therefore replete with semiological and content analysis of advertisements. These are techniques of analysis and synthesis that are thought to be capable of revealing hidden structures and patterns not directly observable in isolated instances of any phenomenon.

The analysis of the literature had, therefore, provided a description of the assumptions which had been deemed necessary for sociological accounts of advertising. This analysis would not have had the breadth and depth it had without the use of the tools by which information is stored, organized and made retrievable. But, having found out what assumptions had been made and mapped them out, it was a short step to ask: what assumptions do we need to make in order to study an advertisement? In other words, what if we subjected the assumptions making up the sociological paradigm on advertising to a thoroughgoing phenomenological scrutiny? Where might this lead? This was not an original tactic; it was advocated by C. Wright Mills:

> Often you get the best insights by considering extremes – by thinking of the opposite of that with which you are directly concerned . . . when you try to contrast objects, you get a better grip on the materials and you can then sort out the dimensions in terms of which the comparisons are made . . . shuttling between attention to these dimensions and to the concrete types is very illuminating. (Wright Mills, 1978: 235)

The phenomenological scrutiny of the methodological assumptions of sociological studies to date on advertising were followed through leading to some of the works of major social theorists such as Husserl, Schutz and Garfinkel. This scrutiny demonstrated that there was something missing in the sociological study of advertising. That something was the topic: advertisements themselves as a pre-theoretical experience. The relevance trees showed that studies of advertising to date had been solely concerned with cause and consequence and had used an explanatory and not a descriptive framework. This preoccupation with the external reality of advertising was augmented by preconceptions about the morality of advertising: not only was advertising approached in terms of external theorizing, but its characteristics and features were defined in advance. The general conclusion was that, although a large body of material in the sociological literature on it showed advertising to be an important topic, analysis of the literature showed that studies of advertising had hitherto only theorized about it as a topic. Advertising had been talked about only in reference to power, ideology, control, alienation and hidden meanings. None of this work could have any purchase if it were not for what we call the mundane reality of advertisements: the ways in which ordinary people read advertisements and the ways in which those working in advertising agencies put together advertisements for the public at large.

Therefore, the question was set: what if all assumptions hitherto made about advertising were placed to one side, where might this lead? What types of research problems might this approach throw up? A research topic was now in the making. The analysis of the literature had shown there to be a hole at the centre of conventional theorizing about advertising. That hole consisted of a disregard for the taken-for-granted aspects of advertisements as a serious topic for sociological description. In short, the analysis of the literature had identified the need for a completely different approach to advertisements. The outcome was that methodological assumptions, moral judgements and methods hitherto used to study advertising were placed to one side.

The task now was to think about the methodological policies and assumptions for the research. The criteria for that approach were that it should be free from the constraints and limitations of looking for hidden structures and free from moral prejudgements. Finding an approach that would be able to describe the experience of an advertisement was not going to be easy. The off-the-peg approach had been rejected. However, some leads had already been identified, rooted in the tradition of phenomenology and methodological indifference – the practice of placing to one side existing approaches and views about a phenomenon. These leads had definite intellectual traditions of their own which might form the starting point for what was required. The next task was to see how the assumptions in these traditions could be applied to produce research. Suffice to say, this was done and formed a part of the methodological story making up a rationalization for a piece of research: a project that would not have been possible without a search and review of the literature.

3

Classifying and reading research

In order to review a research literature you must be able to understand the design issues, methodological traditions and the specifics of research itself. You need to understand the practicalities as well as the conceptual issues of what you are reviewing, and it is only through becoming aware of research design, through practice or reading, that you will be able to undertake a competent review of a research literature. Reviewing research is not, therefore, something that can be done without knowledge. It is not about expressing opinions; it is about evaluating the logical coherence of theories, methodologies and findings in a context of informed scholarship. You must demonstrate understanding of the nature of research; of the ways in which it is presented and of what it means to be scholarly. The aim of this chapter is, therefore, to answer a number of basic questions:

1   What are the elements of research?
2   How does one read analytically?
3   How can information gleaned from reading be managed effectively?
4   What does a review look like?

We begin this chapter, therefore, with an overview of research design, before looking at the process of reading. We end the chapter with some examples of reviews that show the rich diversity of styles and structures that are to be found in the literature.

CLASSIFYING RESEARCH

Research can generally be classified according to its design features and its intended outcomes. Reading a piece of research therefore involves making an effort to understand the reasons why the research was done the way it was and what its outcome was intended to be.

Types of research

The bulk of research in the social sciences is aimed at explaining, exploring or describing the occurrence (or non-occurrence) of some phenomenon. Although some studies combine, to varying degrees, these three purposes, the distinctions between them need to be understood. This is because the different purposes have different implications for the design of research, the ways in which it is presented (its style) and the ways it is intended to be understood. Only by understanding the reason for different styles will you be able to evaluate them on their own merits and in terms of what the researcher intended to produce. Table 3.1 (p. 46) shows some of the characteristics of different types of research.

Within any type of research there can be different types or combinations of the research act. For example, the aim of strategic research (sometimes called pure research) is to provide understanding. The emphasis is not necessarily on producing something pragmatic or even useful. A great deal of historically important research was research done *for its own sake*. Einstein's now famous views on time and space fall into this category. Einstein did not set out to 'invent' relativity or to make possible the building of atomic weapons; he used his imagination to reflect on what it would be like if he could travel at incredible speed. He undertook reflective research. This type of research act aims to examine or explore existing theories, practices or ideas and it does so in the spirit of creativity and imagination. There are therefore many aspects and dimensions to research. Within basic research for example, the research design might be shaped by the goal, which could be exploratory, descriptive or explanatory (see Table 3.2 on p. 47).

In terms of discovery very little research actually discovers anything new. Chance and the ability to make connections between seemingly unrelated factors is what often results in what we call discovery. The Hawthorne Effect (Mayo, 1933) is a common example of chance and observation of related factors. When studying working conditions in a factory it was noted that the act of carrying out the research influenced the behaviour of the workers. Physical conditions, it was observed, were not the only variable in productivity. Workers perceptions of what they thought was happening (even when nothing was happening) were found to be a major influence on their attitude to work.

The distinctions between the different types of research are not always clear or distinct. You will often find informal attitudes to research that grade it according to type. A common example is that of strategic research, which is often seen as superior to applied and other types of research. You need to avoid the fallacy of judging implicitly one type of research as better than another.

Relative standards and judgements

Nearly all subject areas have their own distinctive intellectual traditions, key authors, works and styles. In sociology, for example, Marx, Durkheim and Weber are some of the key theorists and some of their works are seen as classics of the discipline; psychology has Freud, Lacan and Pavlov. In part, it is the approaches which the founders of a discipline took that gives

Table 3.1 *Types of research*

Type	Purpose and features
Basic research	To contribute to theory or knowledge by formulating and testing hypotheses, applying a theory or method to a new area, and evaluating the generalizability of propositions across time and space. Research questions are often of a 'what' and 'why' form. In sociology, for example, the question might be, 'What is society?', in management, 'What is quality?'
Applied research	To produce recommendations or solutions to some problem faced by a specific group of people in a situation. The aim is to take theoretical insights and apply these in real-world situations. Both qualitative and quantitative data are used. Questions tend to be of the form 'how' and 'when'. In anthropology, for example, the question might be, 'How can the structural functional approach explain witchcraft beliefs?', and in organizational studies, 'How can the low motivation of workers be increased through a specific organizational structure?'
Summative evaluation	To summarize and assess the main benefits of a policy, programme or product in order to judge its effectiveness or applicability to a specific situation or in a range of contexts. The aim is to assess the degree of generalizability, therefore abstraction and quantitative data are usually evident. Questions often follow on from some initiative. In management the question might be, 'How did changes to organizational structure change motivation levels?', and in social administration, 'What effect has community care had on voluntary agencies?'
Formative evaluation	To make improvements to a specific programme, policy or set of activities at a specific time and place, and with a specific group. The aim is to focus the research, using case-study method and qualitative evidence. Questions are often focused and specific. In social policy the question might be, 'How can this agency be more effective in meeting the needs of its clients?', and in management, 'How can we maximize the benefits of this computer system for our research team?'
Action research	To help a group to help themselves through the research. The aim is to empower the respondents to 'research themselves and their situation' and on this basis take responsibility for their own situation, make recommendations, possibly implement those recommendations, and perhaps even evaluate the implementation. The focus is mainly on specific problems or issues and involves qualitative evidence. Questions are not usually set by the researcher but are issues subjects feel strongly about.
Illuminative evaluation	To make key behaviours or attitudes in a given context visible for contemplation. The aim is to enlighten policy makers or practitioners to the dynamics of behaviours in comparable situations in order that those behaviours can be understood and attended to in a more appropriate way. A range of evidence, often qualitative, is employed.
Ethnomethodology	To describe the ways in which people make the sense they do in and through the ways they communicate. The aim is to focus on the detail of the commonsense character of everyday life and the practices (methods) by which we make our actions understandable (able to be shared) by others. Close scrutiny of how people do what they do provides an explanation of what those people do and why they do it in the way they do.

Table 3.2   *Goals of research*

Type	Goal
Exploratory	• to satisfy curiosity, provide better understanding or for general interest; • to examine the feasibility of further study by indicating what might be relevant to study in more depth; • to provide illumination on a process or problem. Questions focus on the how, what, when and where. Studies tend to be small scale and often informal in structure, for example, illuminative evaluation.
Descriptive	• to understand a common or uncommon social phenomenon by observing the detail of the elements that make it a phenomenon in order to provide an empirical basis for valid argument. Questions focus on the how and what. Studies tend to be small scale and qualitative, for example, ethnomethodological research.
Explanatory	• to explain the cause or non-occurrence of a phenomenon; • to show causal connections and relationships between variables of the types 'if A then B'; • to suggest reasons for events and make recommendations for change. Questions focus on the why and aim to uncover laws and regularities of a universal nature. Studies can be large or small scale and are often based on hypothetico-deductivism and associated quantitative data.

the shape to the subject knowledge and practices of that discipline. It is the work and ideas of founding theorists that make different disciplines distinct from one another.

As a consequence, each subject area exhibits norms and conventions in research and writing that are particular to it. Different subject areas also have particular views on what is valid research and what the subject is about. This is not to say that all practitioners within a discipline agree about the nature of their subject or about any particular problem that concerns them. Differences exist within disciplines and between subject disciplines. Attitudes to subject areas with which you are familiar need to be put to one side when evaluating research from a discipline with which you are unfamiliar. It is the responsibility of the reviewer to recognize and acknowledge the nature of the discipline from which the work originates. For instance, sociology is essentially an argumentational rather than a knowledge discipline.

Although a considerable amount of empirical work is done by socio-logists, the main debates within sociology are about the subject itself. The argumentational nature of sociology manifests itself in its diversity of positions and approaches, for example, Marxism, functionalism, inter-actionism and ethnomethodology. An example of a knowledge subject might be physics, in which theories about matter progress as more hypotheses are tested and verified. This difference does not mean that physics is superior to a subject like sociology. Rather, the subjects are different and contribute in different ways to our understanding of the world. This pluralism found in and between the nature of different disciplines must be respected.

Implicit in choices about the kinds of issues we have just outlined is the question of comparative judgement. It is tempting for any reviewer to find advantages in one theory or type of research on the basis of their prior assumptions about what should constitute research. As a consequence, research that seems to confirm the reviewer's view of research might attract a favourable assessment. The problem with this is the generalizing tendency (inherent in looking for research) that confirms prior assumptions: both morally and in terms of competent reviewing, the reviewer's credibility can be seriously compromised.

However, this tendency has another implication. In advocating the advantages of one theory or type of research over another, we implicitly make contrasts which can be misleading, and which result in gross oversimplification and severely restrain the innovative pluralism of literature reviewing. Take, for example, the differences between positivism and phenomenology. Where positivism is regarded as objective, phenomenology is, as a consequence, regarded as subjective. Similarly, Marxism is seen as theoretical in contrast to the empiricism of symbolic interactionism.

It is only through reading a piece of research that the developmental character of purpose and type can be teased out of the text. This act of reading is about understanding the researcher's project. We saw in Table 3.1 some of the major goals of research purpose. In many cases it is a matter of horses for courses, but any project can – and many do – involve different kinds of study within the project. It is not uncommon for a study to report, for instance, on both applied and formative aspects of the project. Therefore, it is as important for the reader as for the writer of a piece of research to explicate the rationale of the research purpose and show understanding of the implications of choices made in its design. In the writing of a thesis it is usually the structure that allows the reader to follow the argument, but this is not simply a matter of structure and format. The writer must ensure that the substantive content of the report explicates the logic of the research – and not leave it to the imagination of the reader.

Design features

Very few accounts of a piece of research include the original design plan or proposal. Even master's and doctoral theses omit the original proposal by which the research was designed. It is possible, however, to recover the design features and methodological choices of a piece of research from the published work. Pattern (1990) provides the following summary (Table 3.3) of the main features of research design that the reviewer can look for and evaluate.

The features outlined in Table 3.3 are not prescriptive for all research. They are indicative of the design features from which any piece of research can be constructed, and as such, some of them can be found in all written accounts of a piece of research. It takes a little practice in reading to

Table 3.3 *Issues and options in research design*

Issues	Options
What is the purpose of the study?	Basic research, applied research, summative evaluation, formative evaluation, action research, illuminative evaluation, ethnomethodology.
What is the scope of the study?	What is included, excluded, why and to what effect?
What is the focus for the study?	People, policy, programmes. Breadth versus depth, case study, survey, chronological, comparative and so on.
What are the units of analysis?	Individuals, groups, programme components, whole programmes, organizations, critical incidents, time periods and so on.
What is the sampling strategy?	Purposeful, probability, quota, random, size, representation, significance and level of generalizability.
What types of data were collected?	Qualitative, quantitative.
How were the data managed?	Organization, classification, presentation, referenced, indexed and so on.
What analytical approach is used?	Deductive, inductive.
How is validity addressed in the study?	Triangulation, multiple data sources, multiple study.
When did the study occur?	Currency of findings, long-term investigation, short and snappy, phased and piloted.
How is the study justified?	Literature review and analysis, problem definition, practical outcomes, intellectual endeavour and so on.
How are ethical issues handled?	Informed consent, confidentiality of information, reactivity, data protection and so on.
How are logistics handled?	Access to data and respondents, fieldwork, record keeping, data management and so on.

Source: adapted from Pattern, 1990

identify the design features of someone else's research: effort is required to read research systematically and without prejudice. As some of these features have already been described, the remainder of this section will look at what is meant by focus and units of analysis.

By focus we are referring to the specific dimensions and aspects of the topic that were studied. There are, in the main, three areas that a study can focus on: characteristics, orientations and actions. Characteristics are usually taken to be measurable or recordable attributes, such as age, sex, location and the like. In terms of social interactions these would be the where, how, when, between whom and in what context. Orientations refer to the characteristics of the people, group or organization under study. The orientations of individuals might be their beliefs, attitudes, personality traits and the like. Actions are taken to be what people do. For example, a study that looks at consumer behaviour will be action-focused. While a study into new religious movements might look at either the demographic profile of members (and will therefore focus on characteristics) or at the specific beliefs of the movement (in which case it will be looking at orientations). For the purpose of research design and the analysis of research reports, distinctions can be made between differences in focus. But be prepared for studies which mix and match in terms of what they have focused on at different times in the research.

By units of analysis we mean the specific parameters of what was the subject for study. For example, if the topic is the UK Census, then the units of analysis are statistics based on responses by individuals; it is from decennial questionnaires, filled in by the individual that demographic patterns can be measured. Units of analysis are therefore the units of observation: things we examine in order to study our chosen topic. In broad terms there are four types of units: individuals, groups, organizations and social artifacts. As the unit of observation, individuals might be characterized by their membership of some group or organization. However, if we were interested in the dynamics of the group as a whole, then the group is the unit of observation. This is because we might be aiming to generalize about the typical dynamics of group behaviour. Often in management research it is the organization that is the unit of analysis. Comparisons made between different types of organization in terms of structure, culture, size and the like are the characteristics observed in order to study the larger unit of analysis. Finally, social artefacts such as books, sculpture, pictures and buildings can be the unit of analysis. Also included in this category are other social artefacts such as jokes, songs, scientific experiments and rituals.

Methodological traditions

In many undergraduate courses and in textbooks on research, methods (techniques for collecting data) are regarded as separate from theory (methodology). This division may be practical, but it is artificial. In practice it is your stance on key methodological questions that shapes the character of your research study. For example, if you believe that hard data, such as statistics, are to be preferred to soft data, such as ethnographic data, then a positivistic approach is being taken. If you prefer the rich detail of ethnographic data then you are taking an interpretivistic approach. The distinctions between these two are not always as clear-cut as this, so it is crucial that the origins and implications of both approaches are understood by the reviewer. Methodological issues are not something to be marginalized or ignored, because any serious attempt to understand an aspect of the world is almost inevitably based on some dimension of the intellectual tradition of Western knowledge. These traditions shape the different ways in which different subject disciplines frame their views of the world and how they go about investigating the world. Issues arising from differences between disciplines and methods can best be approached by understanding the connections between philosophical traditions and strategies for investigation. This is because if we aim to acquire knowledge of the world around us we need to appreciate the implications of what we take as the world, and acknowledge that our approach is not universally shared and that there are alternatives from which we can choose.

We might begin by noting that all research originates from some view of reality, which means that there are different ways of gaining an understanding of some aspect of the world and different ways of confirming our understanding (i.e. knowledge). If the two approaches, positivistic and interpretivistic, were applied to, say, atomic particles, then both might be seen to have a coherent logic. Empirically we can't see atomic particles. We 'see' such things through the intermediate use of instruments that measure them. Both accounts are consequently valid even though they are very different. In practice, we might be able to compare them, but we cannot judge them. This is because if we were to judge we would be making a commitment to one or other methodological position, that is, an ontological and epistemological view of reality. In judging, we would make a value-commitment to a position which might compromise our attitude of open mindedness.

In very general terms we can say that it is important to grasp the philosophical meaning of ontology, epistemology and the methodological meanings of validity, reliability and data. This is because alternative views of reality lead to: different propositions about *what reality is* (ontology); different ways of establishing *what can be accepted as real* (epistemology); different strategies for *validating our claims* about reality; and different techniques for *collecting data* (questionnaires, observation, etc.). These dimensions for approaching the object of our research are present in all forms of knowledge whether that knowledge is scientific or common sense. While the kinds of issues and methodological implications of taking one position on ontological status of reality and epistemological status of knowledge are outlined in the next section, you are advised to read further on this topic.

You need to be aware that there are no clear-cut prescriptions about how to translate theoretical ideas into research designs. Similarly, there are no rule books on how to do research. There are types of protocol that guide the researcher and which assist those who would want to validate another's research. As a consequence, the reviewer is faced with the problem of acquiring sufficient understanding of the implications of methodology before beginning to review. Regrettably, there is no simple exposition of the implications of methodological doctrines on research. Added to this is the fact that the philosophical foundations of research are full of complexities and misunderstandings. We come back, therefore, to one of the main points: to assess the competency (rather than relevance) of a piece (or body) of research the reviewer needs to know what competent research looks like in the first place. The competent researcher needs to be able to demonstrate experience with research. Knowledge of research is therefore an essential prerequisite and is not something easily or quickly acquired.

In the research itself, the researcher may not show full awareness of the traditions from which their style or approach originates. It then falls to the reviewer to identify the methodological foundations of a study, particularly if the way in which a topic has been studied is to be mapped out. By mapping out the ways a topic has been investigated, the reviewer can see more clearly the general approaches, usual methods and what kinds of assumptions have tended to be made by an approach. Thus, the reviewer might be better able to identify opportunities for further research, using a methodological approach not yet tried with a particular topic. It is the very fact that the methodological or theoretical traditions underpinning all research can be teased out of an article or book that enable them to be challenged.

Researchers working within a Marxist framework, for example, can be expected to share, to a lesser or greater degree, a set of methodological assumptions. According to Cuff and Payne (1984: 78–9), Marx developed the following methodological assumptions.

- The social world, like the natural world, is always in a process of change.
- Like the natural world, the social world is not chaotic, but ordered by patterns of relationships that can be observed.
- The structure of any society and the forces on it for change can be found in economic relationships between social groups, for example, classes.
- The structure of any society is made up of parts that are interrelated, for example, family, education, religion, media and so on; all of which are shaped by the distribution of economic resources between social classes.
- Human beings are essentially rational and would use their social nature to live in co-operation, but human nature is subverted by the economic structure of society. The economic organization of capitalism makes people selfish, greedy and individualistic, leading them to believe that such characteristics are natural.

Marx also believed that not all people are wholly caught up by the system, and that some, like himself, could transcend the system. Such individuals could rise above the deceptions of capitalism and study the workings of society and explain those workings to others.

Marx employed these methodological assumptions to explain rather than describe the mechanisms of change, social structures and social relationships. These assumptions were neither passive nor randomly chosen by Marx: he developed them through deliberate and systematic thought. His goal was not only to explain the hidden structures of capitalism but to develop a set of ideas that would change society. Marx's assumptions were, therefore, motivated by a moral concern to bring about a different type of social order which he thought would restore the nature of humankind.

READING TO REVIEW

Reading with the purpose of reviewing is very different from reading for pleasure. Reading to review has the goal of producing a product: an analytical evaluation of the research on your topic. This means that you are expected to unravel the reasoning that informs the research and arguments that you find in the literature. Therefore, our first concern must be with the question of what it means to read analytically. Reading analytically is not something that can be done in one reading or in a short time period. It is often the case that three, six or even 12 months might be required for reading and reviewing a literature. It all depends on the level of your postgraduate work and how much time you have to do the work. During this time it is not unusual for the reviewer to pass through several stages in their development as a researcher. The initial difficulties of understanding or of attempting to do too much in too short a time are usually overcome through the experience of reviewing. As a primer to the advice given below we can therefore highlight a few general points about the process and give an indication of what you might expect.

Reading process

Reading analytically is a process that progresses from the general to the particular and, as such, follows that of most other forms of reading. When we read normally we tend to skim through first of all, then pick out some details, skimming before reading more closely the other contents. When reading an article or monograph the procedure is often the most effective. The list below provides a snapshot of the main purposes of reading to review, identifying the information components in a literature that you will be expected to extract.

arguments	concepts	conclusions	definitions	ethics
events	evidence	hypothesis	interpretations	justification
motives	perspective	politics	problem	questions
standpoint	styles	techniques	theory	ways of thinking

Start by reading the title and the blurb on the cover before glancing at the contents list and the preface. A common mistake at this initial stage is to get stuck in and start reading every sentence. Remember that the detail can be looked at later, once you have become familiar with the general layout of the book. At this early stage look at the general structure of the text, making some tentative classifications about what kind of research and theory the author might be using. Remember that this first classification is open to change once more detailed reading begins. If you leave time between the initial read through and the detailed reading, it will give your own intellect time to take in what you have looked at – and will probably enable you to do the detailed reading more effectively. What you are doing is moving from the general to the particular, extracting different levels of detail and information as your reading progresses. Here is a suggested scheme for reading monographs.

1 Initially skim through the book, noting its structure, topic, style, general reasoning, data and bibliographical references.
2 Survey the parts of the book – this means quickly glancing through each chapter to get a general idea of the structure of the contents of the book as a whole and to identify the key chapters.
3 Skim over and then read the preface and introduction, trying to identify the idea, aims and logic for the work. Look for signposts the author provides for the logic of the work. These might be found in overviews of the book.
4 Read the parts of those chapters that you have identified as being important to your needs. You do not need to read the whole book. Chapters to look out for are those which provide the rationale for the study, for example, chapters summarizing theory and method. It is at this stage that you need to extract the main concepts and see how they have been defined and operationalized by the author.

Taking this procedure as our starting point we can now consider what to look for when you are reading analytically. You will need to look for the topic and the aims of the author. Consider, for example, the following extracts from the preface of *The Woman Reader 1987–1914*, by Kate Flint (1993). She uses the preface to explain briefly the origins of her book.

> This book had its origins in a particular act of reading. In 1981, I was invited to write an introduction to Anthony Trollope's *Can You Forgive Her?* (1864–5), . . . I pondered for some time on that title. *Can You Forgive Her?* That interrogative form involves the reader, and provokes a response. The pronoun with which the short query ends suggests, even before we open the novel, that we are to engage our moral judgement with the dubious behaviour, the peccadilloes of a specific, female individual. Assessment of her conduct is necessarily related to her gender. Moreover, the novel proves to be concerned, throughout, with the specific conditions governing a woman's life in the mid-nineteenth century. Very soon, I came to see that gender not just of the title's 'her', but also of the 'you', might matter. To what degree, I asked myself, could one postulate a difference in response between a woman and a man reading this story at the time of its original publication? (1993: preface)

The topic for Flint's research, and subsequent book, came from thinking about the title of a book. She goes on to formulate how she went about exploring the idea that men and women might have read a book, such as *Can You Forgive Her?* (1864–5), differently.

The more evidence of debates about reading which I amassed, the more instances which I gathered of individual reading practices, made me reformulate my initial questions. Asking 'how a woman might read' became increasingly problematical, indeed unanswerable, as I came to recognize the great heterogeneity among nineteenth- and early twentieth-century women readers . . . documentary material tends to suggest that the practice of reading provided a site for discussion, even resistance, rather than giving grounds for assuming conformity. Instead of my initial formulations about the possible relations of women and texts, I came to be fascinated by *why* the polemic should prove so pervasive and long-lasting (for its roots lie way before the Victorian period) . . . so rather than write, . . . a work of critical interpretation . . . I chose to examine the topos of the women reader, and its functioning in cultural debate between the accession of Queen Victoria and the First World War. (1993: preface)

These extracts from the preface provide a quick overview of the idea of the book. To follow these up and add more detail we could look in the Introduction. It is here that we can see that the idea of the book is formulated into a set of aims; for example, 'One aim of the present book is to offer suggestions as to why "the woman reader" was an issue addressed with such frequency throughout the period' (1993: 10).

What this involves is then discussed briefly, followed by a formulation of what the book can offer its reader. For example:

This work offers a dual, though continually intersecting focus. Attempts to legislate about reading and its effects can be seen on the one hand as a means of gaining control over subjectivity, and, on the other, as a means of obtaining access to different types of knowledge, and through this, to different social expectations and standards. . . . It shows how notions about reading fed off attempts to define women's mental capacities and tendencies through their physical attributes, and, in turn, appeared to contribute to the validation of these very definitions. (1993: 11)

Even with this amount of information a reader should be able to summarize the topic and aims of Flint's book. Overall, you should be looking to extract from an item or group of items the project of the author; you will often find that a researcher had a particular motive for doing their research, and from this motive they constructed a project. We are using the term project in a very broad way, to include the motive, moral, political and methodological position that a researcher might have started from and therefore used as the starting point for their research. Your task is to 'unpack' the project in order to identify the logic of what they produced by trying to identify how they produced their research. Figure 3.1 shows some of the main types of elements that make up a research project. You need to put yourself in the role of the researcher and, in particular, stay close to the original materials. Resist attributing motives and methodological assumptions to a work or cohort of authors unless you have clear evidence.

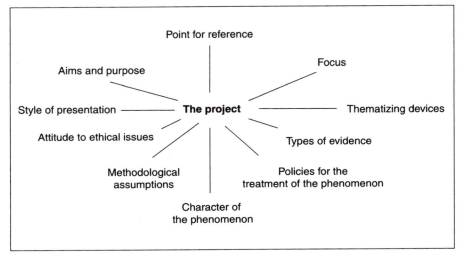

Figure 3.1　*Elements for analysing the reasoning in research*

The aim is to draw out of their work what the author was attempting. This means looking at their work, or pieces of work, to identify the style and structure of their reasoning. If it is a theoretical work this might mean looking for the structure of the argument employed for proposing a particular theory in preference to others. If it is an empirically oriented work it might mean looking at the methodological assumptions and research design that enabled the study to be undertaken. You should therefore be investigating how, and especially why, an author chose a particular theory or tradition and why certain decisions were made concerning the design of their research. You are aiming to make explicit the nature of the connections between the methodological choices an author has made and the data they have collected through to the interpretations they have made of their data. A common starting point for countless reviews has, in fact, been the ability to assess structures of reasoning that different authors use in their work. This ability enables the reviewer to evaluate critically and appraise critically the degree of scholarship an author has managed to attain in their work. Each of the elements identified in Figure 3.1 is explained through reading the text in Example A which we consider next.

REVIEWS OF RESEARCH LITERATURE

In Example A the commentary reflects an analytical reading of Harold Garfinkel's *Studies in Ethnomethodology* (1967). Garfinkel's work has been chosen for a number of reasons. First, Garfinkel's work is cited in many types of work across the social sciences and the humanities as well as the natural sciences. His ideas, like those of Erving Goffman (1959; 1968), have become a common resource across many disciplines. Secondly, Garfinkel's work is not easy to understand. Like the work of Goffman, Garfinkel's work has been subject to some serious misunderstanding about what his project, his work, was about. Finally, an advantage that Garfinkel gives us is that he published several pieces of his work in one volume. We therefore only need to look at one source in order to be able to review a major intellectual figure of the twentieth century.

One of the first things the reviewer is required to do when presenting their review is to outline its aims. In Example A (starting on p. 58) the aim is to show where *Studies in Ethnomethodology* (to be referred to as *Studies*) stands in relation to the development of sociology by arguing that *Studies* represents a radical departure from traditional sociology. Therefore, the short review in Example A has an argument. In order that we may reconstruct the argument, we need to demonstrate that we have understood the meaning, in context, of the key concepts that Garfinkel uses to express his approach to research. This will be one of the objectives of the review: something that can be assessed by the reader of this book. In demonstrating our understanding, we are also attempting to evaluate the reasoning Garfinkel employs when choosing to use the concepts that enable him to do the kind of analysis he reports in *Studies*.

There are then a number of formats that this review could have. It might have the format of a brief history of Garfinkel and his ethnomethodological work, with formal definitions of the key concepts, followed by extracts from *Studies* to show Garfinkel's use of the concepts with a final conclusion that evaluates his work. An alternative format might be to look at the criticisms made of *Studies* in reviews that appeared when it was first published, to see if these early criticisms have continued until the present day. This could then be followed by a critical counter-argument in defence of *Studies* or a critical evaluation of reviews of *Studies*. Hence, discussion of how *Studies* has been understood and misunderstood would form the basis of the account. At the same time, the major concepts and methodological assumptions Garfinkel elected to develop would be explicated. In other words, a review might take a range of formats. Whatever format is decided upon, it should be suited to the aim its writer is attempting to achieve. **Turn now to the reading of *Studies* in Example A.**

Having read Example A, you will find the last two examples in this chapter are rather different. They are two sets of extracts from reviews of the literature. The first, Example B (starting on p. 67), attempts to make a case for a research topic and technique commonly referred to as 'community study'. To do this the author takes a journey through some classic and landmark studies of a diverse range of communities. His main argument is that the study of community is, contrary to popular impressions, a vigorous and rich area of research. The second, Example C (starting on p. 72), is from an actual master's dissertation. It is about the convergence of traditional libraries and information technology. When you read this extract, notice how the student attempts to display his knowledge of the literature. **Read examples B and C now.**

CONCLUSION

The emphasis in this chapter has been the need to teach oneself how to read research. We began by looking at the nature of research. An awareness of the elements that make up choices in research is an important prerequisite to being able to understand an author's argument and research project. This awareness can be practised through reading research and undertaking analysis of that research. A useful resource that will enable this to be done effectively and in a scholarly way is the development of a knowledge about the different methodological traditions that researchers use, but do not always discuss, as the epistemological basis of their research.

In terms of reading research, the ability to analyse and evaluate are very important skills. In a later chapter we will show some ways in which different techniques can be used to analyse and map ideas and arguments. What you need to remember from this chapter is to look for the reasoning an author has employed in their research. This extends to the reasons that are often discipline-specific problems and puzzles. The example of Garfinkel's *Studies in Ethnomethodology* provided an illustration of the need to ensure that when reading research or an argument that is difficult or challenging, sufficient effort should be invested to enable the reader to demonstrate that they have understood (though not necessarily agreed with) what it was that the author was attempting to achieve.

EXAMPLE A   *STUDIES IN ETHNOMETHODOLOGY*

Based on Garfinkel (1967).

Let us begin with a few basic details about *Studies in Ethnomethodology*. *Studies* was first published in 1967; it is not a monograph. It is, in fact, a collection of eight different studies, four of which were published previously. The acknowledgments provide details of prior publications. 'Studies' seems an apt description for these eight papers, because none of them are overtly theoretical or in the style of a text book, nor do they contain long interpretations of traditional debates in sociological theory. Arranged into chapters, each piece is a study of a naturally occurring social phenomenon conducted by Garfinkel and colleagues over a period of about 12 years. The arrangement appears to have little logic to it: the chapters do not provide the reader with a sequential understanding of ethnomethodology, nor do they provide a sequential development of an argument for the method of analysis used by Garfinkel. Hence we might initially characterize *Studies* as a collection of pieces (an anthology) undertaken at different times by Garfinkel. From the contents list, we can see that Chapters 1 to 8 are:

1 What is ethnomethodology?
2 Studies of the routine grounds of everyday activities
3 Common sense knowledge of social structures: the documentary method of interpretation in lay and professional fact finding
4 Some rules of correct decisions that jurors respect
5 Passing and the managed achievement of sex status in an intersexed person, part 1
6 'Good organizational reasons for "bad" clinic records'
7 Methodological adequacy in the quantitative study of selection criteria and selection practices in psychiatric outpatient clinics
8 The rational properties of scientific and common sense activities

Looking at the labelled contents of *Studies* leads to two initial observations. First, the range of topics Garfinkel has looked at is both wide and diverse. There seems to be no common topic. He has looked at transsexuality, decision making in legal settings, and record keeping and selection processes in psychiatric settings. Secondly, the collection makes it clear that this is not a traditional exposition of a sociological approach. The latter observation presents the reader of *Studies* with the problem of where to begin, which is made more difficult when you look through the contents of the chapters. It is immediately obvious that the style (of presentation) in which Garfinkel has written is not familiar: it looks very different from conventional sociological writing. The following short extract gives an indication of Garfinkel's style and the difficulty Garfinkel must have had in attempting to describe a radical departure from conventional sociology.

> Certain versions of Durkheim that teach that the objective reality of social facts is sociology's fundamental principle, the lesson is taken instead, and used as a study policy, that the objective reality of social facts *as* an ongoing accomplishment of the concerted activities of daily life, with the ordinary, artful ways of that accomplishment being by members known, used, and taken-for-granted, is, for members doing sociology, a fundamental phenomenon. (1967: vii)

In such a case, the place to start is from the very beginning, to be exact, start with the preface and acknowledgments. Anyone reading the preface should be able to appreciate that *Studies* is going to be a difficult book to read but, at the same time, the reader will also get the feeling that this is an important book, the outcome of some serious systematic thinking. Having said this, many readers of *Studies* are bewildered about just what it is Garfinkel is trying to say and do. Unlike the work of Erving Goffman (1959; 1968), whose books are an example of lucid sociological writing, Garfinkel can greatly confuse even the most experienced analyst. One of the main complaints in early reviews (Coleman, 1968) of *Studies* was that it would have been much better if Garfinkel had used plain English. Garfinkel's use of seemingly obtuse language makes it difficult to grasp just what he is advocating and why. Coleman's (1968) initial view of *Studies* is a common one, partially due to the fact that he came to *Studies* with an established expectation of what he would find. As a traditional sociologist, Coleman expected to read a sociological work; what he actually read was something very different from what he regarded as sociology. The painstakingly detailed descriptions, the awkward terminology and opaque style appears to Coleman – as to most people – bizarre, bewildering and a little mysterious. These impressions are augmented by the complete lack of critical analysis, interpretation and conclusions and no attempt to explain social behaviours with reference to social structures, or to concepts such as power and control. Therefore, Coleman was left wondering just what *Studies* was all about. This shows the need to put to one side preconceived expectations of what something ought to look like; to take things as they are presented and to try and work out why they are that way. We might begin, therefore, by posing some basic questions for our review; questions Coleman might have found useful.

- What is Garfinkel's ethnomethodology?
- What type of research is Garfinkel's ethnomethodology?
- How does it differ from traditional sociology?
- What is the topic for ethnomethodological studies?
- What are the major concepts used by Garfinkel to do ethnomethodological studies?

Our first question relates to the topic of *Studies*. Each of the eight essays in *Studies* deals with the three major concerns of sociology: social action, the nature of intersubjectivity and the social constitution of knowledge; in short, the problem of social order. Garfinkel does not talk about these concerns, rather he studies them in a particular way that examines the very foundations of what it means to study social order. In Garfinkelian terms his project had the following aims and purpose: *how do people organize their activities so as to be mutually understandable and to be vulgarly recognizable for what they are?* This is just one way of explaining Garfinkel's project, although it is not the only way. However, if carefully constructed such initial characterizations can be useful introductions for more detailed explication and analysis.

Having given a definition we can now make a link to the criticism of *Studies* introduced earlier. The criticism made by Coleman (1968) came from a symposium set up to review *Studies*; Coleman was a member of the panel. On the basis of criticizing the style Garfinkel uses, Coleman missed the concern motivating Garfinkel's research. By commenting that *Studies* would have been more acceptable if written in plain English, Coleman began what has become a common attitude towards *Studies*. It is an attitude that has resulted in misunderstanding of what *Studies* is all about. For example, in the now famous case of 'Agnes' (reported in Chapter 5 of *Studies*), Garfinkel provides an account of a transsexual. He describes the ways in which a person with a penis (Agnes) methodically brings about (i.e. accomplishes) the ascribed status of a 'female'. What methods does this person employ to make 'himself' recognizable (i.e. able to be reported and *accountable*) as female? Garfinkel, therefore, gives a description of the methods Agnes routinely employs to accomplish being taken for a female. His description is of the knowledge people have of how we interpret the methods we use in order to make our actions understandable for what they are intended to be. In this case Agnes employs the methods of action that make 'her' accountably female.

Garfinkel is therefore making an important point about social order ('character of the phenomenon'). If sexual status is something not simply defined by the fact of genitalia but is nevertheless *taken for granted*, then this must be an *accomplishment* by people at a local level, as a part of their everyday interactions with each other. Garfinkel shows that Agnes manages 'her' self-presentation (i.e. her *accountability*) in talk and interaction so as to be routinely taken as a female. Agnes ('type of evidence') is therefore using various common methods of practical reasoning to make herself accountably female. Agnes does not take sexuality as something that is given but something that is readily taken for granted if no other evidence is given during an interaction to suggest that things are other than they seem. Sexuality is thus a naturally occurring feature of social interaction ('point of reference'); we take it for granted that people are the gender they appear to be unless there is evidence for us to raise a doubt. Even in such cases where some doubt might be present, Garfinkel shows that people will routinely try to find evidence to normalize the situation: in this case, to see Agnes as female regardless. This is because Agnes is thoroughly aware of what kinds of methods she can use that others (often without realizing) take for granted, and that accomplish sexual categorization. Hence, Agnes works more than most people would, in an artful way, at methodically producing the practices that will make others recognize her as naturally female.

Thus, the point Garfinkel is making in his description of the methods used by Agnes is very simple. If Agnes is able to produce a categorization of herself as naturally female then those things that we routinely take as objective, such as sexual status, are also a part of the taken-for-granted practices that members (i.e. people) routinely use to make their actions recognizable and able to be categorized, and thereby to make their intention understood ('methodological assumption'). We are all, as members of social groups, engaged in the use of methods that we employ to make our understandings of a situation able to be shared with others (i.e. *reflexive*) – we are continuously maintaining a social order that is intersubjectively shared.

Garfinkel is making a recommendation on what the phenomenon for sociological study might be. That phenomenon is the routine practices members of social groups employ to enable themselves and others to make sense of their social world. Therefore, in each study Garfinkel describes the kinds of methods he has observed that people use to make their actions accountable and the knowledge (i.e. practical reasoning) they assume is shared that enable the meaning of their actions to be seen for what they were intended to be.

However, Coleman believed that Garfinkel had been tricked by Agnes. Coleman assigned Garfinkel's study of Agnes to an instance of medical sociology, criticizing Garfinkel for not looking at the medical decision-making about transsexuality in the context of structural relations of power in society. Coleman therefore utterly missed the point Garfinkel was making in his study of Agnes. By claiming that Coleman missed the point we are showing something of the stance we are taking to a controversial figure such as Garfinkel. We are showing that we intend to be receptive to what he intended in his project. The next thing that we might do in such a review is to reinforce our reading of Garfinkel; to elaborate on what we have already said. This we can do by looking briefly at the relationship of Garfinkel's studies to that of a 'traditional' sociologist such as Émile Durkheim. We might choose Durkheim because it is in his work that the sociological topic of social order was given systematic attention, and because his work is very well known across the social sciences.

For Durkheim, as for Garfinkel, the problem for sociological inquiry is one of order. The patterns that can be found in social relationships and structures of activities are what both Durkheim and Garfinkel are interested in. But the way each approaches the problem is very different. Garfinkel respecifies the problem of order and thus the phenomenon for sociology (the 'focus'). Instead of seeing activities and social knowledge as shaped by external forces (i.e. structures of power), Garfinkel elects to see the orderliness of the social world as something that is generated from *within* activities as they are done by people ('policies for the treatment of the phenomenon'). Therefore, Garfinkel decided to take the methodological policy that recommends that we treat the sense an activity has – its recognizability, intelligibility and typifiability – as an accomplishment of those persons engaged in that activity. Hence no activity, according to Garfinkel, can have its sense pregiven or predetermined by forces independent of the situation in which it occurs. The sense any activity has is, therefore, a feature of the work that members of the activity do (methods) to make it sensible for others to understand (practical reasoning) and its sense is a part of the activity itself (accomplishment). It is the work that members do in any activity that Garfinkel is recommending should be a phenomenon for sociological study.

We are therefore talking about the kinds of methodological policies a theorist can elect to employ when studying the social world. Garfinkel's methodological policies are, however, difficult to understand and even more difficult to put into practice. If we take the central recommendation as being that we treat social facts, such as sexual status, as interaction accomplishments, then this might initially seem familiar; we might think it is a variant on symbolic interactionism. This interpretation might be reinforced by Garfinkel himself, because he never fully provides the reader of *Studies* with a way of fully understanding the radical nature of the implications of what he is recommending. He does attempt, in various places within the book, to explain the meaning of the policy. However, the following extract indicates what the reader of *Studies* is up against.

> Ethnomethodological studies analyse everyday activities as members' methods for making those activities visibly-rational-and-reportable-for-all-practical-purposes, i.e. 'accountable', as organizations of commonplace everyday activities. The reflexivity of that phenomenon is a singular feature of practical actions, of practical circumstances, of commonsense knowledge of social structures, and of practical sociological reasoning. By permitting us to locate and examine their occurrence the reflexivity of that phenomenon establishes their study.
>
> Their study is directed to the task of learning how members' actual, ordinary activities consist of methods to make practical actions, practical circumstances, commonsense knowledge of social structures, and practical sociological reasoning analysable; and of discovering the formal properties of commonplace, practical commonsense actions, 'from within' actual settings, as ongoing accomplishments of those settings. (1967: vii–viii)

The point that we made earlier about the difficulty of reading Garfinkel should now be self-evident. However, it should also be clear now that Garfinkel had something serious and interesting to say. You should be able to see in what we have said that we are attempting to show the serious character of Garfinkel's work, giving it due respect and not treating it as superficial or beyond understanding. This is an attitude that all reviews should demonstrate. However, returning to the review, we have not, so far, answered all the questions that we set. We might still look in more detail at the claim we made about Garfinkel's work being a radical departure from traditional sociology. We might even claim that *Studies* is not sociology but a division of social science in its own right.

If we follow through what Garfinkel is recommending then we can begin to see some interesting implications for research. In the example of Agnes, as in the other studies, we can see just what it is that Garfinkel is asking his readers. He is asking them to consider the ordinary, recognizable world in a way that is different from conventional sociological theorizing. This kind of statement is something we are attributing to Garfinkel; it will therefore need to be explained and justified. This we can do by characterizing some of the ways in which traditional sociology approaches the social world as an object for study. Traditional sociology, such as structural functionalism and conflict structuralism, attempts to make sense of the order observable in the world. Both of these major traditions agree that some general principle can be employed to explain the structures of relationships that constitute social order; but each proposes a different principle. Much of the debate in sociology is about which principle is the right one by which sociology should explain the world. The usual dichotomy is between harmony and consensus, on the one hand, and power and conflict, on the other. Garfinkel's approach steps outside this debate. Instead of asking what the real meaning of an event or occurrence is, he asks a very different kind of question. Garfinkel asks: how is the sense of any occurrence possible in the first place? This simple question makes for a very different approach to social order. Whereas traditional sociology takes for granted the sense available in the world, and aims to produce an interpretation of the meaning of that sense, Garfinkel's policy is to treat that sense as problematic, as something in need of investigation. Therefore, we have two very different types of sociology, because each has a very different point of reference as the starting point.

Once this policy recommendation is employed to study social reality, we begin to appreciate some of the reasons for the style and character of *Studies*. Each study is very descriptive. This is due to the method Garfinkel employs to make visible the character of what people do in order to accomplish the sense of order of everyday life. He employs the phenomenological method of bracketing, which means he suspends acceptance of the attitude we would normally take for granted in our daily life. It is a method equivalent to taking on the role of the stranger in our own culture. It allows us to notice features of activities that are normally too commonplace and mundane to be noticed. It makes visible (rather than reveals) the methods members use to accomplish sense of their activities. By the very nature of this policy Garfinkel could not use a theory developed to explain or compare; nor could he employ someone else's definition of social order. This is what sets him apart from traditional sociology – his respecification of sociology.

Notice that this kind of exposition has a propensity to expand. This is because we are not dealing in turn with each of the questions we set but with different aspects of each question, in differing ways. We are also picking out different ways of describing the various elements of Garfinkel's project. By doing this we are demonstrating our understanding at different levels and our ability to communicate it in a range of ways. Again, the mention of the method of bracketing has a number of uses. We have already noted that the method partially accounts for the style in which *Studies* is written. If we follow this through, we will be able to explain Garfinkel's use, and his reason for using, this method.

To bracket taken-for-granted assumptions means taking a particular attitude to the world that allows study of the foundations of the 'natural attitude'. By natural attitude we mean the cultural framework in which we normally and routinely operate – mundane ways in which we perceive, interpret and decide what the facts of a situation are, and act upon our experiences. Herein lies a possible cause for misunderstanding Garfinkel's project. This method is described in Chapter 3 of *Studies*. Garfinkel calls it the 'documentary method'. This is not the use of documents as data, but refers to the ways in which people interpret the events that they experience in order to make sense of them. It consists of commonly known practices that allow people to make sense of the here and now. Garfinkel was probably aware that this would be difficult to understand. He therefore undertook a number of 'demonstrations' to show the routine use of the documentary method by members. These consisted of attempts to disrupt the usual flow of specific, but nonetheless commonplace, social interactions, by introducing a strange element into it. These demonstrations showed that participants thought more about how they were making themselves accountable; that the co-incumbent had not understood or had mistaken what they had said. Hence, they searched for a means to normalize the disruption by looking for the sense of what was going on. The result, Garfinkel shows, is that social reality is not easily broken; it is not something that can collapse at any time, but is a phenomenon that people continuously work at maintaining through the methods they employ to interpret what goes on around them.

Coleman (1968) failed to realize the purpose of the demonstrations. He approached them with the mindset of Cartesian dualism. This is the approach that assumes there exists a hidden reality behind events that manifest themselves in the world. Therefore Coleman criticizes Garfinkel on two points. First, he criticizes Garfinkel for not telling his readers the real meaning of the actions he describes. He wants from Garfinkel an explanation and not a description. This is because he expects to find inference, generalization and reference to hidden structures, parts of the explanatory framework common to traditional sociology. Secondly, Colemen is critical of *Studies* for not correcting what he considers to be the narrow and partial point of view actors have. If Garfinkel had aimed to provide an explanatory account of the meaning of the behaviours he reports in *Studies* then Coleman might have cause to complain. But Garfinkel had no such aim. His aims are very different from those of conventional sociology, because his phenomenon for investigation and the nature of his interest is not that of traditional sociology. Garfinkel makes no distinction between appearance and reality; he wants no part in providing 'corrections' to actors' views of the world. Hence, a predominant feature of *Studies* is the complete lack of theorizing and interpretation. Garfinkel's interest is in how members themselves theorize about the world; it is this phenomenon that he aims to describe. Hence *Studies* is descriptive, the studies never rise above the phenomenon under consideration; Garfinkel's descriptions are *of* rather than *about* the phenomenon of accounting practices.

We have mentioned in the previous section that an important defining feature of *Studies* is Garfinkel's policy of methodological indifference (attitude to ethical issues). This policy is about recommending that we describe rather than judge actors' views and actions. Garfinkel makes it clear that he is not concerned with validating, criticizing, correcting or providing any other form of warrant to any view of the world. Therefore, we find that there is no moral basis to his work: Garfinkel is indifferent to all kinds of knowledge. For him, all kinds of social activity are a topic for study including the work of other sociologists. This is because his interest is in how members make the kind of sense they do in the way that they do. As a consequence, Garfinkel has no interest in issues that concern traditional sociological research, such as sample size and selection, inference or generality.

Methodological indifference is often mistakenly seen as a refusal to debate methodological issues or take seriously the scientific status of sociology and the problem of data. If we criticize Garfinkel on this policy we, too, will commit the same errors in understanding as Colemen (1968) and the former president (Cosser, 1975) of the American Sociological Association. We will have failed to realize that Garfinkel suspends the general principle explaining social order through generalization. His focus is on the local, *ad hoc* production of social order as it is done by members in natural settings. This focus largely prohibits conventional specification of research design. However, it does not prohibit serious thought about the nature of the phenomenon and what research policies might be useful for its investigation. It is these policies for the study of the phenomenon of social order that we have been discussing.

Up to a point we have provided answers to the questions we set at the beginning of this example and have illustrated the main elements from Figure 3.1 In doing this we have touched on some things rather than others, and we could have gone into more detail than we have. This is because any review, not only a short example like this one, is necessarily selective. We could have explored the distinction we mentioned between explanation and description or sought to provide a history of the antecedent ideas that led Garfinkel to create ethnomethodology. But these were not germane to our purpose, which was to show that even the most difficult of work requires an inquiring attitude to the work other theorists have produced, in order that we may understand the methodological reasoning they have employed. The way in which we have gone about this, as you should now be able to appreciate, was guided by a particular goal and framework. The goal was to produce an appraisal of Garfinkel's sociological reasoning. An important point to note here is that you do not have to agree with the style or approach a theorist uses in order to appreciate what they have done. As we said at the beginning of this section, this is one of the reasons we chose *Studies*: Garfinkel's work, especially his style, is not something many people would naturally take a liking to. In terms of the framework we have used, our review has hinged on the use of contrast. We used the criticisms made by Coleman (1968) as a focal point with which to compare and contrast Garfinkel's sociological reasoning with that of traditional sociological reasoning. Therefore, our brief example has taken the approach of providing therapy to misunderstanding. It has attempted to show the kinds of choices that theorists make when undertaking investigation of the social world, and how those choices have implications for the types of research that is produced, as well as how it is presented.

EXAMPLE B   COMMUNITY STUDIES

Extracts from Payne (1993: 1–6).

Before we can 'revisit' the community study, we have first to locate it, but unlike physical places, the community study is a social construction which is highly adaptable, transportable and indeed, transient. It is one thing to know what and where it used to be: Frankenberg (1966) or Bell and Newby (1971) are useful as original Baedeckers in helping to map and access the early locations. It is another thing to position more recent studies and to understand the research imaginations that create them, and are created by them.

The author sets out the purpose for his review by mentioning some of the problems of defining community. He identifies some starting points and notes that community studies have a history. Some sources are identified that will provide guides to the literature.

Once a sketch map has been drawn, the revisiting can begin. In this brief re-exploration, we shall be less interested in the perennial questions of the definition of community, or the sociological purpose of studying 'communities', as with four questions of research methodology and imagination. Why is it that, from most sociological accounts, communities seem so full of such *nice* people? Why are small settlements apparently so receptive of middle-class sociologists, and yet remain so hostile to other 'incomers'? How can sociologists know if their fieldwork is representative and comprehensive? And how can the sociologist evaluate whether a given finding is characteristic of 'communities', rather than of wider British society?

A tourist map is the analogy for the review, showing different locations and interest points along the way.

A number of questions are asked in order to orient the reader to the terrain.

Rediscovering the community study

After becoming a mainstream strength of British sociology in the 1950s and 1960s, community research rapidly became no more than a backwater interest by the 1970s. The familiar successes of Rees (1950), Williams (1956), Dennis et al. (1956), Young and Willmott (1957), Frankenberg (1957 and 1966), Stacey (1960), Littlejohn (1964), Rex and Moore (1969), etc. found little echo in the following decade. To some extent victims of their own success (what more was there to discover about the social life of small settlements?), criticized for spatial determinism and inadequate theorization by Dennis (1958), Gans (1964), Pahl (1968) and Stacey (1969), they were swept aside by the tide of expansion and specialization of the discipline that began in this country in the mid-1960s (Payne et al., 1981: 95–9).

Subsection title

Chronological arrangement is used along with a contrast structure to show the popularity of community studies, their seeming decline and little impact on future work.

Indication of early criticisms of community studies, and the specialization of sociology is given as part of the reason.

It is important to recognize that community research did not completely cease during this shift in sociological fashion. It also evolved so that we had fewer studies of 'social places', and more accounts of problems studied in a location.

Seeming decline attributed to a change in focus of community studies.

A decade after Newby's observation, Day and Murdock saw little sign of this gap having been filled:

Shows that little was done in over a decade to fill the knowledge gap.

> Bell and Newby's textbook account of this tradition (1971) turned out to be in effect its death knell. Rather than inspiring a new wave of case studies in community research, it seemed to provide ample justification for ignoring past work of the kind. (1993: 83–4)

Beginning to see the use of testimony to shape the map.

They quote a voice from social geography in support: relatively little of social scientific value could be said to have been bequeathed to later generations of researchers either by the concept of community or the methodology of community studies (Cooke, 1988).

Use of sources from other disciplines.

An alternative interpretation can be found at the anthropological end of the discipline. By the mid-1980s, Cohen could reflect that whereas in the 1970s there had been a paucity of studies, things had since improved:

The 'however' movement is used to show that there was an alternative view of what had been happening in the area of community studies.

> the problem we faced on the occasion of this present book was, therefore, quite different: we were confronted by an embarrassment of riches. Research seemed to be going on apace throughout the British Isles, in cities and countryside, on the remote periphery and in commuter villages. (Cohen, 1986: viii)

Bulmer had also been cautiously optimistic the year before, perceiving some sign that the study of localities is being revived (1985: 433). While another study could see 'a lively upsurge of locality and community studies in Britain (Warwick and Littlejohn, 1992: xv).

More testimony using a positive attitude in contrast to the negative attitude of the previous ones.

Are these assessments . . . to be believed? On the whole, the answer should be yes. In the first place, several successful and very recognizable community studies had taken place, such as Brody's work on Inishkillane (1973), Stacey's revisit to Banbury (1975), Strathern's anthropology of Elmdon (1981), Giarchi's description of Troon (1984), or the fifteen or so studies reported by Cohen (1982, 1986). Other, less well-known work includes Stephenson (1984), Holme (1985), Fraser (1987), Morris (1987), Macleod (1990), Dean (1990), Goudy (1990) and Borland et al. (1992). These range over communal patterns of kinship, housing, migration, politics, drinking, religion, social control, localism, identity and cultural survival – for the most part the familiar themes of the earlier tradition of the 1950s and 1960s. In addition, there were several studies that were arguably not quite community studies, but which examined issues by looking at their manifestations in particular localities and which took these localities very

A question-and-answer is used to take the side of the positive view of community studies. More citations are given to provide evidence.

Links shown to previous studies; themes are said to be the same.

Citations to studies that have interesting titles, that are said to be about community, but are not classified as community studies.

seriously. Examples of this trend are Moore's 'The social impact of oil' (1982), Davies's description of 'The Evangelistic bureaucrat' (1972), Dennis's concern over 'People and planning' (1970), Pryce's report on the 'Endless pressure' of ghetto life (1979), MacKinnon's study of 'Language, education and social processes in a Gaelic community' (1977) or Wengler's account (1984) in rural Wales: 'The supportive network'.

Next door to the community study

On this brief and by no means exhaustive review, it seems reasonable to claim that the community study is tolerably alive and well, and living in British sociology (albeit in a less fashionable or visible part of town). One reason for this survival has been that wider sociological concerns could be examined in specific sites (Moore, Davies, Dennis, Pryce, MacKinnon, Wengler). Another reason is that processes external to sociology put community back on the research agenda, as in the work of Martin Bulmer. On the one hand, his contributions can be seen as a development of his early career experience in the sociology department at Durham (Bulmer, 1978), a department which produced a series of local studies such as Moore (1974), Taylor (1979), Williamson (1982), and also Bulmer (1975). On the other hand, his work in the mid-1980s (e.g. Bulmer, 1986, 1987) was also related to the fresh stimulus of Peter Wilmott (1983, 1986) and Clare Wengler (1984) which marked the rediscovery of local systems as a potential basis for 'community care'. The setting of a new political agenda for social policy, in which a government that did not believe in the existence of society, set about decanting the mentally ill and others into the care of 'the community' sharpened interest in kinship, networks and neighbouring.

A parallel political stimulus led to the rediscovery of the mining community, namely the miners' strike in 1984–85. Drawing on the experiences of strikers and their wives, a number of sociological and polemical accounts appeared in the following years: Gibbon and Steyne, 1986; Parker, 1986; Samuel et al., 1986; Seddon, 1986; Allen, 1989; Winterton and Winterton, 1989; Gilbert, 1992 and Warwick and Littlejohn, 1992 (who also record the growth of something of a 'Featherstone history industry'; see Evans, 1984; Berry and Williams, 1986; Clayton et al., 1990). These are neither all 'conventional' community studies nor produced within normal canons of social scientific work, but draw on the idea of the community, communal sentiment, and in some cases specifically on contrasts and continuities with the classic study, 'Coal is our life'.

A third area of development was the shift away from the community *per se* towards the idea of 'locality'. This has taken two forms. One is in the field of social geography, where there has been less antagonism towards space as

The point of the previous section is emphasized: community studies is still a major form of research. Note how studies classified on the fringe of the category are cited as a reason for the continuation of community studies research.

We see an adaptation of the definition of community studies to include studies of locality. In the next paragraph note how the notion of locality study is consolidated as an important development of community studies.

The miners' strike of the early 1980s is used to chronologically locate studies of locality. The gender dimension is mentioned. However, strong links are made with a classic community study, 'Coal is our life'.

These studies are said to have revived awareness of the concept, community.

We are taken further into the notion of locality with a subdivision.

a variable in social action. Although there have been debates about the status of space as a causal explanation of social relations, interest in where things happen has not weakened. Space and locality are seen as elements within broader and more general social theory, which call attention to the kinds of sub-cultural variation that Newby sought (above). The work of the Changing Urban and Regional Systems Initiative (e.g. Cooke, 1989) and others like Soja (1989) kept locality on the research agenda in social geography.

Other concepts are introduced such as space. But emphasis is given to broader social theory that is used to explain geographical variation.

The second source of interest in locality within sociology was the study of the restructuring of industry and employment. This included work that connected directly with the social geographers (e.g. Gregory and Urry, 1985) as well as the explorations of economic life funded by the ESRC. For example, the study of economic change and labour market suggested how through the notion of 'occupational communities' (e.g. Salaman, 1974)

Variation in social relations between different localities is linked to economic change, which is one of the factors underpinning studies of mining areas.

> change in industrial structure affects the nature of community. . . . Historically and in certain locations, such as mining and textile townships, the job recruit-ment process creates a strong link between work and residence and between work relationships and commu-nity relationships. An aim of research is thus to explore the nature of the link between work and community under contemporary conditions. (Roberts et al., 1985: 7)

The idea of communities linked to occupation is followed.

The Social Change and Economic Life Initiative (SCELI) was also concerned with changes in production, work patterns, and household formation and strategies because . . . SCELI concentrated on studies *in* localities, rather than *of* localities (Aberdeen, Kirkcaldy, Roch-dale, Coventry, Swindon and Northampton), but these included 'household and community' surveys and some locally specific studies. It would be wrong to call these community studies: rather we see that in these and similar studies, the physical location of social relations is not irrelevant to those social relations, nor to the development of our ideas about the interconnection of work, the informal economy, households and networks (e.g. Pahl, 1984; Bell and McKee, 1985; Morris, 1988; Beynon, 1992; Stanley, 1992; etc.). Their emphasis, however, is on the interconnections with wider social forces, and to a large extent these researches based in a locality represent the alternative and evolved perspec-tive that has replaced the more traditional community study as a sociological fashion.

A distinction is made between studies in, and studies of, localities. The question is why this distinction made.

The answer provided is that recent studies are in localities and form an alternative to, not a replacement for, traditional community studies.

Relocating the community study

'Community' is more than just the inclusion of space in the analysis of social relations. One can think of the studies discussed above as ranged on a continuum from the single researcher doing an ethnography of an isolated (rural) settlement – such as the contributors to Cohen (1982); Brody, (1974); Macleod, (1992) or Giarchi,

The map given of the terrain now allows for the major statement that the author wants to focus on – what he has classified as 'pure' commu-nity studies.

(1984) – to the team using social surveys to explore the manifestation of economic restructuring in a given location or region (e.g. Roberts, 1985 or Gallie, 1988b). In between are a variety of studies which to a greater or lesser extent are issue-based (e.g. Moore, 1984), localized (Stacey et al., 1975), ethnographic (Gibbon and Steyne, 1986) done by individuals or teams (Warwick and Littlejohn, 1992) and explicitly related to the origins of the idea of community (Strathern, 1981).

This sketch map suggests four characteristics with which to locate studies about communities.

(a) is the research carried out by a large team or one or two researchers?
(b) is it predominantly qualitative or quantitative in style?
(c) is the 'community' an identifiable settlement or simply an administrative creation?
(d) is it concerned primarily with aspects of community *per se*, as against wider social processes which just happen to be manifested locally?

There is nothing absolute about these four questions. Their function is to provide a framework for thinking about a large number of differing studies. In the case of this paper, for instance, we wish to concentrate more on a 'purer' type of community study. In connecting Dennis et al. or Frankenberg to Cohen, one does not wish to exclude other studies but rather explain why one subset can, for particular purposes, be more relevant than another.

The inclusion of methodological style illustrates the flexibility of the framework. Key studies like Young and Willmott used a range of methods: indeed the first edition made great play of the latest technology of the IBM card counter/sorter (Platt, 1971; Payne et al., 1981). Brody's sensitive account of Inishkillane starts with a review based on historical and literary documents. Warwick and Littlejohn draw both on surveys and historical statistics, and pull together medical researchers, archivists, adult education classes and SCELI support (1992: xiv–xv). There is no reason to ignore their valuable contribution just for that, even if the main concern here lies in the research carried out by individuals using qualitative methods.

One purpose of this orienting framework is to explain how this paper concentrates on the more 'typical' community study, making links between some of the classics and some of the more recent studies. The observations which follow arise directly from doing that kind of single-handed ethnography, but to some extent they can be generalized to the other kinds of study. Two examples of such generalization are the interconnected ideas of visual appearance, and the way the immediacy of issues changes over time.

At the same time he wants alternative studies to be recognized as important, but different from his interests.

A summative formulation is provided as a means for the reader to characterize the different types of research identified as community studies.

This acts to reinforce the authors' classification and differentiation of what he has categorized as 'pure' community studies.

With the case made, due consideration for the treatment of other studies is emphasized.

A short adjoiner: emphasizing the flexibility of the approaches to community studies reinforces the author argument about the value of community studies research.

Conclusion of what the review has attempted to achieve.

Although the single researcher is mentioned the link is again made to generalizability of single researcher and their work.

GENERAL COMMENTS

The structure of this review displays an argumentational purpose. The author has the intent of persuading his reader that community studies are an important and productive avenue of research. This he does through a technique that we might call the 'implied reader'. By this we mean that Payne seems to imply that some people hold to the assumption that community studies are a thing of the past, with no relevance for research today. Hence he sets up an argument to correct this implied assumption by an implied reader. The review, therefore, uses the stance of 'contrary to popular belief. . .'. The reader is taken through a range of material that cites many works which are classified to show a continuity in the study of community. The use of definition is a major resource in achieving the sense of continuity. The term 'locality' is used to argue that studies of locality are studies of communities.

EXAMPLE C   LITERATURE REVIEW: CONVERGENCE OF LIBRARY AND COMPUTING SERVICES

Extracts from Bolton (1997).

Historical perspective

Convergence emerged as a theory in the mid-1980s. However, Sutherland suggests that its real birth place can be traced back to the 1960s in the United States.[4] The period witnessed the development of a number of co-ordinated approaches in schools and educational training institutions. Reflective of this early evolutionary period was the article written by A.D. Veaner in a 1974 issue of the *Journal of Library Automation*. The article highlighted what proponents of convergence claim to be is one of the primary reasons for its attraction; the growing similarity in the roles of both the library and computer departments within academic institutions.

The subheading sets out the historical focus for this section of the review.
The point is made that convergence is not a recent development.

Some definitions of what convergence is might have been helpful even if definitions had already been given elsewhere.
In the citations there is no need to use initials.

> 'Close examination of the library and computer faculty gives evidence that both deal with the same commodity: information. . . several institutions have recently coalesced the library and computer centre organizational.'[5]

In long quotations there is no need to use quotation (speech) marks.

Note the use of the numerical system.

Veaner correctly identified that primary to the movement towards converged support services was an appreciation that with the developments made in the field of networking, a greater commonality existed between computer and library departments. Whilst computer departments ran the technical side of the network, the library should control what information

The author shows agreement with the position being described. But the reason for this is not explained.

The use of the word should is a

was put over it. American institutions, being more technologically advanced than their British counterparts, realized the potential more quickly as a result. It was not however until 1986, that a marked shift towards the development of converged support services started to happen in earnest. It began with the implementation of a converged support service at Carnegie Mellon University, Pittsburgh, as part of the university's high cost in technological investment programme: Computing by Immersion. Patricia Battin followed suit at Columbia University with the mapping of a new Scholarly Information Centre and the merger of the library and the academic and computer service departments. In an article published in the EDUCOM Bulletin 1984, Battin called for: '. . . the information of a scholarly information centre by merging libraries and computer centres to provide an information infrastructure that will provide a one-stop shopping community and a stabilizing mechanism for effective and flexible response to rapidly changing technologies'.[6]

value statement that either ought to be avoided or be clearly explained with the use of evidence. This is because a claim is part of an argument.

The international contrast is a demonstration of reading, helping to focus attention onto events in the UK.

The year 1986 is put forward as a key year. The claim that American university libraries converged services earlier than their British counterparts is given substance with the use of verifiable examples.

A key author is mentioned along with a simple analogy.

In 1986 Barbara Higginbotham produced an article that supported the work and doctrine of Molholt and Battin. The article concluded with a prediction of the likely duplication of resources available in both computing centres and libraries because of the increasing similarity in each other's role. This would almost certainly cause confusion to their customers about which service to use and for what purpose. The net result was predicted to be an ineffective and inefficient support service. Higginbotham finished by suggesting:

Reference to a supporting article is used but the use of the word doctrine *may be misplaced. However, how Higginbotham's article supports prior views is difficult to see given that it seems to be critical of those views.*

> Academic institutions should provide a single support service of professionals knowledgeable about a variety of information resources, as well as the technologies and software that will help them organize or manipulate the information.[7]

The description of Higginbotham's work, if it is supposed to be significant, is insufficiently explained.

1987 witnessed Diane Cimbala's publication of her vision for the scholarly information centre based loosely on staff patterns outlined by Higginbotham. She considered however that, due to barriers created by the different service cultures, and practical obstacles over skills and professional structures, any change would be within a long evolutionary process.[8]

Following the chronological arrangement succeeding work is introduced. There is no need to use an author's first name. In a short paragraph a substantial amount of information is provided that requires amplification.

Whilst the debate in America forged on, it is not surprising that the issue in Britain did not take shape until 1988. The efforts of Colin Harris at Salford University, Ivan Sidgreaves at the University of Plymouth, and Patricia Kelly at Limerick in reorganizing support service structures within their respective institutions along converged lines, went some way to prompting the debate in Britain.

Institutions where convergence took place are mentioned, but the relationship between them and the names included are not explained.

A.G. Williams cites the publication of the British Journal of Academic Librarianship (BJAL) in 1988 as holding

The use of an author's initials is incorrect. Identification of a

special historical significance in being the first journal edition devoted to the topic of convergence.[9] It included an excellent exposition of the issues involved by Bernard Naylor and a series of case studies from converged institutions at Plymouth, Limerick, Salford and Carnegie Mellon. The case studies were written by senior protagonists and reflect on how and why converged structures were introduced. The decision-making process is articulated and major obstacles are highlighted. The studies published are highly relevant as primary source data but do not go into any real depth on the problems faced and how they were resolved.

professionally oriented journal that had a special edition shows the ways in which debates tend to be published in journals before they are published in monographs. The journal's title might have been italicized.

Insufficient attempt is made to assess the importance of articles found in the journal.

The key period within the debate in Britain however is from 1992 to 1994. The period witnessed the publication of a number of key studies, articles and conferences in this area. In 1992 Sutherland[10] published what is considered to be the most extensive study on this issue. The research was initially undertaken on behalf of the then Middlesex Polytechnic. Middlesex Polytechnic was considering a convergence of a number of their support services and felt that a broad ranging investigation into the experiences of other institutions in this area would be advantageous. The investigation was undertaken through a literature review and interviews at a number of institutions. Especially pertinent to this dissertation is the inclusion of recommendations and guidelines for institutions considering a structural re-organization of their support services. Many of these issues will be reflected on during the discussion document.

A period is identified as being important. This is justified in terms of the increase of publications on the topic.

A key landmark study is identified, but insufficient details are given about it, especially any implications it may have had on the debate. A discussion (critical evaluation) of the recommendations said to be included in the appendix would have been useful.

In 1992 the second IUCC/SCONUL conference took place. Williams cites this event as being significant, not for the number of papers published referencing convergence (only three), but because it illustrated how seriously computing and library managers were considering service re-organization.[11] In addition, for the first time in Britain, senior figures within the computing service aired their views on the subject.

Presumably the abbreviations were explained at the beginning of the dissertation. The number 11 needed to go after the reference to Williams, e.g. 'Williams[11] . . .'.
The reference to senior figures needed explaining. References were needed along with an indication (signposts) as to the nature of their views.

Further indication of the growing interest in convergence were the seminars held in September 1993 and 1994 for library and information service managers of conveyed support services. Figures from Sidgreaves[12] indicate that in the first year fifteen managers attended. By the following year the figure had risen to twenty five, with a further five unable to attend.

The review continues to employ a chronological arrangement. The use of increasing numbers attending conferences is effectively used to indicate the growing interest in the topic.

Recognition from established bodies came with the publication of the Library Association's Guidelines: Implications of Convergence for Academic Libraries in October 1992, and the Fielden report published in 1994 as part of the major review undertaken by Sir Brian Follett into library provision within the higher education sector.

Recognition of the topic by a professional body is shown as being important. The title of the document could have been italicized. A key landmark document for higher education is also mentioned showing awareness of the larger picture.

The guidelines produced by the Library Association were extremely broad and lacked any real detail. The three page document provided little that could not be found in more detailed expositions in one of the journal articles. However, it is worthy of recognition for symbolic purposes, if only by the fact of its production. The Library Association felt that the issue of convergence held such significance for its members that it had to make its official position known.

Presumably this is a reference to the British Library Association. As the main professional body for the library profession, more needed to be said about the Association's position by critically evaluating the content of their document.

The Fielden report was significant however, not only for its symbolism, but also for its substance. It is the document that has probably had the greatest impact on the provision of converged support services. It draws on a large amount of quantifiable data extracted from a variety of sources: a major library and information service university survey, a literature review, and visits and interviews with senior post-holders within the academic library environment. Whilst only one section is solely devoted to the convergence of information support services, other areas within the report, such as staff implications and training, do directly relate to the issue. The report initially identifies key issues and developments within the academic library environment, then goes on to outline convergence as an organizational theory. Whilst outlining a variety of converged support service models, Fielden simply breaks them down into sweeping definitions; operational and organizational convergence. Operational convergence is described in terms of the merger of two or more services through a mutuality of roles and responsibilities within an informal, non-converged management structure. Organizational convergence is in practical terms non-converged. That is to say that services are not merged operationally although they are integrated within a management structure.

The claim that the Fielden report has 'symbolism' is not explained.

The report is, however, given sufficient space for explanation including an overview of the research on which it was based.

Fielden makes a series of broad assumptions based on the experiences of British, American and Australian institutions. The prime assertions for consideration are the increase in the number of converged services, and the use of para-professionals. One of his principal suppositions is that professionals will spend more time in consultation with academic staff, producing learning packages and other material, and tutoring in information skills. This will create a void, leading to the employment of more para-professionals, with both side ranging computing and library skills, to fill the gap. The three major groups affected, and their re-aligned roles outlined are: senior managers, professional/subject librarians, and library assistants/para-professionals.[16]

The claim is made that the Fielden report makes assertions. These are identified but not critically assessed.

The reasons why the Fielden report makes certain suppositions is not explained and hence not evaluated.

One of the most interesting trends predicted is the transference of the theory into the area of teaching, with the anticipated convergence of support services with the academic community. An increased emphasis has already been placed on user support and the teaching of information skills by library professionals.[17]

Far too much (too many ideas/topics) is contained within this paragraph. The individual topics needed to be distinguished using separate paragraphs.

Encouragement from the state, for a greater emphasis to be placed on the role of the professional librarian outside the library and into the classroom, has seen a parallel trend emerging within the school education sector in recent years. Schools will find this of increasing importance with the education sector placing a greater emphasis on the medium of technology, and with the growth of material published over the internet. The logical result is that libraries, as information specialists, will become more extensively utilized by the teaching establishment. It is not unreasonable to expect a similar evolution to emerge within the higher education sector.

Claims are made that are said to be interesting, but insufficient reason and material are provided to substantiate the claims. This might have been achieved by expanding on the implications that are mentioned.

Finally during the 1992 to 1994 period came the publication of the 1994 Relay edition on convergence.[18] Its publication was inspired directly by the heightened interest in convergence. Evidence of this came from the spate of letters to the *Times Higher Educational Supplement* in response to a strongly worded letter from Fred Ratcliffe and David Hartley,[19] criticizing the trends toward converged support services. The edition of Relay included an excellent exposition of the prominent issues within the debate by Ivan Sidgreaves. It also contained a series of lucid replies from several quarters of the higher education sector, two librarians and one academic. The replies offered a number of differing viewpoints within the debate due to the varying background and experience of the correspondents.

The chronology is brought up to date with a useful reference on how the debate has entered the public arena.

References critical to the policy of convergence are mentioned. The character of the criticism could have been outlined to signpost what they were about.

Issues

One of the things to be drawn from the review of the literature was the recurrence of a number of the major themes on both sides of the debate. We shall now examine these to provide the necessary overview for the discussions and interviews which follow in . . .

The subheading 'Issues' implied that the brevity of the history section will now be expanded on, to look in more detail at the arguments and implications of differing positions within the debate. The expectation is, therefore, that now some ground work has been done, what will follow will be analysis, evaluation and synthesis.

One of the major issues to arise within the debate, and expanded upon by Veaner and Battin, concerns the usage, and rapid developments, made in technology. Proponents of converged services, such as I. Sidgreaves,[20] suggest that the rapid development in information technology, and its increasing transference into the library, has effected a fundamental change within the information environment. Automated library systems for housekeeping, CD-ROMs, and networked access to the internet have become commonplace in academic libraries. The library has subsequently become increasingly dependent upon information technology. The internet for example, has gripped the imagination of the information environment because of its tremendous storage and retrieval opportunities. Linked to this is the emergence of the 'access versus holdings' debate; is it more effective and practical to provide remote access to information sources rather than maintaining the traditional physical collection in the library itself. The debate has been prompted by four factors:

This and the next four paragraphs give an indication of the reasons for convergence. This is done through the use of short lists and quotes.

The use of a simple example acts as an illustration. This might have been more effective if some numerical data could have been given that indicated quantity.

1 an explosion in the volume of global information
2 technological advances and the realization of the potential that networked information holds
3 lack of storage space in many libraries
4 rising costs of printed materials

Short lists, like this one, can be effective and efficient devices to emphasize factors.

Change has been significant for the library community. For many librarians, the need to develop technical skills in the manipulation of information technology has meant undergoing a re-learning process.

Mirroring this change has been the development of the role of the computer specialist. It has meant a move away from pure data computation, or 'number crunching', on a large, specialist mainframe,[21] towards a more user-focused approach through advancements made in the desktop PC and campus network.

It has been argued by proponents of convergence such as Veaner, that the roles of the services have become closely entwined and will increasingly lead to demarcation concerns over precise areas of service responsibility. In 1990, a survey conducted by Woodsworth and Maylone[22] into issues which were affecting the organizational structure of academic libraries in the USA found that:

> Work is no longer readily identifiable as naturally belonging either in the library or the computer centre. . . . The study found a bell curve; a small number of jobs that were identical, many that were similar in part, and another small number in which there were no similarities.[23]

It is therefore argued that there is a greater necessity for maintaining good communication links between both sets of specialists. If both services were subsumed under one departmental structure, problems over communication and differing priorities would diminish.

The reasons that underpin the argument for convergence are summarized before opponents to the argument are introduced.

Opponents of convergence such as Ted Smith,[24] Pat Crocker[25] and Fred Ratcliffe,[26] claim that the theory is ill-conceived. They maintain that a narrowing of roles should necessitate the convergence of services. For example, a user will still need different elements from each service, requiring both technical and information handling skills.[27] Ted Smith reasons that Fielden's predication of the development of a new 'multi-skilled' support operative, with both specialist library and computing skills, is naive.[28] The problem for both types of specialist is the expanding knowledge base in their respective areas combined with spiralling global information and a rapid increase in the amount of hardware and software packages available.

First names of authors are not needed.

This paragraph gives a succinct overview of the key points in the argument against convergence. It would be expected that each of these points would be explained and amplified in relation to what proponents of the argument have said.

Another major concern that re-occurs throughout the literature is neatly expressed by the sub-heading of Bebbington and Cronin's 1989 article on convergence, 'A clash of cultures'.[29] Sach, in 1986, maintained that a

The use of a heading found in an article provides an idea of the kind of assumption that opponents of convergence use

significant differences in skills, attitudes and cultural outlook, would make any closer working relationship difficult to achieve.[30] This philosophy was backed up the following year by Cimbala who suggested that staff would resist attempts at integration because of historical and practical differences over their respective professions.[31]

as a starting point for their arguments.

GENERAL COMMENTS

The structure of this review shows a concern to map out the growth of interest in developments affecting academic libraries. It uses chronological arrangement to organize the materials selected for inclusion. Unlike the previous literature review we have been critical with this one. We have attempted to point out places where the author might have developed his own argument, provided explanation for claims that he has made and expanded on debates that have been mentioned. This might be the first time that the author has attempted to write a review of literature. As such, he has been careful to use a familiar arrangement and to subsection the material that he has chosen for inclusion. The review, however, assumes too much on behalf of the reader. The descriptions of what those contributing to the data have claimed are too brief and key assumptions, although mentioned, are not examined. Therefore, the review provides only the minimum amount of evidence of critical thought, because it stays too close to the surface of the arguments made. Regarding presentation, certain conventions could have been followed. These include citing all ideas that have been paraphrased rather than just the main ones, not using speech marks on indented quotes, and omitting the initials or first names of authors. These are all small points that can easily be rectified; they otherwise distract from a satisfactory but not good review of the literature.

4

Argumentation analysis

Argument is the spirit of many disciplines. An academic seeing fault, error or other possibilities in the work of another and making suggestions for improvement or change is what makes for what we call progress in the ideas of the social sciences. Being able to recognize the structure and substance of an argument is a necessary ability in everyday life but is especially so for the successful academic researcher. If you cannot see the logic of even the simplest argument then you cannot justify developing the work of another, or suggest alternative courses of action or other ways of explaining something. In this chapter we look at the following questions.

1 What is an argument?
2 How can we understand the structure of an argument?
3 How can arguments be analysed and evaluated?
4 How do arguments relate to the nature of debate in the social sciences?

This chapter is about how to analyse an argument, in particular, those types most commonly found in the social sciences. As can be demonstrated by a visit to the library, almost any article in a social science journal is based on argument and most research is based on one or other position that the researcher has chosen to use as a starting point. Such positions are usually based on what the researcher believes to be the methods for acquiring knowledge about, and a standpoint on, a range of debates. There are, for example, a number of questions social scientists face when undertaking work. Should the researcher inform subjects that they are being studied? Should the researcher remain impartial when the research has a moral element? Should the views of subjects be taken into account? There are many more questions like these that social scientists have to deal with in their work. The main concern in this chapter is with methods for analysing and understanding an argument.

Before looking at two useful approaches to evaluating arguments we will look at what we mean by argument and explain why argument is so important for the social sciences.

An argument involves putting forward reasons to influence someone's belief that what you are proposing is the case (Hinderer, 1992). Whichever way someone makes an argument they are attempting to convince others of the validity (or logic) of how they see the world and convince us that we should see it the way they do. An argument has therefore at least two components: a point and a reason:

- making a point (or statement)
  by
- providing sufficient reason (or evidence) for the point to be accepted by others.

These elements are related and the movement can go either way to form the argument:

- a movement from either a point to reason
  or
- from evidence to conclusion (the point).

The movement from one to the other can be supported by other components called inferential devices. These are rules or principles which permit the making of a claim on the basis of some evidence (or warrants). We will be looking more closely at these later.

In our definitions of the types of argument given below, we exclude arguments based purely on what is called formal logic. Our concern is with those types of arguments most commonly found in the social sciences, based on supposition, inference and assertion. These are much less structured and often more difficult to analyse than arguments based on formal logic. Fisher, whose work we will be looking at shortly, illustrates this point. He defines argument as consisting in 'giving reasons for some conclusion: the reasons are put forward in order to establish, support, justify, prove or demonstrate the conclusion' (1993: 140). He also shows that there are elements in formal logic which are useful to the analysis of assertion and supposition. He states that:

> Every argument . . . contains its reasons and its conclusions: the reasons presented for a conclusion are usually called premisses of the argument. The question the logician is interested in is whether they are good reasons for the conclusion; if they (the premisses) are said to entail or imply the conclusion, and the conclusion is said to follow from the premisses or to be implied or entailed by them. (Fisher, 1993: 140)

Regardless of how many components an argument has or how complex it may be, all arguments are open to question and can be challenged.

Definitions: Inference, assertion and supposition

Inference	An assertion made on the basis of something else observed or taken as knowledge; used in deductive and inductive arguments.
Assertion	A declaration made on the existence or cause of something with or without the use of evidence.
Supposition	An assumption made about what is or is not a case or state of affairs.

THE IMPORTANCE OF ARGUMENT IN THE SOCIAL SCIENCES

Words such as *logic, valid, premiss, reliable, reason* and *conclusion* make up the vocabulary of argument. A whole discipline has developed, dedicated to logic and the search for undeniable propositions. It is not necessary to be an expert in formal logic or philosophy to construct and analyse arguments. But why should social scientists take an interest in logic and argument? There are so many reasons for understanding argument that we could write another book. However, the main reasons are outlined in the following list.

- A great deal of research is done in the social sciences by researchers who might, for the sake of illustration, be classified as interactionist, linguist, feminist, Marxist, ethnomethodologist, post-structuralist, behaviourist and so on. Researchers working within these and other approaches tend to hold different or differing opinions on the nature of reality (ontology) and how knowledge can be acquired of that reality (epistemology), and therefore what counts as valid knowledge. Hence, we have the basis for debate and argument in the social sciences.
- Many social scientists are particularly knowledgeable about the complexities and implications of holding one view rather than another about what counts as social science. Hence, they are able to understand the different types of argument and the implications of different standpoints. This enables them to be active participants in the debates that characterize the social sciences.
- To many people the debates that go on between social scientists seem esoteric and this often leads to bewilderment and confusion. Social scientists often do not make clear the origins of their ideas or explain the rationale of them. Students are left wondering what a debate is *really* about and why people invest so much time and effort into them. However, if we take the premiss that differences of opinion over matters such as the interpretation of data, the meaning of concepts, the validity of knowledge, and the topic for inquiry, are the basis of scientific progress, then there is a need to be able to understand and analyse argument.

An understanding of the origins of logic can be a useful knowledge base from which to start argumentation analysis and understand the importance of debate to the social sciences. In this section we look at the classical traditions of argument and at some of the forms that debate has taken in the social sciences.

INDUCTIVE AND DEDUCTIVE LOGIC

For the Greeks logic was not a theoretical or abstract pastime. Aristotelian logic aimed to set criteria for proper scientific thinking. The approach was essentially one of deduction (as opposed to induction).

***Definition*: Deduction**

It is commonly a statement or theory whose truth or falsity is known in advance of experience or observation (a priori: prior to experience) – referring to instances of reasoning in which the conclusion follows from the premisses. Deduction (or inference) can proceed from the general to particular, general to general and particular to particular.

***Definition*: Induction**

This is commonly a statement whose truth or falsity is made more probable by the accumulation of confirming evidence (a posteriori: based on experience) – referring to instances of reasoning in which statements are made about a phenomenon based on observations of instances of that phenomenon. It consists in arguing that because all instances of *a* so far observed have the property *b*, all further observations of *a* will also have the property *b*.

The deductive approach dominated until the sixteenth century when challenges were made to it, and other forms of systematic thinking began to develop. One of the more pervasive forms was positivism. This led to a more abstract approach to logic, based on mathematical concepts. Twentieth-century philosophers such as Bertrand Russell and Alfred Whitehead aimed to construct universal systems of logic. Positivism however, failed to provide the basis for a universal scheme of fundamental descriptive laws from which predictions could be made.

Positivism

The idea that logic could be used as the basis of a method for investigating the nature of the world took hold during the Enlightenment in the eighteenth century. From the aim to uncover the laws that governed the workings of the universe a view of what constituted reality (ontology) and of knowing about that reality (epistemology) developed into a standpoint that we commonly call the attitude of scientific inquiry. In part, this involved a particular doctrine applied to the method of science, which consisted of a set of principles about how scientific (i.e. valid and reliable) knowledge could be acquired. Table 4.1 shows the main principles and what they mean.

It was the logical positivists (e.g. Carnap, 1929; Ayer, 1946; Hempel, 1965; Schlick, 1949) associated with the Vienna Circle of the 1920s who are mostly responsible for the debate on and about positivism, along with Wittgenstein (1972) and Popper (1959). For the logical positivists, science was concerned with the problem of verifying, using reliable methods, the meaning or existence of something. They tried to limit inquiry and belief to those things that could be firmly established. Hence, ideas about aesthetics,

Table 4.1   *Principles of the scientific method*

Principles	What they mean
Observation	Only that which can be observed can be measured. All basic concepts must be clearly defined, for example, what is meant by length and what is to be measured, before they can be used (operationalized). Systematic observation is therefore necessary for science.
Hypothesis formulation	On the basis of systematic observation, the scientist formulates a hypothesis (a proposition) that explains what has been observed.
Experimentation	The hypothesis is tested to ascertain its truth. This involves attempting to verify the hypothesis by trying to show the hypothesis is wrong (i.e. falsifiability). Hence if the hypothesis cannot be shown to be wrong, it must be true.
Scientific laws	From the results of experimentation, general explanations (or laws) can be developed that wholly or partly explain particular phenomena, for example, the law of gravity.
Theory formulation	The discovery of particular laws can lead to the development of more general theories (or models) that enable more things to be explained using a unified approach.
Flexibility	If new evidence is found that falsifies or changes an explanation the scientist should acknowledge this and change the law and theory.
Replicability	The procedures used, including definitions of main concepts along with data, should be open for other scientists to scrutinize, thereby enabling others to replicate the work.
Objectivity	Scientists should be neutral observers of the world and not concern themselves with morality or ethics, nor should they be motivated by anything other than the pursuit of knowledge.

morality, ethics, judgement and religion were assigned to metaphysics – as being outside the interest of, what they took to be, proper logical empirical science (see Hospers, 1988; Trigg, 1993).

Debate in the social sciences

The standpoint that positivism (especially logical positivism) demanded from science was questioned by scientists wanting to investigate the social world. Many social scientists were particularly keen to rid themselves of the stricter forms of positivism. Social order, patterns of social relationships and modes of thinking did not fit with the belief that there was only one absolute logic and one form of approach to rational understanding (i.e. truth). The connection between human reasoning and the procedures of positivistic science therefore came to be a subject for debate. In opposition to this position called absolutism, it was proposed that there were many logics. This counter-position, known as relativism, found expression in such areas as linguistic semantics and psychology. For example, Piaget and Inhelder (1955) argued that the variety and complexity of natural language and behaviour implied that there was no single logic, but that there might be a range of acquired rules, encoded in the brain, that people follow. Hence, what could be considered rational, logical and even the truth are matters for debate.

Logic became seen as normative: that standards of behaviour follow cultural conventions rather than ideal standards of rationality established by formal logic (Turner, 1984). In economics, for example, models and theories were developed to describe real life decision-making (Simon, 1957). Examples and illustrations were devised and case studies undertaken to show how real decision-making deviates from rational models: what actually happened compared with what ought to have happened in an ideal situation. The aim was to improve decision making by identifying key variables that all effective decisions needed. In this way some theorists, such as Cohen (1986), maintain the usefulness of normative logic because it provides what they consider to be an ideal standard for comparison.

Not all social scientists, however, aimed to produce comparisons of everyday logic with that of science. The anthropologist Edward Evans-Pritchard (1902–73), for example, undertook a study of the Azande people from southern Sudan (1937). His interest was with the mental life of what were then commonly called 'primitives'. Contemporary views held the position that tribal peoples tended to have a primitive mentality: they were intellectual inferiors to Europeans. Comparing Western scientific logic with the superstitions and myths of tribal people was the norm for research. Evans-Pritchard's fieldwork refuted this comparison and belief; it demolished the divide between 'us' and 'them'.

Evans-Pritchard did this by focusing on the mythical beliefs and practices of the Azande. The defining feature for Azande life was the pervasive belief in witchcraft and sorcery. For example, no Azande would venture out on a journey or similar undertaking without first consulting an oracle. The purpose was to see if any misfortune would be likely to befall them on a journey, or to see if anyone had bewitched them. To European science, this kind of belief was not a religion or the basis of logical thought; it was a measure of the primitiveness of tribal societies. Evans-Pritchard opposed this view. He showed that the metaphysical ideas of any society could be treated with the same seriousness as those of any of the great world religions. Added to this he showed that the logic of such beliefs was *situational*, being dependent upon the cultural conventions or ways of viewing the world of particular groups.

Hence Western science, according to Evans-Pritchard, is just one way of understanding the world and although successful in terms of technology it is not the only or dominant form of understanding to be found in human cultures. If we want to understand such beliefs as Azande magic, we need to understand the use and nature of them as experienced by the Azande in their everyday lives. Trying to compare and measure notions about intellectual superiority were, according to Evans-Pritchard, inappropriate due to the fact that Western science and Azande witchcraft are incomparable: they are two different ways of thinking about the world and of organizing daily activities.

Therefore, in terms of our debate, we can identify two key points. The first is that Evans-Pritchard argued that non-literate peoples' apparent irrational (illogical) beliefs formed a coherent and logical system of ideas. The second point is the approach Evans-Pritchard took to understanding the logic of Azande belief and practices. His approach was informed by science. It was based on close observation, questioning and inquiry into what was going on in Azande culture, leading him, and us, to a more balanced, unprejudiced and even objective view of such beliefs. Hence, the procedures of science can help us understand science itself, as well as non-scientific based phenomena, and what could be considered logical.

Through this potted and condensed history of logic we can see how some social scientists have been classified into different camps depending on their degree of allegiance to particular (and somewhat idealized) methodological traditions. Another point to note is that when we talk about different positions we are entering the grey area at the boundary of social science and philosophy: the place where understanding not only becomes difficult, but reveals the reasons for many of the fundamental differences within the social sciences. That locale is the realm of philosophy where questions about the nature of reality and how we can acquire knowledge are the subject-matter.

Many social scientists, however, still hold to a notion of the possibility of positivism. Even those theorists who want to counter the extremes of positivism still have to enter into the debate over positivism. Positivism therefore still exerts a strong influence on the aims and structure of social science thinking and the nature of argument. So we can reiterate our point about the nature of debate in the social sciences by saying that differences are based on different approaches and answers to questions and issues related to methodological policies, perspectives and standpoints to do with research. Table 4.2 (overleaf) summarizes some of the issues for the design of research.

A continuing debate exists, therefore, between many different camps about what we should use as the standpoint for thinking about and investigating the social world. We can clarify this debate without over-simplifying it by saying that there are two main protagonists, realists and the anti-realists. Realists take the positivist line that there is a world to be investigated which exists independent of human belief, perception, culture and language: reality and truth are therefore to be uncovered or dis-covered. Anti-realists take a different view. They believe that the world exists, but its character and the ways we understand it are constructed and shaped by the language we use to describe it. What we take as reality is, according to anti-realists, not something that is universal but plural: there are many or multiple realities, each separate and based on different assumptions for understanding.

Table 4.2 *Issues for research design*

What is reality?	*Ontological issues* concerned with what we believe to exist and able to be investigated. For example, what is the subject-matter for psychology? Is reality singular and objective, existing apart from me and my perceptions and cultural biases? Or is reality shaped by my prior understanding and assumptions?
What procedures can be used to establish what can be accepted as real?	*Epistemological issues* concerned with how we can know anything. For example, is my knowledge wholly gained through senses and is therefore objectively real or is my knowledge a matter of how I perceive the world? Can I include intuition, personal experience or only the data to make claims?
What is the process of research that can ensure valid knowledge?	*Methodological issues* concerned with how we can validate what we claim to be knowledge. For example, how can we have a logic of inquiry that gives us assurance in our knowledge? Should we use a deductive or inductive process; aim for generalization and explanation or context-based description aimed at an emerging design, categories and theories? Are we interested in prediction, explanation or understanding?
What is the role of values and ethics?	*Axiological issues* concerned with the personal values, morality and ethics of the researcher. For example, whose side should a researcher be on, if any, the underdog or elite? Should I aim to ignore the moral issues of the subject-matter and my own feeling or use these as part of my research?
What are reliable techniques for collecting data about claims?	*Data-collection issues* concerned with which techniques are the most reliable and which kinds of data the more accurate. For example, is the survey questionnaire better than the observational case study? Shall I use quantitative data rather than qualitative because people regard it as more objective? Or is qualitative evidence better because it will show that all data is dependent on interpretation for its meaning?
What is the language of research?	*Rhetorical issues* concerned with how to talk about and write up research. For example, is writing in the third person more objective than the first person? Should I be formal, precise with definitions and aim to quantify or use informal language that is easier to understand and show how understanding evolved?

Logic, in the broad sense of the term, refers to various forms of reasoning over why one position rather than another should be the one used to study a particular subject-matter. There is no one absolute logic by which universal truths can be determined. In social science, logical reasoning takes a range of forms and is presented in many different styles. The logic of a piece of research or school of researchers is not always explicit, it can be based on unstated methodological assumptions. These assumptions shape the ways in which such researchers approach the social world and how they investigate it and eventually report on their investigations.

Methodological assumptions, like those we attributed to Marx in Chapter 3, are important to understand. This is because they orient a researcher towards certain ways of thinking about the subject-matter in which they are interested and help them to make decisions on how to undertake research. These assumptions frame the view a researcher will have of the meaning and operationalization of concept and influence what they regard as the goals of social science. In this case the dominant goal for Marxist researchers is structural analysis of covert forces and relationships that give rise to manifest inequalities and forms of oppression; theoretical explanatory analysis therefore dominates many Marxist-inspired studies. By understanding the methodological assumptions from which a researcher works you can analyse the use of these in any particular study that claims to have used them. You could compare, for instance, how different Marxist studies have used the concept of alienation. The comparison might seek to analyse the different arguments put forward for why the concept has been used differently from other studies. In this way all approaches, whether they have an explicit argument or not, are open to analysis.

ANALYSING AND EVALUATING ARGUMENTS

If our objective is to analyse and then evaluate an argument we need some methods for doing so. Whatever method we use it needs to be clear, consistent and systematic. It is these qualities which give coherence and intelligibility to analysis and evaluation. They can also help with the main difficulty of producing an explicit evaluation: laying out the steps and reasons for what has been done. We need these kinds of ground rules because of the divergent nature and styles of argument in the social sciences. We will shortly be looking at two methods on how to deal intelligently and fairly with whatever argument we come across. They have been chosen because of the flexibility they offer and because they can provide a systematic approach to analysis and evaluation. The first method, argumentation analysis, was developed by Stephen Toulmin (1958) during the 1950s. Toulmin developed an approach to argumentation analysis that was rooted in the practice rather than the theory of logic. Toulmin provides a flexible approach to the examination of actual procedures used in practical argument. Complementing Toulmin's philosophical approach, Fisher (1993) provides a method for a systematic reading of texts. This initial reading technique enables the reader to systematically extract the main elements of any argument for the purposes of evaluation. These flexible but explicit approaches to argumentation analysis are especially useful to the social scientist in that they allow both analysis and evaluation of arguments based on assertion and methodological commitment.

Toulmin's method of argumentation analysis

In his book, *The Uses of Argument* (1958), Stephen Toulmin sets out a model of argumentation and provides a method for its analysis. The basis of

Toulmin's approach is relatively simple. He proposes that an argument can be broken up into a number of basic elements. Figure 4.1 shows these elements and the relationships that exist between them such that they form an argument.

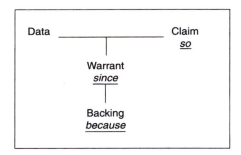

Figure 4.1   *Toulmin's structure of an argument*

For example, if we were to say, 'performance at university depends on age and gender', we would be making a claim. It is a contentious claim that is open to challenge. It is claiming that a relationship exists between academic performance, age and gender: hence we have three variables. What evidence (data) would allow us to accept such a claim? We might possibly expect such a claim to be based on empirical research by reliable researchers using reliable methods. If this were so, the claim would be based on evidence. The evidence would be made available in the research report. The pedigree of the reports might be shown in who produced them, that is, who undertook the research. If those who had undertaken the research were respected academics, then backing will have been provided for the initial claim.

A challenge can be made to any or all elements. Is the claim justified? Are the evidence, warrant and backing justified? Added to these we can ask whether the claim stands up to major challenges? Is it sufficiently robust or does it need to be reworded? For example, a challenge to the warrant might be made on any or all of these grounds: the research was out of date; the conclusions in the reports did not logically follow from the data collected; the evidence was inappropriate; or the data-collection techniques were unreliable.

Therefore we have claims, evidence, warrants and backing.

- *Claim*   an arguable statement.
- *Evidence*   data used to support the claim.
- *Warrant* (or *permit*) an expectation that provides the link between the evidence and claim.
- *Backing*   context and assumptions used to support the validity of the warrant and evidence.

Figure 4.2 is an example from everyday life. In dry summers consumers are asked and expected to save water through careful and limited use. This is normally taken to mean water should only be used for essential things – watering lawns, filling swimming pools and washing cars are prohibited. The argument for this could have the following structure.

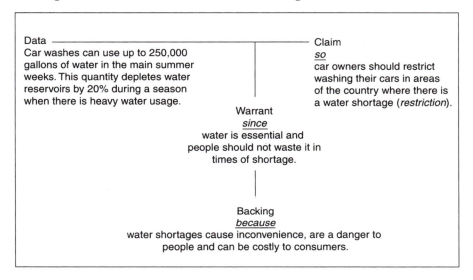

Figure 4.2   *An argument for saving water*

There are a number of ways in which these main elements can be assembled to produce an argument. There are also variations on the use of each element. Claims, for example, come in five main types: *claims of fact, claims of value, claims of policy, claims of concept* and *claims of interpretation*; these are explained in Table 4.3 (overleaf).

The range in the types of claims from which an argument can be constructed shows that almost everything is arguable. Facts can be verified, but their interpretation can be a matter of dispute. Opinions over an interpretation also require substantive support in much the same way as any structured argument. But facts alone are not always sufficient or available. Intellectual debate also employs scenarios, illustrations, analogies and models to provide substance and backing to an interpretation.

Other difficulties arise in distinguishing opinions from personal preferences, judgements and inferences. There may little dispute about the ingredients of a pint of Guinness, but a great deal of dispute can arise over, say, whether it tastes sweet or bitter, or whether it is acceptable to consume alcohol and so on. There is no methodical or prescriptive way of resolving such disagreements.

Inference and personal preference can, however, be identified and analysed. An inference is an interpretation we make on the basis of

Table 4.3 *Different types of claim*

Claims of fact	are statements that can be proven to be true or false. For example, statements such as, London is the capital of England, or, there are three universities in Manchester, are either true or false: they can be verified or refuted using evidence such as an authoritative reference (e.g. encyclopaedia). The difference between a claim based on facts and other forms of claim is that others require additional warrants and backing for their acceptance.
Claims of value	cannot be proven true or false: they are judgements about the worth of something. For example, someone might make the statement that watching *Coronation Street* is a waste of time: this is a judgemental statement. To back it up they might add a qualifying standard, such as watching soap operas does nothing to improve the mind or enhance understanding of the world around us. One might agree with the value claim or make a challenge through the counter-claim that modern living is stressful, that people need relaxation, and that watching *Coronation Street* is a form of relaxation and is therefore good for people.
Claims of policy	are normative statements about what ought to be done rather than what is done. For example, someone might claim that public libraries are an essential part of the culture of a civilized country and should therefore be protected from budget cuts. In this case we see a claim of policy combined with a claim of value.
Claims of concept	are about definitions and the recognizability of the language used. For example, when comparing views on abortion or euthanasia, the way the claim was worded would be important. Some organizations, such as Life, would claim abortion was murder of an unborn child. The claim employs particular definitions that are not only restrictive but emotive. The use of words is not therefore as given in dictionary definitions, but is a matter of interpretative use.
Claims of interpretation	are about proposals on how some data or evidence are to be understood. Facts mean nothing without interpretation and interpretations can and often do differ.

observing something else. For example, we might see a student standing on a chair in the library shouting 'Fire!' and infer that there was a fire in the library. This is because people *do not usually* stand on chairs shouting 'Fire!' In Example A at the end of this chapter you will see how Karl Marx tackles an argument based on inference and assertion to produce an interpretation dialectically opposed to that proposed by another (fictitious) economist.

Like claims, there are also different types of warrant (or permits). The two main types of warrant are stated warrants and unstated warrants. The function of all warrants is to link or provide a bridge between a claim and what is presented as support (backing) for that claim. Warrants are therefore about basic assumptions underlying claims: they are basic beliefs or fundamental premisses about something from which a person makes a statement. For example, in the American Declaration of Independence Thomas Jefferson made it clear what his assumptions are by stating that 'all men are created equal, that they are endowed by their creator with certain unalienable Rights, that among these are Life, Liberty and the pursuit of happiness'. He prefaces this declaration (claim) with the warrant, 'We hold these truths to be self-evident . . .'.

In the social sciences most approaches have sets of methodological assumptions about social order. We can take an example from sociology to illustrate what we mean here. Sociologists working from within a structuralist approach tend to regard social order as an outcome of relationships between institutions and dominant values. How they perceive of this relationship makes for a significant difference between them. Structural functionalists perceive the relationship as based on consensus while conflict structuralists perceive the relationship as based on domination. While each of these approaches has a long and complex philosophical backdrop it is the basic assumptions that theorists in each approach use that shape the nature of the warrants they use for their claims about the world.

A more commonplace example can be seen in the attitude many British people have towards their elected representatives in Parliament. The broad assumption among the electorate and press is that elected members of Parliament should be accountable, honest and exhibit high standards of ethical behaviour, but in practice this is not always the case. In Toulmin's terms, the situation would look like this. Some members of Parliament have behaved in ways not becoming to their position by taking money to ask questions in Parliament: this is the data for which concrete examples could be given. The claim could be: members should not be permitted to take money or other incentives to ask questions in Parliament (a value claim). This is based on the warrant: members should be honest and act in the best interests of the general public and not a minority of vested interests.

The excerpt from the Declaration of Independence is an example of a stated warrant. But not all assumptions are stated in an argument. There may be a number of reasons for this, including that the author assumes the reader is familiar with the assumptions of the argument or that the author wishes to disguise the assumptions used. The following extract shows an argument from an unstated assumption: Vickie Shields (1990) is writing for the converted.

> Any critical study of visual communication must necessarily address the question of how meaning is communicated through visual images. Meaning is not found intricately woven into the fabric of the text to be unearthed by a trained scholar, nor is the meaning of a text to be defined solely in individual psyches. The ability of a visual text to communicate meaning involves an intricate interplay between the codes and messages encoded into the text at the time of its production and the cultural experience of subjectivity the spectator brings to the viewing of that image. The production of visual texts takes place within

dominant ideological structures. Texts therefore, have the ability to reflect or reproduce dominant cultural discourses about such things as gender, race, ethnicity, class, age, education and sexual preference. (1990: 25)

This extract is from the introduction of an article. What we have here, is, in the first instance, a text aimed at a friendly audience of like-minded people. The language and concepts used are vague and without reference. But to the converted these concepts and words will be familiar. The author also expects her main statements, for example, 'Meaning is not found intricately woven into the fabric of the text to be unearthed by a trained scholar, nor is the meaning of a text to be defined solely in individual psyches', to be meaningful and expects the reader to know to whose work she is referring. This might be taken to be Judith Williamson's *Decoding Advertisements* (1979), which is a major milestone in the feminist analysis of advertising. Similarly, the statement, 'The ability of a visual text to communicate meaning involves an intricate interplay between the codes and messages encoded into the text at the time of its production', has a literature behind it. This might be the semiological approach of Ferdinand de Saussure (1966) and Barthes (1967); and the ways in which it has been employed by academics such as Nichols in *Ideology and the Image* (1981) and Sut Jhally in *Codes of Advertising* (1987). Hence, our investigations would take us into some interesting areas of cultural studies, providing us with the opportunity to read and understand some of the major developments, arguments and applications of methodologies and techniques used over the past decade and more.

Some other things to note about this short extract are its general methodological approach and polemical character. References to broad social concepts such as class, race, age, education, ethnicity and gender tend to show a bias towards a structuralist approach within cultural studies. You could therefore expect many of the methodological assumptions of structuralism to be part of Shields's general argument, and if we wanted to inquire further into her argument we would need to become familiar with those assumptions and styles of discourse used by structuralist theorists. We would need to learn about the conventions of the approach – the styles of presenting argument and analysis about the broad as well as subtle differences between sub-schools within the approach. More particularly, it can be seen that these assumptions are motivated by a standpoint or perspective originating in the works of Marx. This can be seen in the vocabulary of 'dominant ideological structures' and reference to the notion of 'reproduction of cultural discourses'. Therefore, from this basic starting point, the reader could begin to describe the assumptions of this argument as motivated by a moral standpoint. These are not stated, but are apparent in the language of this extract.

Whether it is easier or harder to write for a readership that has pre-digested your position and found it agreeable is open to debate. There is no reason why you should not agree with the moral, political, religious, or

methodological attitude of an author. But it is your responsibility to analyse first, to think about the argument you read and then evaluate it. The
act and process of argumentation analysis involves a reflective attitude:
you must put to one side (i.e. bracket) preconceived allegiances and
preferences as well as prejudice and political opposition to approaches.

Some prejudicial forms of assumptions can originate from ethnocentrism
– the belief that one's own culture is more important and better than any
other. Many of the founding theorists in social science, such as Durkheim,
Tönnies and Simmel, made ethnocentric assumptions. They assumed that
modern industrial urban society was superior to rural non-industrial
society, that is, people in industrial society were mentally and socially
more advanced than so-called tribal peoples with their primitive mentality.
Much of this kind of armchair ethnocentrism was challenged by anthro-
pologists such as Bronislow Malinoswki and Evans-Pritchard, who actually
lived among other cultures. Nevertheless, the notion of cultural development in terms of a hierarchical contrast remains a major tradition in
Western social thought.

Along with the task of identifying warrants, the reader must also look for
qualifiers and restrictions. Some arguments use words such as *probably*,
some, *many* and *generally*, which often indicate a qualifier. A qualifier functions to limit the scope of a claim in order to make it more acceptable and
to place limits on its application. For example, in Britain there is an
ongoing debate about arming the police force. Some people have made the
claim that the majority of police officers should be armed. The word
majority is a qualifier: it limits the scope of an armed police force by
allowing for exceptions. The claim is stating that not all, only the majority,
of police officers should be armed. The claim has allowed for a possible
restriction. This might be that only police officers trained and psychologically able to use firearms should be allowed to carry them.

The other major element of arguments is backing. This can take the form
of additional information, perhaps an account of personal experience or
hypothetical scenario. In the example of the British police force, the backing
might include recounting incidents in which unarmed officers were faced
with armed criminals. Concrete illustrations are usually much more convincing than hypothetical or generalized scenarios. However, the main and
most common form of backing is the legitimacy conferred on an argument
through the use of academic style.

Fisher's method of critical reading

Fisher (1993) provides us with a systematic technique for reading analytically. His technique enables the evaluation of any argument to be done
by analysis of its formal structure. Words that are used to structure an
argument are the focus for the analysis. Words such as *thus* and *therefore* are
highlighted, because they are used to link evidence with claims and suggest
inference, reasons and conclusions. From this, the structure of the argument

can be seen or even rewritten as an argument diagram. Like Toulmin's approach, Fisher's technique can be very effective because it allows you to think through the argument you are analysing. Fisher's approach differs from Toulmin's in that he provides us with a systematic set of procedures for the analysis and subsequent evaluation of an argument. We will look first at his method for systematically extracting an argument.

The purpose of the following procedure, adapted from Fisher (1993), is to extract the conclusions (C) and reasons (R) of an argument.

1 First look quickly through the text in order to get an initial sense of the author's project and purpose.
2 Read the text again circling ⬭ any inference indicators (thus, therefore, etc.) as you read.
3 Look for conclusions and any stated reasons for these. Underline the conclusions and place in brackets < > any reasons.
4 Attempt at this stage to summarize the author's argument. If there is no clear argument, ask what point(s) the author is trying to make and why.
5 Identify what you take to be conclusions by marking them up with a C – remember that there may be interim conclusions as well as the main one. Typical indications of a conclusion are the use of the following words: therefore, thus, hence, consequently, and so on. Be careful not to assume that a summary or formulation provided by the author of their argument so far must be the conclusion.
6 Taking the main conclusion, ask yourself what reasons are presented in the text for believing this conclusion or why you are being asked to accept this conclusion. Typical indications of reasons are words and phrases such as: because, since, it follows, and so on.
7 The reasons provided for the argument can be ranked into a structure. Go through each reason (R) asking whether it is essential or secondary backing for the argument. From this, you will be left with the core reasons for the argument. You will then be able to construct an argument diagram with the following structures:

R1 + R2 = (therefore) C [for joint reasons]

R1 or R2 = (therefore) C [for independent reasons]

Variations on these structures are common. For example, a main conclusion might be supported by an interim conclusion and several basic reasons. So, taking the first equation above:

R1 + R2 = (therefore) C1 (interim conclusion)

C1 + R3 = (therefore) C2 (main conclusion)

This is a relatively simple method to use and depends only on close reading. We are not yet asking whether the reasons identified make good (i.e. sound) reasons; this stage is about analysis, not evaluation. It is not a prescriptive method that will instantly reveal an argument. This is especially the case in the social sciences, where many arguments are based on assertion and hypothetical statements and it is important to become practised in recognizing such arguments in order to avoid committing the fallacy of taking for real a hypothetical scenario. Typical indicators of hypothetical and assertive arguments are: if, suppose, provided that, and so on. Finally, the extent to which you can adequately analyse and evaluate an argument depends on your grasp of the subject-specific language and its problem definitions. Bearing these points in mind we can now look at the evaluation of an argument.

Practice with Fisher's notational technique should enable most competent research scholars to extract the details of any argument. It is essential to have the structure of the argument laid out before you can evaluate it. When evaluating an argument you are attempting to assess not only the logical but also the contextual structure of the argument as a whole and of its parts. Fisher's method for argument evaluation can be applied to most forms of analysis. His method is based on what he calls the assertability question. This is a method involving questioning both the premises and conclusions of an argument. The main assertability question is: what argument (what *you* would need to believe) or evidence (what *you* would need to know) would justify the acceptance of the conclusion?

Note that this question is not attempting to establish truth. It is about establishing justified reasons for accepting an assertion. The question is not therefore delving into the realm of philosophical scepticism where truth, reality and meaning are all open to abstract debate and doubt. Fisher's method is about using normal everyday standards of evaluation and judgement. For this reason his method should be usable by any competent person. In practice, therefore, the assertability question assumes that most people can apply an appropriate standard and that such a standard will need justification and will be open to critical scrutiny. Hence, Fisher personalizes the evaluation of an argument thereby avoiding a prescriptive dogma, because a prescriptive method would stifle imagination and lateral thinking. Returning to the assertability question we can now treat it as a practical approach to evaluation in that real arguments are evaluated by questioning the relationship between the premises and conclusion.

For most arguments you should ask whether the conclusion follows from the premises. For a conclusion to be acceptable the following conditions must be satisfactorily established by the analyst:

- therefore, its conclusion must follow from its premises,
- its premisses must either be true or, if suppositions, justifiable.

Even if the premises of an argument could be true or justifiable the conclusion could be false or doubtful. Similarly, the conclusion could be acceptable, but one or all of the premisses doubtful. In a more complex analysis you might find the premises to be justifiable, but the conclusion able to be inverted, that is, the consequences of the premises seen in two ways. Putting this into practice, Fisher claims that clarity can be achieved through addressing the following kind of question to an argument: could the premises be true and the conclusion false judging by appropriate standards of evidence or appropriate standards of what is possible?

Therefore, you need to ask what argument or evidence would justify your acceptance of the conclusion. It is because standards are not universal, but historically, culturally and subject specific, that care is needed here (see Turnbull, 1971, for an interesting example of a description of a culture that through a change in the physical environment changed radically). Different cultures, like different disciplines, differ in what they accept as standards of proof. When dealing with subject-specific disciplines ask what should be taken as proof and why. However, avoid taking for granted what the discipline accepts as justification for asserting a conclusion or what its adherents assume to be knowledge. You should, in other words, think about and think through for yourself the arguments and assumptions you are dealing with. In this way you will understand more because you will have applied a healthy natural scepticism. Turning this into practice is not too difficult.

Many standpoints and perspectives in the social sciences have their origins in moral, political and ethical positions. For example, very early on in his life, Karl Marx was politically committed to the idea that capitalism was morally perverse and should be replaced. He spent the rest of his life developing a methodological approach to show how and why this should happen. All of his work was therefore an immense effort to elaborate the basis of his original position. By asserting a conclusion, someone puts forward a proposition they take to be true. The basis therefore of some arguments is assertion. This does not mean such arguments are wrong. Rather they need to be constructed very carefully; paying attention to their reasoning, using evidence systematically, and coherently, and relating ideas in as rigorous a way as possible. You can, therefore, develop an argument from assertion and analyse one by the same approach. Example A at the end of this chapter shows how an argument based on assertion can be analysed for evaluation. In the example the notational system based on Fisher's procedure, looked at earlier, is demonstrated. Inference indicators are marked to make the structure of the author's argument clear. **Read Example A now, starting on p. 99.**

From a great exponent of the technique of argumentation, we turn now to a rather different aspect of argumentation, that of fallacies.

FALLACIES IN ARGUMENTS

The term fallacy comes from the Latin *fallere*, which means to deceive. It is important to note that it is not normal for academic authors to deceive their readers, although there have been some notable exceptions to this norm (e.g. the Cyril Burt scandal, see Beloff, 1980). Therefore your first working assumption is that the author is genuine and has not set out to hide information, distort facts or slander opponents in order to make a more convincing case for their own argument. It may sometimes be the case that the author has made a mistaken assumption, or not examined the assumptions that have been made, or has not noticed the faults in their reasoning.

There are two types of fallacies: fallacies other people make in their arguments and fallacies you can make when evaluating other people's arguments. What we will do here is to look at some of the most common errors people make when constructing arguments. We begin by listing some simple fallacies before describing an example.

A number of authors have highlighted the main fallacies common in arguments. Hinderer (1992), for example, discusses how some of the main fallacies result from confusion, while Thouless and Thouless (1990) provide a long list of tricks often used to make an argument convincing. Of the 37 tricks identified by Thouless and Thouless (1990: 139–44) the ones shown in Table 4.4 (overleaf) are the most likely to be encountered when reviewing a research literature.

Look now at Example B (starting on p. 102), which describes a debate over method, using a critique of Judith Williamson's *Decoding Advertisements* (1979). This brief discussion of the work of Williamson and Francis demonstrates something of the ways in which debates in the social sciences are riddled with arguments.

CONCLUSION

Argumentation analysis and evaluation to a lesser or greater degree deconstructs and then reconstructs differently the ideas of other people. Inevitably some things will be lost or cannot be included, while other things might suffer in translation. What I am saying is that any analysis and evaluation of a body of literature will incur some costs: certain things will have to be sacrificed in order to obtain other things. Clarity, consistency and coherence are not easily achieved; to make an analysis intelligible not all the detail and contexts analysed can be included in the final synthesis. It is not necessary, however, to short-circuit this problem by presenting things as if simple choices could be made: different ideas as competing rivals. To do this would most certainly be committing the error of oversimplification and gross comparison.

At the heart of this problem is the fact that you cannot read everything on all approaches relevant to your topic. For example, if you were to research the topic of economic determinism this would entail reading both Marx and Weber, amounting to tens of thousands of pages of difficult and sophisticated argument and analysis. There would also be a very wide secondary literature to read. If you were interested in the history of social thought on

Table 4.4 *Fallacies in arguments*

Fallacy	What it is and how to avoid it
Implied definition	Referring to something without clearly defining it; always define what you refer to, especially concepts.
Illegitimate definition	Closing down alternatives by giving a restrictive definition.
Changing meanings	Defining something as A, then using A in a different way, B.
Emotional language	Using value loaded or ethically loaded terms.
Use of all rather than some	Using bland generalization to incorporate all variables and thereby minimize contradictory examples.
Ignoring alternatives	Giving one interpretation or example as if all others could be treated or categorized in the same way.
Selected instances	Picking out unusual or unrepresentative examples.
Forced analogy	Using an analogy without recognizing the applicability of other contradictory analogies.
Similarity	Claiming there is no real difference between two things even when there is.
Mere analogy	Use of analogy with no recourse to examples from the real world.
False credentials	Exaggerating your credentials or experience to convince others of your authority.
Technical language	Deliberate use of jargon intended to impress the reader and/or hide the lack of a foundation to an argument.
Special pleading	Claiming a special case to raise your argument above other similar positions. This is often associated with the use of emotive language.
Playing on the reader	Telling readers what they want to hear rather than challenging their thinking and assumptions.
Claiming prejudice	Attributing prejudice to an opponent in order to discredit them.
Appealing to others for authority	Claiming some other in authority has made the same argument as yourself in order to strengthen your own position.
False context	Giving examples out of context or using nothing but hypothetical scenarios.
Extremities	Ignoring centre ground positions by focusing only on the extreme ends of a spectrum of alternatives.
Tautology	Use of language structures to get acceptance of your argument from others. This is often in the form of 'too much of X is bad' therefore X itself is good.

Source: adapted from Thonless and Thonless, 1990

economic determinism this task might not be a problem. But if you were interested in looking at the applications of ideas about economic determinism, the task would be too large: it would prevent you from getting on with the job of empirical work. Therefore, a certain amount of ignorance is inevitable. Practical considerations mean some texts cannot be closely read, while others can only be read selectively and casually. Some texts might not be read at all. It is for these reasons that Anderson et al. (1985) make a number of recommendations, of which one is maintaining an attitude that allows us to recognize our own limitations and to approach a work with the modesty and understanding characteristic of good scholarship.

This really means 'playing fair' when assessing the strengths and weaknesses of other people's ideas. Although this might sound like an old notion, fair play is an important part of scholarly activity. Having an inquisitive attitude to different ideas and seeking other ways of looking at the world and approaches to researching the world means you are exercising an intellectual attitude from which differing ideas can be synthesized into new and exciting ideas. The value of this attitude repays many fold the effort needed to exercise it. One major benefit is that it can save us from making victims and fools of ourselves. Social science is replete with articles claiming discovery: a new idea has been developed or a new breakthrough made enticing us to dump existing ideas and follow this new one. All too often we find that the breakthrough is another case of what Anderson et al. (1985) call (after Sorokin) the Christopher Columbus Complex: going to Disneyland and believing one has discovered America. The main causes of this complex are laziness and an inflated ego, making us believe that as part of the contemporary world we have a greater degree of insight and intellectual understanding of society. As a consequence, the works of now dead, social theorists such as Sorokin go unread or are only understood through derivative sources. Ideas by predecessors are therefore glibly criticized for what is perceived to be their weak purchase on current issues or problems of the discipline. As Anderson et al. point out: 'victims of such a complex tend to overestimate our contemporary achievements because they underestimate those of our predecessors, the tasks they faced and perhaps failed at, largely because victims of the complex have not tackled those tasks themselves' (1985: 70). We need to remember that, done properly, argumentation analysis and evaluation is not only a rewarding, but an intellectually stimulating activity, resulting in genuine developments of which a research scholar can be justifiably proud.

EXAMPLE A   KARL MARX: LOGIC OF ARGUMENTATION

Based on Marx (1950).

The following extract is from Marx's 'Value, prices and profit' (1950). It is an argument well known to scholars of Marx. It has been used extensively to demonstrate the impeccable logic of his argumentation analysis: especially the kind of analysis he uses in much longer and sophisticated texts like *Capital*. The target for Marx's analysis is the assertion that working people act irrationally when they combine (i.e. unionize) in the pursuit of higher wages. Marx attributes this assertion to 'Citizen Weston'. Marx skilfully dissects Weston's argument. He shows how Weston's premises do not follow from each other and how his conclusion does not follow from the premises. Added to this, Marx takes Weston's own premises and recasts them into a logical argument to show the rationality of unionization for higher wages. A possible way to approach this extract is to read it through first. Afterwards read the notes, adapted from Fisher (1993), that accompany it. Note that Marx's analysis is not linear but combinational: Marx expects his reader to re-read the argument, moving back and forth through its different sections.

Citizen Weston's argument rested, in fact, upon two premises:

firstly, <the *amount of national production* is a *fixed thing*, a *constant* quantity of magnitude as the mathematicians would say;> secondly, the <*amount of real wages*, that is to say, of wages as measured by the quantity of the commodities they can buy, is a *fixed* amount, a *constant* magnitude.>

In this first paragraph Marx sets out the premises of Weston's argument as: (1) production is a fixed thing therefore (2) wages are fixed (as measured by what they can buy) therefore given (1) + (2) the conclusion is: the working class cannot gain higher wages through combined struggle (e.g. unionization). In the next two paragraphs Marx sets out to show that (1) and (2) are false, that (2) does not follow from (1), and even if the conclusion was true, it is not true because of (1) and (2). Marx's analytical reasoning looks like this:

Now, his first assertion is evidently erroneous. <Year after year you will find that the value and mass of production increase, that the productive powers of the national labour increase, and that the amount of money necessary to circulate this increasing production continuously changes.> <What is true at the end of the year, and for different years compared with each other, is true for every average day of the year.> The amount or magnitude of national production changes continuously. It is not a constant but a **variable** magnitude, and apart from changes in population it must be so, because of <the continuous change in the accumulation of capital and the productive powers of labour.> It is perfectly true that if a *rise in the general rate of wages* should take place today, that rise, whatever its ulterior effects might be, would, by itself, not *immediately* change the amount of production. It would, in the

The value of production and the productive power of labour increases every year, and the amount of money in circulation is variable (changes) because increased production requires changes in money circulation. Therefore, national production and circulation of money are variables and not constants. Presumably, national production can decrease as well as increase. Therefore, Marx is claiming that Weston's assertion is false. To show the validity of his point Marx would need to produce sufficient historical evidence that shows variability of national production, labour output and amount of money in circulation.

first instance, proceed from the existing state of things. But if *before* the rise of wages the national production was variable, and not *fixed*, it will continue to be variable and not fixed *after* the rise of wages.

But ⟨suppose⟩ <the amount of national production to be constant instead of variable.> Even then, what our friend Weston considers a logical conclusion would still remain a gratuitous assertion. <If I have a given number, say eight, the absolute limits of this number do not prevent its parts from changing their relative limits.> ⟨Therefore,⟩ <if profits were six and wages two, wages might increase to six and profits decrease to two, and still the total amount remain eight.> ⟨Thus⟩ the fixed amount of production would by no means prove the fixed amount of wages. How then does our friend Weston prove this fixity? By asserting it.

But even conceding him his assertion, it could cut both ways, while he presses it only in one direction. If ⟨suppose⟩ <the amount of wage is a constant magnitude> ⟨then⟩ it can neither be increased nor diminished. If ⟨then,⟩ in enforcing a temporary rise of wages the working men act foolishly, the capitalists in enforcing a temporary fall in wages would act not less foolishly. Our friend Weston does not deny that, under certain circumstances, the working men can enforce a rise in wages, but their amount being naturally fixed, there must follow a reaction. On the other hand, he knows also that the capitalists can enforce a fall of wages, and, indeed, continuously try to enforce it. According to the principle of the constancy of wages, <a reaction ought to follow in this case> not less than in the former. <The *working men,* ⟨therefore,⟩ reacting against the attempt at, or the act of, lowering wages, would act rightly.> They would, ⟨therefore,⟩ act rightly in enforcing a rise of wages, ⟨because⟩ <every reaction against the lowering of wages is an action for raising wages.> According to citizen Weston's own principle of the constancy of wages, the working man ought, ⟨therefore,⟩ under certain circumstances, to combine and struggle for a rise of wages.

Marx points out through an illustration that Weston's position is an assertion and not a logical argument. He points out that even if (1) was true there is no reason to accept the conclusion. Marx uses the illustration to show that the total amount of the whole may be constant but the elements making it up, that is, national production, wages, labour output and money in circulation, are variable in quantity. The elements can change relative to each other without affecting the whole. Therefore, Weston's conclusion is, as Marx points out, an assertion. Marx has therefore dealt systematically with Weston's reasoning and shown it to be flawed. But Marx does not stop here; he continues his analysis before making his claim, which is based on Weston's own rationale. This is the clever bit.

In this paragraph Marx asks the 'what if . . .' question. He asks what if one accepts Weston's assertion that wages are a constant? In asking this Marx's motive is to show the dual nature of the assertion. If working people act irrationally in pursuing wage increases, then, capitalists in pressing for lower wages act equally irrationally. This is Marx's first step. His second leads him to his main conclusion. Marx points out that if capitalists force a reduction in wages, working people will be acting rationally in resisting such pressure. This is because the working people would be abiding by Weston's assertion in trying to maintain wages as a constant.

Marx makes his main conclusion but it emphasizes a restriction, 'under certain circumstances . . .'.

If he denies this conclusion, he must give up the premises from which it flows. He must not say that the amount of wages is a constant quantity, but that, although it cannot and must not rise, it can and must fall, whenever capital pleases to lower it.	*In typical Socratic style, Marx presents his opponent with the reality of his own reasoning. Weston would presumably have little choice in accepting Marx's argument because Marx has left him with no logical basis for argument.*

As you can see, Marx's main conclusion is 'the working man . . . ought . . . under certain circumstances . . . to combine and struggle for a rise in wages'. The clever thing about this is that Marx bases this conclusion on Weston's own premise of the constancy of wages. Following through the reasoning of the extract one can see not only the systematic logic but the impeccable style of Marx's argumentation.

Although the exposition of this extract (in the right hand column) has worked in a linear direction, one could have started from the conclusion and worked in multiple directions. From that conclusion, 'working men . . . would act rightly in enforcing a rise in wages' working backwards will reveal how Marx came to this conclusion. To do this we read deductively, looking for a structure of reasoning that supports this main statement or conclusion. However, whichever way you read Marx's argument it reaches the opposite conclusion to that of Weston.

There is another point also to note in this short example – the ways in which Marx's methodological assumptions underpin his analysis of Weston's argument. In Chapter 3 we outlined what are generally taken to be the methodological assumptions Marx developed. We can use these to show once again (Table 4.5, p. 104) the importance of methodological assumptions and how they are used as the starting point for a challenge.

EXAMPLE B   DEBATE OVER METHODOLOGICAL FALLACIES

Analysis from Francis (1986).

In his analysis and subsequent critique of Judith Williamson's *Decoding Advertisements* (1979), Francis (1986) provides a good example of the kind of debate over fallacies and understanding that arises in the social sciences. His analysis also shows an example of the use of the phenomenological reading technique. Before we look at the debate we need to understand two things: why Francis chose to look at *Decoding Advertisements* and what we mean by phenomenological reading.

Francis chose to look at Williamson's book because in the early 1980s it was a major development in feminist analysis of advertising; it showed the kinds of work that could be produced using a feminist standpoint within the methodological assumptions of structuralism and psychoanalytical analysis. Choice of which works to critique is therefore important; especially if you are making a critique of a major argument. Francis chose a

Table 4.5 *Marx's methodological assumptions and Weston's assertions compared*

Marx's methodological assumptions	Weston's methodological assertions
Everything is in a process of change therefore change is rational.	Structures in the world are fixed and therefore change is irrational.
Singular events only appear chaotic because we do not look for the structure of relationships that connect events into a whole, therefore look for what connects events and situations.	Challenges to the status quo must be challenged and prevented to avoid chaos.
The force for change resides in the economic relationships between social classes, therefore look at the relationships between the classes for an explanation for change.	Social classes are related but ought not to be in conflict as conflict is irrational because it will not change anything for the better.
People are encouraged to see their situation in isolation rather than in terms of broader structures of social inequality, therefore they may act in ways contradictory to the good of society.	People should accept the status quo because it cannot be changed for the better. Change would lead to chaos.
People are essentially rational but the individualizing force of capitalism makes them selfish. Therefore certain forms of community (society) are better than others because they encourage the essential rationality of human nature.	People are essentially irrational and therefore need to be controlled by people who know better. Selfishness and individualism encourage self-help, innovation and enterprise which are good for society as a whole.

landmark study for his critique. So, whatever else he aimed to do in his analysis, he needed to be very careful as to how he analysed the argument in *Decoding Advertisements* and how he argued that it is based on a number of methodological assumptions that are fallacies.

Phenomenological reading technique

In his analysis Francis used what might be called the phenomenological reading technique. The basis of this technique has its origins in the work of the philosopher most commonly associated with phenomenology, Edmund Husserl (1859–1938). Although his work is complex we can get an understanding of it through some simple illustrations. Take, for example, the interest that experimental psychology might have in the relationship between hunger and the image of food. Husserl would not be interested in the relationship between the image of food and hunger but with a more fundamental (or a priori) question. He would ask: what exactly is it that is to count as an image of food? Husserl is interested in a pure description of the phenomenon (noumena) that humans experience. He is not interested, therefore, in the causation of such experiences or the history of the phenomenon. Husserl is recommending that if we want to know what a thing is like, what its essential features must be in order that it can be recognized as an example of that thing, then we must place brackets around the assumptions and understanding that we take for granted. Issues about the ethics, morals, politics, consequences and especially reality (ontology) of a thing should not, Husserl recommends, be of primary concern.

When used by sociologists like Francis, Husserl's phenomenology places a priority upon describing the different ways in which the intention people have influences the ways they understand everyday life. For example, the drawer in a jeweller's shop might be full of rings, some of which are classified as wedding rings. Once purchased, these wedding rings might come to have an emotional meaning for the wearer, symbolizing love and commitment. To the jeweller they mean something different: they are a commodity for sale. Hence, the same object can be constituted in different ways depending on the intentionality of different people. The main point to note here is that both realities are equally valid.

Applying this attitude to science, the mathematical approach of, say, physics, and the analytical approach of, say, semiotics, are only two from many ways in which the world can be understood. This leads to a second point that is important for Francis. The scientific approach, whether in the natural or social sciences, takes for granted that there is a world having prior existence to the world of causality and relationships between things that scientists aim to describe. The mundane world in which we all exist (*Lebenswelt*) is the one from which the scientific approach is derived.

Hence, following Husserl's ideas, Francis takes the position that the kinds of analysis produced by scientists are abstractions and idealizations about the world in which we live and have little to do with the properties of the things that we experience in everyday life. What we see in accounts about the world are the operation of procedures for analysis, based on assumptions subscribed to by the analyst about the intent of the phenomenon studied. Hence, those things that are classified as belonging to this or that class of things (phenomena) are not a matter for study as things in themselves. Added to this is the point many phenomenological social scientists make: the 'correctness' of any scientific analysis of a phenomenon is not validated by comparing it with how it is usually experienced in everyday life. Rather, the issue of validity is looked at from within science by ensuring that the procedures used were correct and rational. Ironically, when the world of everyday life is used, it is used with the intent to provide a correction to what is assumed to be our partial view of reality. Hence, one of Husserl's followers, Alfred Schutz (1967), argued that the procedures and intent of science are incomparable with the procedures and intent used by people in everyday life.

Although there are many ideas here, we should be able to see that Francis is working within an approach that is different to that from Williamson. Francis is interested in two main things. The first is the assumptions Williamson accepts about advertising and how she employs a set of procedures to arrive at her analysis of advertising. The second is what it might take to describe the essential features of an advertisement. This approach can be seen in the following list of questions that Francis might be seen as asking about *Decoding Advertisements*.

1   What assumptions have been made that enabled the account to be made?
2   What are the consequences of these assumptions for understanding the thing (i.e. phenomenon) itself?
3   What happens if we suspend these assumptions?
4   What assumptions would we need to make in order to analyse the phenomenon as a thing in itself rather than as an instance of something else?
5   What consequences might these have for our understanding of that phenomenon?

Francis's reading of Decoding Advertisements

Francis subjected *Decoding Advertisements* to a critical reading. He claims to have identified a number of major fallacies in the assumptions made about advertising, products and viewers which impact on the status of several methodological assumptions within structuralism and its use to analyse advertising. Francis argues that there are three main fallacies on which *Decoding Advertisements* is based. He calls these the description fallacy, the technical reading fallacy and the formal knowledge fallacy.

The description fallacy, according to Francis, is assuming that the function of an advertisement is to describe the details of the product. Williamson, claims Francis, criticizes advertisements for not describing products: this criticism is based on her assumption that the function of an advertisement is to describe a product and advertisements that do not do this are deceptive. As a case in point, she cites a perfume advertisement for Chanel No. 5 in which Catherine Deneuve (a French model and actress) is pictured with a bottle of Chanel. Williamson claims that advertisements like those for perfume are 'hollow referent' images – they are used because no real information can be given. Francis observes, however, that 'if we cease to conceive of descriptions as essential to the nature of advertising, the basis of Williamson's charge of deception disappears' (1986: 209). He follows this up with: 'I assume Williamson is not suggesting . . . that we cannot describe smells. In everyday life we routinely do so' (1986: 209). What Francis has done here is to show the fallacy of making an assumption about the function of something, in this case, an advertisement. He has also shown that if one changes or drops (suspends) that particular assumption, the substance of much criticism about advertisements disappears.

A second fallacy, the technical reading fallacy, made by Williamson is that of assuming viewers of advertisements have insufficient mental ability to see the structures by which she believes an advertisement works. She assumes that advertisements have hidden structures that cannot readily be perceived by looking at the manifest image. On the basis of this she criticizes advertising agencies for hiding the technical work that went into the production of an advertisement. Williamson has, Francis observes, conflated 'two different perspectives on advertisements. She has conflated the everyday and routine viewing of adverts with a technical interest in adverts. It is because of this that Williamson is able to claim that "we" the general viewer do not "see" the "real" structure and purpose of advertisements' (1986: 210). Williamson fails to realize, Francis argues, that the whole objective of the technical construction of an advertisement is aimed at the production of an 'object that can be understood . . . by anyone' (1986: 221).

The third fallacy Francis finds in *Decoding Advertisements* is the formal knowledge fallacy. On the basis of assuming advertisements convey messages, Williamson proposes that these are structured and work at a level where most people are unaware of them. Viewers of advertisements do not know they are receiving a powerful advertising sales pitch. Referring to the work of Toulmin, Francis points out the formal tautology in this. In attributing objective existence to unconscious and covert structures of ideas, Williamson is attributing concrete reality (misplaced concreteness) to an ideational notion. But for the notion to hold she must continue to assume that viewers cannot see how advertisements are structured. She therefore claims that the only way to get at these structures is through analysis and uses elements from psychoanalytical theory to do this. But as Francis makes clear, 'unless we clearly distinguish between the phenomena and the representations we use to picture them, our theories will remain self-sustaining tautologies' (1986: 213). In short, what *Decoding Advertisements* does is to claim the existence of formal structures and then apply formal analysis to demonstrate the adequacy of the approach: it does not describe advertisements or products, it describes the procedures of its own theory.

We can see that Francis intends to approach advertising, not as a phenomenon, but to examine properties as the phenomena. It is this difference of project that sets the two appart. There is no reason why we should see Francis's critique as negating the work of Williamson. We might even want to look at what criticisms could be made of Francis's reading of *Decoding Advertisements*. Assessing the original argument and the critique is a common theme in the social sciences. In terms of Francis's critique we might see a counter-argument develop on the lines of a clarification of what Williamson intended, thereby attempting to correct the reading Francis gives us. For example, it might be claimed that Williamson did not criticize advertisements for not describing products. If this is the case – and we can only see if it is by reading *Decoding Advertisements* for ourselves – then Francis's claim about Williamson regarding advertising as deception might be thrown into doubt. But let us assume Williamson did argue that advertisements contain no real information, we have the issue of what we mean by information. This takes us back to Husserl's phenomenology: we need to inquire into what makes information what it is in order to be able to recognize it as such. Williamson might therefore have an idea about what information should be and it is this that Francis is criticizing. It is these kinds of problems that can often lead to new topics for research. Again, following this through, we might then show in defence of Williamson that she thought some products, such as perfume, were difficult to describe. Hence, what she is critical about is the association of perfume with certain images. It is this association, not the product or even advertising as an institution, that she is interested in. Williamson is therefore concerned with the issue of persuasion. If this is the case her analysis is of the strategies used by advertising to persuade. But does this clarification distract from the original critique made by Francis? From a phenomenological approach there are strong grounds for claiming that Williamson is more concerned with procedures of analysis than with the thing in itself, whether an advertisement or information.

But why should Williamson be interested in a phenomenological approach? As with most research, the answer is that it is up to the researcher to make choices about what their topic is to be and how they are to study it. However, Francis might observe that a researcher also has the responsibility to understand the consequences of the choices they make. In this case, he might claim that the choices Williamson made had more to do with demonstrating preconceived views about advertising than with describing the properties of advertisements. Here, then, Francis would be looking to show the motivation for Williamson's interest in advertising. Again a correction of this might be attempted by saying that Francis has misunderstood the methodological tradition within which Williamson is working. As a consequence, he misunderstands her arguments about how smell is packaged as a perfume and how this has meaning for consumers. This line might therefore take us towards another aspect of the debate, that of understanding the traditions within which different researchers work.

The importance of this cannot be overestimated. We have already shown something of this in our explication of the origins of the phenomenological reading technique. The same, therefore, could be done for the tradition within which Williamson worked. Again, it is such inquiries that can form the basis of further research. It is finding these unexplained areas in arguments or assumptions that have not been defined that can often be the starting point for a new piece of research. For example, we have just seen that Willaimson might, it could be claimed, be interested in the symbolic and cultural meaning and signification of perfume. If this is the case, then Francis's criticism could be the starting point of research into perfume, such as the question of what makes particular smells perfume.

This takes us back to the debate. Francis might be criticized for not defining what he takes an advertisement to be or what he takes to be the essential properties of perfume. He might therefore have made a number of fallacies, principally of referring to something without clearly defining it. But is this serious criticism of the critique Francis has put together? There is no definitive answer to this question. It depends on how you, the reader, want to understand the argument; and this itself might be based on your prior interests, concerns and ideas about the role of social science. It is in many ways the different idea that Williamson and Francis each have about social science that makes their positions incompatible. Williamson works within a tradition that seeks to apply semiological theory, a tradition that aims among other things to show the ways in which messages are structured to convey certain meanings. Her book *Decoding Advertisements* was a major step in synthesizing work in structuralism and psychoanalysis from a feminist perspective. Francis, however, works from within a different tradition. As we have seen, his interests are with foundational issues that centre on the general question of *just what* rather than how and why. He wants to redirect our attention to the question of just what is an advertisement: to think first about what it is that we are going to research.

5

Organizing and expressing ideas

Once you have undertaken a comprehensive literature search you will need an array of tools for a comprehensive analysis of its content. Obtaining numerous items relevant to your topic should not be too difficult. What tends to be difficult is subjecting the literature to a thorough analysis. There are some very basic tools which enable analysis and which are essential for the application of more sophisticated methods. Without an understanding of these tools and the techniques for using them, a great deal of time and effort can easily be wasted. The previous chapter examined how arguments might be analysed. In this and the next chapter, we go on to look at some of the techniques of analysis which many authors use to arrange and structure their arguments and which can be used to map ideas in a body of literature. An understanding of the ways in which ideas are structured is an essential prerequisite for systematic analysis and critical evaluation of ideas and arguments. At the same time, as analyst-cum-evaluator, you will be seeing how others have managed information and ideas in order to construct what they take to be a plausible argument. This chapter looks at the following questions:

1 What is meant by analysis and synthesis?
2 How are analogy, metaphor and homology used to present ideas and theories?
3 Why is definition important in the social sciences?
4 How can definition be used to determine the topic for analysis?
5 How can we compare and contrast the ideas of different theorists?

The aim is to show you ways in which you can undertake competent analysis, evaluation and assessment of the literature in order to be able to: map out the main issues on a subject; examine the use of concepts and the ways in which comparisons have and can be made; see how complex ideas can be described; and to understand the role that methodological assumptions have in shaping the ways in which ideas and arguments are presented. At the same time, the objective of analysis is not only to understand, but it is also about seeing if you can make connections between ideas, and find a gap in the literature that can become your own topic or even produce a new synthesis. What follows is an overview of what we mean by analysis and synthesis, in the context of what knowledge is and what it means to comprehend the literature.

ANALYSIS AND SYNTHESIS

Analysis is the job of systematically breaking down something into its constituent parts and describing how they relate to each other – it is not random dissection but a methodological examination. There is a degree of exploration in analysis. You can play around with the parts, rearranging them in various configurations to explore possible leads. You should not be afraid to try things out purely to see how they fit together. Nevertheless, when it comes to analysing several items, such as a batch of articles, you should attempt to be systematic, rigorous and consistent. If a range of arguments is being analysed, you will need to explicate the claim, data and warrant for each argument. In this way, the identification of the individual and similar elements in a range of items can be compared and contrasted.

In any literature review the data for analysis is information; that is, the interpretations, understandings and arguments that others have proposed that they want you to accept as a plausible story. These can come in a variety of structures and formats, styles and mediums. Although text is currently the most prevalent form, statistics, film, images and diagrams, both in print and on computer, are now being used more frequently as ways to present an interpretation or as the materials for research. The point to note here is that the information we are dealing with is not data collected via a research instrument, such as a questionnaire, but published materials relevant to your topic.

The kinds of analysis relevant to literature reviewing are those which systematically extract key ideas, theories, concepts and methodological assumptions from the literature. For this reason, techniques such as discourse analysis, conversation analysis, content analysis, semiological analysis and the like are beyond the scope of our interests.

Synthesis, therefore, is the act of making connections between the parts identified in analysis. It is not simply a matter of reassembling the parts back into the original order, but looking for a new order. It is about recasting the information into a new or different arrangement. That arrangement should show connections and patterns that have not been produced previously. Table 5.1 (overleaf) outlines some of the connections between analysis and synthesis and gives indications of what we mean by knowledge and comprehension.

Synthesis requires you to have a comprehensive knowledge of the subject and a capacity to think in broad terms, because a range of viewpoints, methodologies and stances often require connecting. This means that as an analyst you will usually find yourself battling to keep control of a large amount of information. Also, you should not refrain from considering ludicrous suggestions and generalizations, or dealing with eccentric ideas in the literature. In some cases it is the seemingly novel position that is the most interesting and with greater potential than the conventional and familiar one. New, interesting and potentially useful ways of looking at some aspect of the world can be generated at all levels and in all subject

Table 5.1   *Analysis, synthesis, comprehension and knowledge*

Analysis	Select, differentiate, dissect, break up.	Unpacking a thing into its constituent parts in order to infer or determine the relationship and/or organizing principles between them; thereby isolating the main variables.
Synthesis	Integrate, combine, recast, formulate, reorganize.	Rearranging the elements derived from analysis to identify relationships or show main organizing principles or show how these principles can be used to make a different phenomenon.
Compre-hension	Understand, be able to explain, distinguish, interpret.	Interpreting and distinguishing between different types of data, theory and argument; thereby being able to describe, discuss and explain in various ways the substance of an idea or working of a phenomenon.
Knowledge	Define, classify, describe, name, use, recognize, become aware of, understand, problem solve.	Perceiving the principles, use and function of rules, methods and events in different situations; classify, characterize, generalize, analyse the structure of, and learn from experimentation on the meaning of, concepts and their application.

fields. The subsequent synthesis does not have to be outstanding or in a class in which we might place the ideas of Copernicus, Newton and Einstein. It does, however, need to be coherent and explicit. This means providing a clear exposition on the origins of the elements in the synthesis and showing how the connections were made. The latter is about describing and showing how a batch of ideas compare and differ, and how they can be related to a problem.

Apart from looking for a topic, a researcher undertakes to analyse and synthesize ideas in the literature for a number of other reasons, one of which is to practise and develop competence in the skills of analysis. Through practice you will develop a style of your own and begin to enjoy the confidence it will give you in your own competence. A second reason is the need to gain knowledge of the subject area. The foundation for analysis is thinking in various ways about what you are reading. This process will enable you to dig beneath the surface of an argument and be able to see the origins of a piece of research or theory. In this way you will be able to make direct mental connections between what would appear at face value to be separate arguments or articles. In other words you will come to know the typology of origins and assumptions which most authors on a subject employ, but rarely state, in their work. With practice you can become an expert and be able to assess critically a piece of work in a broader context rather than merely regurgitating it as a single item in a list. As a researcher at postgraduate level, you will be expected to demonstrate these capabilities; this requirement is often stated in criteria as: 'a critical exposition of previous work' and 'an ordered presentation of knowledge of the subject'. Adequate demonstration of an appropriate level of analytical thinking is therefore very important.

ANALOGY AND HOMOLOGY

In the eighteenth century there was a relatively manageable stock of theories about the world and many academics had an understanding of ideas in both the natural and social sciences, because disciplinary divisions had not yet fully emerged and the academic community was still relatively small in number. However, with succeeding generations the academic disciplines have proliferated and diversified – manifested in the range and scope of the many ideas, concepts and theories in the social sciences. Many of the approaches to understanding society have developed into very complex disciplines in their own right and to become competent in at least one major approach, say feminism, can take several years of hard work.

Two techniques which social scientists use to overcome some of the initial difficulties that they think others might have in understanding their theories are analogy and homology. An analogy compares one thing with another. For example, you could describe the workings of the human brain as similar to that of a computer. This analogy, originally developed to explain the working of a computer, is now used interchangeably to describe the brain and computer. Analogies, therefore, help us to understand what is being talked about. They can give us a starting point: a reference to something with which we are familiar in order to help us grasp the complex and unfamiliar. Homology is used to look at one phenomenon in terms of the structure of another, very different, phenomenon. The particular structure of social-class relations at a given period in history might, for example, be used to explain the structure of messages found in the writing of an author. Those messages might be said to have a structure that is related to the structure of social-class relationships of the society in which the author lives. A homologous relationship will have been proposed to exist between two separate things. Homology therefore takes as the starting point that the ideas of an individual can be explained by reference to social structures and social relations.

Using analogy

One of the major reasons for the use of analogies is that the social sciences have very particular vocabularies. A feature of all academic disciplines is the unusual and often abstract vocabulary needed to converse in that discipline. For example, a student of information studies might use the term *dialog*. The student is not referring to the common use of the term *dialogue* in the sense of people conversing or exchanging views, but to an organization (Dialog) that provides access to on-line databases. You should not be put off by the difficulties in understanding the language of a subject. Nor should you be overcritical of a discipline that seems heavy with jargon. Most discipline-specific terms have been developed for good intellectual reasons – they help us to describe concisely very complex ideas and theories about society. It is your responsibility as a research student to work at understanding the language of a subject – if you cannot understand the vocabulary of a subject then you cannot analyse and evaluate the relevance of that research to your work.

Those unfamiliar with sociology often find difficulty with the lack of agreed definitions of key concepts. The specific meaning of a concept is usually dependent upon which particular strand of the discipline you are studying and, without a standard definition, comparisons in the use of any concept can be difficult. Added to this is another problem: just as you think you have grasped a concept and have pinned it down by a definition, it soon begins to elude you again. Unlike facts, ideas and concepts are not static; they shift and re-form their meanings in whatever way a theorist determines. Defining most concepts is therefore like trying to nail custard to a wall. This is why analogies are common in the social sciences – they help us to describe the intangible in ways that make them more concrete. If you are to analyse the use of any concept, theory or idea you must be able to evaluate the use of analogies. Some common analogies used in the different disciplines in the social sciences include:

- *Sociology*   the 'living body' of society.
- *Management* the 'pyramid' of organization.
- *Economics*   the 'flow' of currency.
- *Librarianship* the 'web' of information.

One of the oldest and most pervasive analogies in the social sciences is the organic analogy. Although it originated in the sociological work of Herbert Spencer (1820–1903), it has been used across many disciplines. Spencer's basic concept was that evolution was a unifying principle. He contended that society, like nature, undergoes evolutionary processes of transformation into higher and more advanced forms. The general principle behind this is the development of complexity from simplicity and differentiation from homogeneity. Whatever exists, according to Spencer's concept, is in constant struggle – a struggle between the forces of change and forces attempting to maintain equilibrium. Spencer therefore viewed society in the way he viewed nature. He described this conceptualization through analogy, claiming that society could be viewed as a living organism. **Example A (pp. 114–114) in this chapter shows the main concepts in Spencer's organic analogy – read it now.** As you do so note how he is careful to point out the similarities as well as differences between a living organism and society.

EXAMPLE A   THE ORGANIC ANALOGY

Based on Spencer (1969) and Radcliffe-Brown (1952).

In this first extract we can see how Spencer defines society in terms of the properties of living organisms.

Societies agree with individual organisms in four conspicuous peculiarities:

1 That commencing as small aggregations, they insensibly augment in mass: some of them eventually reaching ten thousand times what they originally were.

The idea of simple to complex through expansion: the continuum of development. The implicit notion of progress.

2 That while the first so simple in structure as to be considered structureless, they assume, in the course of their growth, a continually increasing complexity of structure.

Increasing size leads to the development of structures. The implicit notion that some societies are 'simple' and others 'advanced'.

3 That though in their early, undeveloped states, there exists in them scarcely any mutual dependence of parts, their parts gradually acquire a mutual dependence; which becomes at last so great, that the activity and life of each part is made possible only by the life and activity of the rest.

Gradual rather than sudden change from 'sameness' and independence to 'difference' and dependence. The implicit notion of labour division and individuality.

4 That the life of a society is independent of, and far more prolonged than, the lives of any of its component units; who are severally born, grow, work, reproduce, and die, while the body-politic composed of them survives generation after generation, increasing in mass, in completeness of structure, and in functional activity.

The whole and the parts: the whole is greater than the sum of the parts. The implicit notion that society has a life independent of its parts but influences those parts.

In analysing this analogy we can see that Spencer preferred and advocated a systems model of society. He argued that society was made up of parts that were interdependent; the relationship between the parts was structured into determinate patterns and each part had a function in the maintenance of the whole. We also see the idea of the whole (society) being larger or greater than the parts from which it was composed.

Spencer's organic analogy is interesting in itself as a piece of sociological reasoning. It is also interesting for the influence it had on empirical work in the discipline. Thinking about society as a body made up of organs led others, such as the anthropologist Radcliffe-Brown (1881–1955) to look at the functioning of the parts of society in relation to each other and the whole. Like Spencer, Radcliffe-Brown (1952) analytically divided a society into parts such as the kinship system, political system and belief system. In the following extract from his work we see how he uses the organic analogy to develop a metaphor for thinking about the function of the parts of a social structure. This functionalist theory enabled him to go beyond a description of activities observed to explain how these activities functioned to maintain society. This you can see in the following extract.

As the word function is here being used, the life of an organism is conceived as the functioning of its structure. It is through and by the continuity of the functioning that the continuity of the structure is preserved. If we consider any recurrent part of the life-process, such as respiration, digestion, etc., its function is the part it plays in, the contribution it makes to, the life of the organism as a whole. As the terms are here being used a cell or an organ has an activity and that activity has a function. It is true that we commonly speak of the secretion of gastric fluid as a 'function' of the stomach. As the words are here used we should say that this is an 'activity' of the stomach, the 'function' of which is to change the proteins of food into a form in which these are absorbed and distributed by the blood to the tissues. We may note that the function of a recurrent physiological process is thus a correspondence between it and the needs (i.e. necessary conditions of existence) of the organism.

Here we see some of the essential features of organic life described. The focus is on continuity of the organism.

An example is given that is intended to apply to all processes and organs in a body. Radcliffe-Brown is arguing that every activity found in the body has a function in contributing to the maintenance of the body as a whole.

Repeated definition of activity is used to emphasize the point that to uncover the reason for an activity, look for its function in terms of the larger structural whole.

The idea of 'needs' is introduced: that the body has functional needs that are required to be fulfilled in order for its survival.

To turn from organic life to social life, if we examine such a community as an African or Australian tribe we can recognize the existence of social structure. Individual human beings, the essential units in this instance, are connected by a definite set of social relations into an integrated whole. The continuity of the social structure, like that of an organic structure, is not destroyed by changes in the units. Individuals may leave society, by death or otherwise; others may enter it. The continuity of structure is maintained by the process of social life, which consists of the activities and interactions of the individual human beings and of the organized groups into which they are united. The social life of the community is here defined as the functioning of the social structure. The function of any recurrent activity, such as the punishment of a crime, or a funeral ceremony, is the part it plays in the social life as a whole and therefore the contribution it makes to the maintenance of the structural continuity.

Having described an organism, Radcliff-Brown turns to a comparative description of society.

The idea of the whole being greater than the sum of its parts is maintained. The parts are thought to be organized into patterns of social relationships that are a part of general structures.

The idea of continuity is followed through to emphasize the role of social structures.

All activities are seen as a part of the structure of social relationships, from court cases to funerals are to be seen as recurrent activities and, as such, having some function in the maintenance of the structures making up the whole.

The functionalist view of society, noted in Example A, was developed by others such as Parsons (1951), Merton (1938), Erikson (1966) and others. By the time Parsons was developing his systems approach, the organic analogy was no longer in popular use. Nevertheless, it allowed social researchers to analyse any society in terms of the functional needs of all societies. Each part was looked at as if belonging to one of three groups: a group which fulfilled regulatory functions (e.g., political-power arrangements), a group which fulfilled sustaining functions (e.g. agriculture) and a group that fulfilled distribution functions (e.g., money). The parts of society included language, religion, morals, beliefs, stratification and agencies of education and socialization. Any regular and routine phenomenon was treated as an institution for analysis in terms of the function it fulfilled for the maintenance of the whole.

The organic analogy is therefore a way of expressing a number of assumptions about the nature of any society. These assumptions can be and have been operationalized in a range of empirical studies, for example, Erikson's (1966) famous functionalist study of the Salem witchcraft craze. Whether you are dealing with an empirical study or theoretical development within the functionalist approach, the assumptions being used can be extracted from both for evaluation. The assumptions in the organic analogy are now well known and include the following: all societies grow and their growth is inevitable and cannot be prevented; social change in the arrangement of the parts is therefore ever present, hence, growth is associated with increasing specialization of parts (i.e. an increased division of labour) and this entails increased interdependence – each part needs the others even though there may be no direct link between them:

- in order to maintain regulation between the parts – to prevent the society fragmenting because of extreme individualism – moral boundaries are erected and maintained;
- a range of institutions constantly maintains boundaries and standards of acceptable behaviour, and this maintenance can be overt but is mostly covert (e.g., shaming rituals undertaken by the media show others what will happen if they too engage in certain types of behaviour).

In the research literature analogies are found in various forms and guises, organic and non-organic. Some theorists use extensive analogy to communicate the principles of their theory; others use relatively simple phrases, for example, 'the white heat of technology' and 'the cutting edge of research', which are metaphors. Metaphors are usually used for the purpose of quick illustration and most are part of some analogous conception of the world and therefore shape a theory's standpoint and perspective. For example, 'the white heat of technology' implies that lack of technology is cold, and possibly backward looking. A writer using such a phrase is expressing an argument about how we should see the use of technology: bright, dynamic, and extremely 'hot'. They are also setting up an implicit structure for a contrast, in that the use of technology is seen to be preferred and lack of technology is seen as a poorer alternative. Of course, context (including the purpose of the writer) influences the impact of the metaphor and will need to be taken into account.

Analogies are used to communicate to others certain views of the world. As such they are either a standpoint or perspective on the world, which makes them open to question: an analogy, the assumptions upon it is based and the consequences it might have, are all open to question, analysis and evaluation by the researcher. There are certain ways in which analogies can be analysed. The starting point is understanding the principles of good and bad analogies. The basic principle of analogy is comparison of one thing with another, which means that when someone uses an analogy they are arguing that what is true of one thing will also be true of another. In the organic analogy 'growth' is regarded as applicable to both living things and societies. Analogies have the following structure: x is like y; y has many features common to x; therefore, what is true of x will also be true of y: y can be described like x. This logic can be analysed through an interrogation technique similar to the one developed by Fisher (1993). The following are questions you can address to assess the usefulness of an analogy:

- Is it apt; is it valid?
- Are the claims made in the reasons for its use plausible?
- If so, in which respects are they comparable and to what degree?
- Are there more features or principles which are similar than dissimilar?
- If so, are these key features or not?
- What are the consequences of this for the analogy?
- To what kind of research and theorizing does this commit its use?
- Is this kind of research acceptable?

If we look more closely at the organic analogy we can see that there are some serious reasons for the careful use of analogy. The first point to note is the tendency of the organic analogy to encourage the assumption that what exists in a society must have a function. Even though something may seem to have no function or be dysfunctional (i.e. disruptive) for the whole, it is nevertheless regarded as being functional. The analogy encourages the analyst to look for or uncover the hidden rationality, and thereby a function for everything. Analytical attention is tied to the positive functions rather than negative functions of institutions and behaviours. In the human body, however, some organs appear to have no positive function or even no function at all; the appendix, for example. This kind of counter-evidence from the analogy could pose a challenge to the conventional bias inherent in the assumptions of the organic analogy.

A second point to note is the assumption of societal needs. A society or social system is assumed to have needs, and if these needs cannot be fulfilled then the social system will, it is assumed, 'die'. There is a certain attraction in assuming that all societies have certain prerequisites, but it can lead to some unusual and doubtful conclusions. For example, religious belief is often assumed to be a prerequisite of all societies. In societies rooted in religious beliefs, it is assumed that religion provides the moral basis for behaviour and therefore holds the society together. But what of those societies where there appears to be no formal religion, as in the former USSR? This assumption (or proposition) can only be maintained if a surrogate for religion is found – an assumption which could result in non-religious cultural movements being identified as fulfilling the function of formal religion. In the case of the former USSR the claim could have been made that communism was a form of religion. Similarly, one might claim that television and pop culture are forms of religion – these are things that people follow and engage with. However, claims that religion helps to maintain social order are propositional. They are claims made on the basis of a particular theoretical standpoint, and so are open to debate and challenge – as are alternative interpretations about the phenomenon of religion itself.

These points about the organic analogy are also applicable to other analogies, including any that you, as the researcher, deem appropriate to devise for your own ideas. Analogies are, nevertheless, very useful and, like some models, can save a great deal of time and effort when describing the principles of a theory or process. As in the case of the organic analogy, however, no conclusions or claim can be accepted on the basis of, or with reference to, an analogy, regardless of how good the analogy is. This is because analogies are not evidence or data; they are devices used to make complex ideas and theories more understandable. Therefore no analogy is proof of anything claimed or evidence for any proposition; if it is proffered as such, then that claim would be invalid.

In your research you need to look for the ways in which analogies are misused by authors, either deliberately or mistakenly. In particular, look for analogies used to induce belief or mitigate critical evaluation or negate alternative possibilities. Picturesque metaphors (ways of thinking about society) and similies are what induce belief in or acquiescence with a claim and the reader is more likely to accept them without critical questioning. Try to question all metaphorical turns of phrase used by an author. Ask what alternative metaphor could have been used; then ask what difference these other forms or analogies would make to the picture being proposed. Always bear in mind that an analogy or metaphor is an abstraction and that care needs to be taken in order to avoid mistaking it for reality. Through the use of this technique you can build up a critical attitude and a bank of typical metaphors and analogies with corresponding recipes for their analysis and evaluation.

Using homology

Homology is a word not often used in the social sciences even though, as a methodological principle, it is the basis of some notable studies. Much of the work done by the structural anthropologist Claude Lévi-Strauss (1963;

1964–72), the studies of classic literature by Lucian Goldman (1964) and studies of scientific knowledge by Shapin and Schaffer (1985) all employ the notion of homology. Homology might be seen as having a tenuous relationship with analogy and metaphor, each being distinct positions on a continuum. At one end, analysis using analogy looks for similarities between different phenomena, and the use of metaphor takes the line 'think about one thing as if it were the same as another thing' (Law and Lodge, 1984: 104–20). Homology takes a position at the other extreme, that there are direct and corresponding relationships between structures existing in the natural world and structures existing in culture and the human mind. A short example might help here.

Investigations (Russell, 1983; Shapin and Schaffer, 1985) into the work and thought of the famous scientist Robert Boyle (1627–91) claim that he looked on the laws of society in much the same way as those of nature. He believed that matter was innate and irrational, by which he meant that matter could not organize itself because it had no free will. Using this as a starting point, Boyle, it is argued, looked for the determining factors that shaped matter, such as air pressure, heat and weight leading to the corpuscular theory of matter. This was radical thinking in the seventeenth century. Previously even Boyle himself had subscribed to an animist theory of matter, which involves the personification of the natural world. In attempting to account for Boyle's transformation from an animist position to a corpuscular position, Shapin and Schaffer (1985) argue that a structural homology existed between the political context, religious belief and ideas in science in the seventeenth century. Politically, the period was one of radicalism that questioned traditional social and religious hierarchies. Radicals such as Gerard Winstanley, leader of the Diggers, believed that people and not the Church were responsible for the organization of society.

Alarmed at the growth of such radical religious-cum-political movements, a counter-position developed, called Latitudinism. The Royal Society, of which Boyle was a key figure, advocated Latitudinism. This was the belief that knowledge was not God-given, but had to be acquired and accumulated through hard work. Added to this was the assumption that the pursuit of knowledge was to be guided by men of learning such as ministers and gentlemen. Therefore what we have here is a homology. On the one hand were the radical movements and on the other the Royal Society and the Church. The radical movements advocated self-activity by the masses to organize themselves. Followed through, this might mean revolutionary change in the structure of society. Boyle reversed this view. He insisted and demonstrated through experimentation on gases that matter was inert and he then applied this to social structure. In homologous terms Boyle claimed that differences in nature were equivalent to differences in society. Nature could not organize itself, therefore society could not change itself. For inert matter read people, for active principle read Church, and for natural hierarchies read social hierarchies. In short, Boyle is said to have thought about the science of chemistry in the same way as he thought about the politics of society, applying the same structures of thinking to both. This is characteristic of the use of homology in the social sciences.

Assessment of argument based on homology (or its variant, correspondence theory) is not an easy task, because arguments based on the notion of homology or correspondence are usually very complex. There are, however, a number of levels on which any argument based on homology can be assessed. The goal of many theorists who use homology in their arguments is to give what they believe to be a scientific explanation of the social world, so we can use this as our starting point. The focus of any assessment would be the theory of the relationship said to exist between phenomena in the natural world and phenomena in the social or mental world. In short, examine first the plausibility of the theory itself in the light of the evidence, then see if there is sufficient evidence for the argument and what kind of evidence it is. If there is both necessary and sufficient evidence, then an argument based on homology might be a powerful validation of the methodological assumptions used. Conversely, if the evidence is thin or counter-examples have been ignored or dismissed as not relevant or not as good, then the plausibility of the theory can be doubted.

In a similar way the significance attributed to individual thinkers can also be questioned. Was Boyle, for example, as influential on the thinking about social organization as it is claimed; or does the claim rely on extrapolation from the evidence? Finally, you could look into the role of the analyst, asking how have they been able to see this connection when others have not? In most cases analysts take on a position of special status; one in which they claim their analytical framework has enabled them to show us the real picture. When this kind of self-attributed status is used in conjunction with a political starting point, the result is often like the work of the evangelist: converting us by encouraging us to see the world as they do. Therefore their work is motivated by the urge to change some state of affairs that they regard as wrong. Given these pointers you should be able to explore the plausibility of arguments based on homology. More important you should be able to reflect on your own preconceptions about the use of analysis and what kinds of goals motivate your own research.

CONSTRUCTING MEANINGS: DEFINING

In order to be able to think and express your ideas clearly and systematically it is important that you use words and concepts in appropriate ways. Conversely you will also need to know how to analyse the ways in which others have used words and concepts; especially in defining the subject-matter. Therefore to think clearly and to make sound arguments you will need to understand how to deconstruct the ways in which a word or concept has been used in an argument, and also how to follow the development of an argument based on definition. The aim of this section is to raise awareness of the use of words in order to avoid sloppy and avoidable misuse, equivocal meaning and misinterpretation.

Defining is about placing boundaries around the meaning of a term; it comes from the Latin *definire* – to put boundaries around. The boundaries relate to the way in which a term or word is used in a given context. There are different types of definition, such as formal definitions and stipulate definitions, which we look at later. One of the main things to notice at this stage is the way in which a definition can have different focal nodes. In her work on academic writing and reading Giltrow, (1995: 187–96) maps out the nodes of three main focal groups to show how a definition can be developed though different phases (Table 5.2).

Table 5.2   *Focal nodes of a definition*

Focus	Nodes
on the phenomenon itself, isolated for scrutiny	formal definition reflection on the word itself comparison division
on the 'career' of the phenomenon	examples account of variation associations
on the phenomenon's situation in a broader context	role in system cause and effect frequency

Source: adapted from Giltrow, 1995

When the definition focuses on the phenomenon, the thing itself is made different from other things. The phenomenon is isolated from similar phenomena and potentially grey areas are clarified. This may be done by making it clear what is and what is not included in the definition, a procedure which limits the phenomenon and therefore helps to focus attention on the topic of analysis. The same procedure can be used to extend what is to be included in the definition (i.e. classification) and thereby what is to be the topic. For example, if our topic was broadcasting we might want to look at a specific kind of media or all types of broadcast media. Either way a formal definition could be used to limit or expand the class of media for our study. We might, for instance, want to differentiate terrestrial from satellite broadcasting; then a formal definition of terrestrial broadcast media would differentiate it from satellite broadcast media. Conversely, we might want to look at the effects of broadcast media; in this case our definition might place media into a larger class, say agencies of control, along with other agencies, such as education, the courts and psychiatry. Formal definition, therefore, is based on differentiation and classification. Although many are offered as authoritative, you need to remember that all formal definitions are offered as plausible proposals and are, as a consequence, open to critical analysis.

Another technique associated with a focus on the phenomenon is reflection on the word itself. Focusing in on a word draws attention to that word.

This means that a concept or word can be analysed into its constituent parts and those parts defined as the features of the phenomenon. For example, broadcasting might be defined in terms of different technology, the production process, message encoding and decoding and message consumption. Similarly, focusing attention onto the word itself means that you can differentiate it from other words in the same class. For example, television broadcast media might be differentiated from radio broadcasts by reference to the visual aspect of television.

When we focus on the career of a phenomenon, we are defining the context and history of a thing in order to give it a location as a topic for research or theorizing. This can be done by tracing the history of the phenomenon by looking at the preconditions which indicate its development. Key landmarks and examples are often a feature of the career definition. Examples and instances can also be used to show variation from a theme or core; to show the ways in which a phenomenon splits into various strands of sub-development, each with its own career and special features. The idea of the career itself is largely a process of selection and therefore abstraction; it is the analyst who proposes what is to be seen as the key features and developments of the phenomenon. As such, key features are selected for their associative and contrasting relevance between other elements that might also be associated and which might be used to construct a different career definition. Therefore, career definitions are propositional and are also open to critical analysis.

In contextual terms a phenomenon and its parts might be defined in relation to the function or role each plays in a larger system. For example, the notion of the 'professional' can be applied in numerous situations. If a common definition is given to the concept of professionalism then its use across different contexts can be proposed. If defined as the power of the expert, professionalism can be placed into the class of phenomena associated with power and control; its frequency and different forms of manifestation can therefore be measured. You may often find, as many student researchers do, that it is economical to use pre-existing definitions and views of a phenomenon. If, however, the point of the research imagination is to be analytically creative, you should resist passive acceptance of traditional and habitual ways of defining phenomena.

There are a range of methods you can use (individually or in combination) to construct and analyse definitions or the use of words including the following.

- *Etymologies*   tracing the development of a word.
- *Dictionary*   stating the dictionary meaning of a word.
- *Writing formal definition*   showing the meaning of a word through the use of examples.

The most obvious thing at this stage is the use of dictionaries and encyclopaedias. Figure 5.1 shows some examples of what information you can expect to find in dictionaries and encyclopaedias.

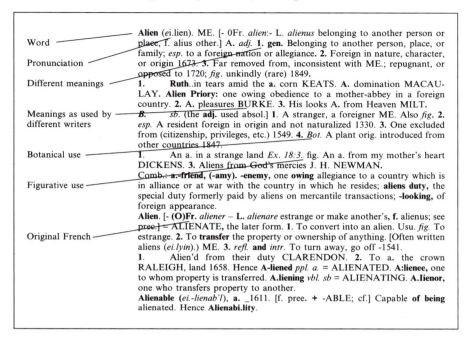

Figure 5.1 *Dictionary use*

Source: *Shorter Oxford English Dictionary of Historical Principles* (3rd edn, 1944).
By permission of Oxford University Press

- *Definition by example and counter-example* listing the things to be associated with a word.
- *Listing attributes* explaining the everyday use of a word.
- *Lexical or reportive definition* stating how you intend a word to be understood.
- *Stipulative definition* eliminating a particular meaning of a word or showing inaccurate uses of a word in order to emphasize a more precise or different use.
- *Defining by negation* using words to give an emotive slant (either positive or negative meaning) to something.
- *Definition by elimination* excluding particular events, items or explanations from a defintion to emphasize a specific argument.

Some concepts in the social sciences have relatively long and complex histories. Tracing the ways in which a concept has been defined and operationalized is called etymological analysis. In Table 5.3 (overleaf) different uses of the concept community are mapped and chronologically arranged.

Table 5.3 *An etymological summary of the concept 'community' 1880–1990*

Author	Period	Key points	Framework	Seminal works	Argument
Durkheim, Marx, Tönnies, Weber	1880s	Rural–urban continuum. The Great Transition. Positivism.	Theoretical Positivist	*Gemeinschaft and Gesellschaft* (Tönnies, 1887); *Division of Labour* (Durkheim, 1888)	Social change affecting traditional social bonds and community life. Community based on the notion of will. The Great Transition establishing a new basis for the division of labour. Social intervention to rebuild community will eventually be necessary.
Burgess, Lloyd Warner, Lynd, Park	1920s	Empirical research. Chicago School of Sociology. Outsider community studies.	Ethnographic Naturalistic Inductive	*Middletown* (Lynd, 1922) *Local Community Fact Book of Chicago* (1923)	Importance of fieldwork as a method to examine social structure. Importance of social statistics in community studies. City life has an ecological structure/base.
Harrison, Shaw, Wirth, Young	1930s 1940s	Mass observation of British society. Community within an urban setting. Participant observation. Research method description.	Ethnographic Descriptive Inductive Deductive	*The Jackroller* (Shaw, 1930) *Yankee City Series* (Lloyd Warner, 1937) *Urbanism as a Way of Life* (Wirth, 1938) *Street Corner Society* (Whyte, 1943) *Scientific Social Surveys and Research* (Young, 1944)	Urban life weakening traditional social bonds, subsequent decline in family life. Chicago School has had a positive impact on community study methodology. It is possible to map out concrete community study methodology.
Arensberg, Dennis, Hillery, Janowitz, Nisbet, Reiss, Stein, Wirth	1950s	Problem of community definition. Questioning community theory. Consideration of alternative concepts e.g. neighbourhood.	Empirical Spatial Evaluative	*Community Press in an Urban Setting* (Janowitz, 1952) *The Quest for Community* (Nisbet, 1953) *Towards a Description of Community Areas of Agreement* (Hillery, 1955)	Need to rethink approach to community and community studies. Ninety-four separate definitions, only commonality is the inherent idea of people. Searching for community based on Tönnies's concepts will prove fruitless.

Authors	Decade	Description	Category	Key texts	Commentary
Arensberg, Frankenberg, Nisbet, Stacey, Vidich, Warren, Wilmot and Young	1960s	British community studies. Myth of community. Questioning methodology. Insider community studies.	Empirical Analytic	*The Sociological Tradition* (Nisbet, 1967) *Community and Conflict* (Arensberg, 1968) *Communities in Britain* (Frankenberg, 1969) *The Myth of Community Studies* (Stacey, 1969)	Community based on shared traditions most fundamental of sociology's unit ideas. Continuity of community life. Sociologisgists are not studying community, they are studying area and locality.
Bell and Newby, Benson, Bernard, Elias, Filkin, Gusfield, Macfarlane, Plant, Scherer	1970s	Rethinking the concept of community. Comparative community studies. Community in social policy.	Theoretical Normative Summative	*Contemporary Community: Sociological Illusion or Reality* (Scherer, 1972) *The Sociology of Community* (Bernard, 1973) *The Concept of Community* (Gusfield, 1974) *The Origins of English Individualism* (Macfarlane, 1978)	Need to redefine community. Anomalies in models for understanding community life today. Paradigm in crisis. Community has taken on so many meanings as to be meaningless.
Bulmer, Clark, Cohen, Cooke, Kingdom, Marion Young	1980s	Loss of community as a result of 1980s boom. Alternative conceptions such as locality. Symbolic community. Gender and community.	Rhetorical Postmodernist	*Resurrection of Community Studies* (Bulmer, 1985) *The Symbolic Construction of Community* (Cohen, 1985) *Ideal of Community and Politics of Difference* (Marion Young, 1986) *No Such Thing as Society* (Kingdom, 1987)	Postmodernist acceptance of diversity in conflict with the idea of community. Community is an invention in the eye of the beholder. Ideal of community privileges; unity over difference.
Allen, Atkinson, Crow, Day and Murdoch, Etzioni, Hedges, Jones, S., Keith and Pile, Payne	1990s	Resurgence of community and community studies. Virtual community. Communitarianism. GIS and community.	Theoretical Idealistic Homogenic	*Identification with Local Areas* (Hedges, 1992) *The Spirit of Community* (Etzioni, 1993) *Place and the Politics of Identity* (Keith and Pile, 1993) *Community Life* (Crow and Allen, 1994)	Community can be reconstructed through government intervention. Community is about rights and responsibilities. Heterogeneous nature of modern life demands a new spatial vocabulary.

Source: adapted from Jones (1997)

The first thing that strikes you is the widespread use of the concept throughout the history of the social sciences. But also note the way in which the origins of the concept lie in the late 1880s, in the works of the classic studies produced by Marx, Tönnies (1955), Weber (1965a) and Durkheim (1984). The etymological map proposes that the concept of community, although widely used in many different ways, has a common frame of reference (or paradigm). That frame is made up of the assumption that a major transition from a rural way of life to an urban one occurred in the mid-nineteenth century.

Hence, running through these studies is the methodological assumption of contrast. This is the belief that industrial society can be compared and contrasted with pre-industrial society in respect of the kinds of community that characterized each mode of living. Rural, pre-industrial society is thought to have been characterized by a qualitatively different kind of community from industrial society: one in which social relationships were much closer and family bonds much stronger. The works of Tönnies (1855–1936), Weber (1864–1920) and Durkheim (1858–1917) along with that of Marx (1818–83) have all shaped the development of social theory in the twentieth century and will probably continue to be an influence on the social sciences in the next millennium. They all used a framework that assumed the break-up of community. Tönnies refers to *Gemeinschaft* and *Gesellschaft* (community and association), while Durkheim termed non-industrial society, mechanical solidarity, and industrial society, organic solidarity.

What community has been taken to mean may therefore differ between the different studies but, as the etymological map shows, a set of methodological assumptions is common to all uses of the concept. The map shows the approach to community: the ways in which a key conceptual construct, although subject to much debate, has distinct methodological boundaries.

Hence, if you were undertaking a study of community Table 5.3 shows the relevant literature you would look at. As a consequence you would be working within and with a long-standing framework of methodological assumptions. Breaking free from these assumptions would be a difficult task because the framework is historically established and has enjoyed widespread use throughout the social sciences.

Definition: Paradigm

In social science, the concept of paradigm derives from the work of T. Kuhn, in particular, *The Structure of Scientific Revolutions* (1970). It is used to describe how scientists work within accepted (usually unquestioned) ways of defining, assigning categories, theorizing and procedures within disciplines and during particular historical periods. Different eras of science are characterized by particular world views (paradigms) that are taken as knowledge, and are used as standard forms of solutions to problems, of explaining events and of undertaking research. Paradigm shifts occur when the dominant paradigm is successfully challenged by another paradigm able to incorporate the existing paradigm and also offer wider explanatory power and understanding.

Working within the framework has advantages; you would be relatively safe because you would not be attracting attention by doing something different. Paradigm shifts do some times occur, for example, the Ptolemanic paradigm was incorporated into the Copernican paradigm. Those who do step outside established and cherished paradigms, however, often have their work marginalized. For example, the historian Alan McFarlane in his work, *The Origins of Modern English Individualism* (1979), cast doubt on the methodological assumptions about the idea of the transition from rural community to urban individualism. Even though his argument is systematic, it has not been incorporated into the popular expositions that disseminate the stock of knowledge underpinning the social sciences.

Challenging an established position – a position many other theorists take for granted – is not something to be done lightly. It requires a thorough knowledge of the consequences of using different assumptions and the ability to construct carefully reasoned argument. But having produced this kind of map you will be able to see more clearly, in global terms, the concepts you are using. Hence, you will give yourself a choice over which definitions you might find useful, because you will have analysed how others have defined and operationalized the concept in their studies.

However, even within the tradition itself we see a great deal of healthy debate. As a key concept within the social sciences, community has attracted considerable attention. The concept of community, its meaning and ways in which it can be operationalized is a major source of debate, criticism and research. As such, its literature is massive, running into hundreds of items, and has considerable potential for analysis. However, a major problem with such a concept is that most researchers who have sought to give a definition of community have done so by adding more examples or seeking more information about the concept. This has led to more confusion than illumination of just what is meant by such a nebulous concept. Table 5.3, however, attempts to summarize the main developments in its use by showing the historical continuity of interest in the topic. It also shows the ways in which different theorists at different times have re-evaluated the use of the concept and at the same time argued against previous definitions and ways of operationalizing it.

Example B looks at a very familiar work to see re-evaluation of another topic. In his classic work, *Suicide: A Study in Sociology* (1970), Émile Durkheim demonstrates how to construct a rigorous argument through the use of definitions. Durkheim's aim was to demonstrate the scientific status of sociology. **Turn now to Example B below.**

EXAMPLE B   DEFINING THE TOPIC FOR ANALYSIS

Source: Durkheim (1970) *Suicide: A Study in Sociology.*

In the three books (all in one volume) that make up *Suicide* Émile Durkheim demonstrates through definitional analysis the existence of a social reality as a phenomenon for serious scientific study. In order to show conclusively the importance and distinctiveness of social, as opposed to psychological and biological, explanations of behaviour, Durkheim chose suicide as his topic. We can see why Durkheim chose suicide in the statement that is his hypothesis: 'Suicide, perhaps the most intimately personal action that an individual can take, is a phenomenon which is nevertheless, not to be understood in terms of individual psychology, biology or physiology, but in terms of social forces wholly external to the individual' (1970: 46).

In this hypothesis we see Durkheim defining the subject, as he saw it, for sociology. In identifying the pattern of suicide rates among peoples of different European countries Durkheim is insisting that he is not concerned with suicide as an individual action. He wanted to show that the rate of suicide was a social phenomenon (a social fact) and that it could be explained in terms of the social relations to be found in different societies and cultures. The evidence he uses for this initial statement is the invariability of the suicide rate for a number of nationalities. Using statistics showing the number of suicides in European countries, Durkheim makes a number of interesting observations.

> [T]he statistics for one and the same society are almost invariable. . . . This is because the environmental circumstances attending the life of peoples remain relatively unchanged from year to year. To be sure, more considerable variations occasionally occur; but they are quite exceptional. They are also clearly always contemporaneous with some passing crisis affecting the social state. (1970: 46)

Durkheim's argument is that social rather than other factors are largely responsible for the invariance in the rate of suicide: the suicide rate of a society or community 'is not simply a sum of independent units, a collective total, but is itself a new fact *sui generis*, with its own unity' (1970: 46). Durkheim's topic was therefore the distribution of suicide. It was this topic that he had distinguish from the circumstances of particular individuals who commit suicide.

To do this, in book one of *Suicide* (*Extra-Social Factors*), Durkheim attempts to show that explanations relying on factors other than social ones are inadequate. He does this through a systematic elimination by definition, that is, eliminating other possible explanations, in this case, of suicide. In this book Durkheim eliminates the following: insanity, gender, geographical location, alcoholism, race and heredity, cosmic factors, and imitation. He begins this by building up his own definition of suicide and he starts by showing the need for a definition:

> Since the word 'suicide' recurs constantly in the course of conversation, it might be thought that its sense is universally known and that definition is superfluous. Actually, the words of everyday language, like the concepts they express, are always susceptible of more than one meaning, and the scholar employing them

in their accepted use without further definition would risk serious misunderstanding. (1970: 41)

Durkheim is therefore claiming that everyday language is too imprecise for serious scientific argument. This is because, he argues, words as used in everyday conversation are indefinite and are likely to vary in meaning from one situation to the next. Therefore, Durkheim is arguing for a precise definition of suicide before any serious study of the topic can be made. He approaches this task by proposing a series of formulations of suicide. His first formulation is this: 'the term suicide is applied to death which is the direct or indirect result of a positive or negative act accomplished by the victim' (1970: 42).

He then amends this definition because he shows that it is incomplete and could be ambiguous. The same definition of suicide could, argues Durkheim, be given to individuals suffering from hallucination who throw themselves out of a building, as to those who do so knowingly. Similarly, he argues that a person's motive cannot simply be inferred, because motive cannot be observed. Moving through such examples, Durkheim turns to the problem of how to classify the deaths of people who sacrifice themselves for others. In the following extract we can see what he means by this problem.

> In general an act cannot be defined by the end sought by the actor, for an identical system of behaviour may be adjustable to too many different ends without altering its nature. Indeed, if the intention of self-destruction alone constituted suicide, then the name suicide could not be given to facts which, despite apparent differences, are fundamentally identical with those always called suicide and which could not be otherwise described without discarding them. The soldier facing certain death to save his regiment does not wish to die, and yet is he not as much the author of his own death as the manufacturer . . . who kills himself to avoid bankruptcy? (1970)

Durkheim continues with such examples in order to show that there is a need to study suicide as a social fact rather than as a psychologically or personally motivated action: although people commit self-destruction for a variety of reasons, whatever the reason 'scientifically this is suicide' (1952: 44). It is through this kind of reasoning that Durkheim is able to reach his conclusive definition of suicide: 'the term *suicide is applied to all cases of death resulting directly or indirectly from a positive or negative act of the victim himself, which he knows will produce this result*' (1970: 44).

Note that this definition already excludes certain types of suicide, for example, the suicide of animals, victims of hallucination, alcoholics who drink themselves to death, dare-devils who accidentally kill themselves and scholars who work themselves to death.

Having constructed and explained his definition of suicide, Durkheim goes on to show, through careful analysis, that existing explanations of

suicide are inadequate. He proceeds by a process of elimination by argument, through the use of a range of quantitative data such as statistics and
maps to substantiate his arguments. He rules out factors such as insanity,
gender, alcoholism and race. He eliminates alcoholism by comparing a
map of prosecutions for alcoholism with one of suicide rates in areas of
France and Germany (1970: 77–81). He found that there was no significant
connection between them. He therefore concludes that a 'society does not
depend for its number of suicides on having more or fewer . . . alcoholics'
(1970: 81). In a similar, way Durkheim eliminates insanity as a cause for the
invariance of the suicide rate. By definition, if all those who commit suicide
are classified as insane, then there would be little case for a social
(structural) explanation. But, as Durkheim points out, there is an enormous
difference between certifiable madness and the depression of an otherwise
'normal' balanced person. Yet both may commit suicide. From available
statistics, Durkheim shows that more women than men were to be found
among the populations of asylums for the insane (in the late nineteenth
century), but in society at large, more men commit suicide (1970: 71). He
also shows that insanity rates peak at about the age of 35 years of age
remaining constant until about 60 years of age. However, Durkheim shows
that suicidal tendency increases regularly from childhood to the most
advanced old age (1970: 73), suggesting again that insanity is an unlikely
cause of suicide. As a consequence of using the available data Durkheim is
able to conclude that:

> as insanity is agreed to have increased regularly for a century and suicide
> likewise, one might be tempted to see proof of their interconnection in this fact.
> But what deprives it of any conclusive value is that in lower societies where
> insanity is rare, suicide on the contrary is sometimes very frequent. (1970: 76)

Suicide shows how definitions used as the basis of an explanation, once
scrutinized, can be shown to be ambiguous: if they are treated in strict
stipulative terms the evidence that could be used to support them often
shows an inverse relationship exists. For example, when examining the
claim that insanity was the cause of suicide, Durkheim takes the rates of
insanity not generally but for three different religious groups: Protestant
faith, Catholic faith and Jewish faith. He shows, contrary to the opinion of
his day, that in this case 'suicide varies in inverse proportion to psycho-
pathic states, rather than being consistent with them' (1970: 73).

There have been, over the course of the twentieth century, many critical
evaluations of Durkheim's famous study. Nevertheless, most are agreed
that Durkheim's style of argument is a classic illustration of how definitional analysis combined with comparative data can be used effectively to
eliminate explanations. Systematically questioning the evidence of any
explanation or argument can therefore be an effective method of analysis. It

helps to clarify your understanding of those arguments and also to show (or not, as the case may be) the strength of the arguments you are proposing.

COMPARING AND CONTRASTING

A common practice in the social sciences is to make comparisons between the works and ideas of different authors. This usually involves finding common points of interest between, say, definitions of main concepts, kinds of data collected and the interpretation of findings. The practice can be useful in identifying common areas of interest and differing positions on similar topic areas. Figure 5.2 shows that comparing and contrasting can be done at several levels. The point to note, however, is that comparing theorists has inherent difficulties, mainly to do with the selection of criteria or points of reference that are valid and comparable.

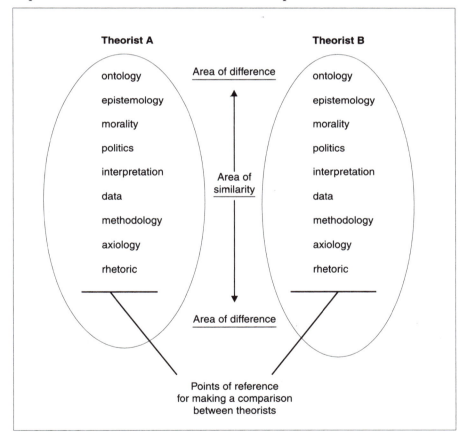

Figure 5.2   *Identifying locations for comparison*

Not all things can be compared with all other things. Any number of phenomena belonging to the same family of things (e.g., methodological assumptions) can usually be analysed in a comparative framework, but rarely can all the elements in one phenomenon be compared to those of another with equivalent degrees of similarity and difference. There will be certain elements in one phenomenon not present in others and vice versa (see Figure 5.2). Selectivity, therefore, is essential to any successful comparative analysis.

One of the requirements of selection is that choices made need to be clear, explicit and justified, because the choice of which elements to compare might affect the degree to which the reader agrees with the analysis. The detail required for a justification (i.e. argument) depends on the audience and the degree of novelty of the comparison. Taking account of, and writing for, a particular hypothetical readership is important. When setting out on the analysis you need to have in mind just what type of person will read the research report. Try to think about the level of knowledge you can reasonably expect from your potential readers. Similarly, the more novel or even radical the comparison, the greater the need for detailed explication. Conversely, the more familiar the comparison, the less will be the need for explication.

In their small but very enlightening book called *The Sociology Game*, Anderson et al. (1985: 60–9) make a comparison between the ideas of Karl Marx and Max Weber. Their short explication demonstrates the kind of attitude that we have been looking at throughout this book. The first is the need for an interpretation that is open-minded, clear and based on demonstrating understanding. They show how the relative ideas of Marx and Weber (1965a, 1965b) share certain assumptions, but differ in others; but the differences are not necessarily a reason for championing one of them to the detriment of the other – a preference for one does not invalidate ideas of the other and cannot be used to this end. The second approach the authors show is the need to understand the consequences of the differences and similarities in the ideas of Marx and Weber. They do this by discussing some of the more moderate and non-controversial interpretations of Marx and Weber and contrasting these with more extreme and controversial interpretations. Through this method they show that a reader can make choices about how to interpret a theorist, but in doing so the reader needs to be aware of the logical consequences of choices. **Bearing these points in mind, now read Example C below.**

EXAMPLE C   COMPARING MARX AND WEBER

Based on Anderson et al. (1985).

We begin this example by looking at how the authors set out what it is they are attempting to achieve. They start with the ideas of Marx: 'any theorist can be interpreted in many different ways . . . if the recent . . . treatments of Marx have done much to improve our understanding of his work, it has done nothing to make him any more conclusively interpreted' (1985: 60).

In order to focus on the main themes in the work of Marx and Weber, Anderson et al. examine a number of places in which Marx and Weber are commonly assumed to be different, such as the questions over economic determinism and idealism.

Economic determinism

Both Marx and Weber had proposed arguments based on the role of economic relations and modes of production. Anderson et al. begin by outlining what they see as the main points in Marx's thesis.

> Marx gives economic relations an important position in the understanding of society and its working. Irrespective of how this is eventually worked out, there is no question that for Marx understanding the structure of economic relations is fundamental to understanding the nature of society, and it is at this point that the fullest range of interpretations have centred. The range stretches from the readily acceptable claim that economic relations limit the possibilities of social life to the stronger claim that there is a specific causal connection between economic structures and other elements of social structure. (1985: 60)

That Marx emphasized the importance of economic relations in the formation and shape of society is not in doubt. However, as Anderson et al. also point out, at the time Marx was writing, people might have found it difficult to make the connection between economic forces and art, culture, religion and activities like literature. The fact that theorists have made connections between the economic conditions of a society and cultural activities shows that Marx's initial thesis has been developed in ways not developed by Marx himself. This development is therefore an area open to debate. For instance, have Marx's ideas been developed in ways consistent with what Marx himself would have recognized and agreed with? Or have Marx's ideas been used in ways not consistent with his original aims? Either way the ideas of Marx, and how they might have been used, are open to comparative analysis. However, Anderson et al. make another important point about the methodological strategy Marx suggested: 'We can . . . read Marx as making what is now an inoffensive "heuristic" suggestion about a strategy social inquiry might adopt for understanding a wide range of social phenomena, including many which might seem far removed from economic spheres of life' (1985: 61).

It might therefore be the different methodological strategies that different theorists suggest which can be a point for comparative analysis. In the case of Marx, Anderson et al. suggest that the role of economics might therefore be seen as the base of society. Such things as religion, art, education and the family can therefore be treated as the superstructure. In terms of methodology the superstructure can be described as determined by the base. This thesis, as Anderson et al. point out, is a much more contentious thesis than merely suggesting that the economic base has an important role for society. Although a contentious claim, it is also a claim that is bold and original but less plausible than saying that the economy is a precondition for the cultural aspects of social life. As Anderson et al. mention it is 'not uncommon a situation in sociology where often the interest in a claim is inversely related to its plausibility' (1985: 61). This difference between the bold and less bold thesis is, according to Anderson et al., the basis of a difference between Marx and Weber:

> [I]f we take Marx as advancing the less bold thesis, the more plausible one, that economic relations are important in social life, then there is little difference between them. Weber is no less convinced than Marx that economic relations are important for our understanding of society and its workings. He also emphasizes that there cannot be a simple and one-sided connection between economic and other social phenomena. . . . But if we use the Marx of the bolder thesis, namely, as advancing the position of 'economic determinism', then there is a wide gulf between him and Weber. Weber does deny that economic relations are the only determinate and influential forces in history, though this denial is not one intended to minimise their contribution, but to deny that they have exclusive sway. (1985: 62)

There is no need to cast Marx's ideas in terms of an either/or, as if we had a choice between extremes. Anderson et al. emphasize that the analyst has other choices and can impose limitations on an interpretation:

> [Marx could] be interpreted as concentrating on those aspects of social life in which economic relations are influential, so imposing . . . self-constraints on his theorising; that is, being interested in phenomena only in so far as they can be seen as influenced by economic relations. Restricting theorising in this way to certain kinds of influences does not have to deny other kinds of influences. (1985: 62)

Idealism

A second area in which Marx and Weber are often contrasted is the question of idealism. Where Marx is often said to have been a materialist, Weber is said to have been an idealist. In contemporary social theory, materialism is a label that connotes superiority over other positions, especially the idealist position. This simple and hierarchical contrast is a case of naive labelling. Marx and Weber were, of course, far too sophisticated in their thinking to have opted for a simplistic position. So any comparison needs a much more sensitive and informed treatment. To understand fully the nature of thinking in a materialist or idealist conception, a degree of knowledge about the history of ideas is required. One way to do this is to refer back to the work of the German idealist philosopher Hegel (1770–1831). Anderson et al. provide a succinct summary of the relationship between the thought of Marx and that of his tutor Hegel.

> Hegelian Idealism . . . postulated history as the development of thought which meant, in practice, the development of art, religious thinking, and, especially, philosophy. Thought developed, or so Hegel could be uncharitably understood to be saying, as if it were something which existed independently of human beings in some ethereal world of its own. Marx, however, was sceptical of Hegel's Idealism or, more accurately, the idealism ascribed to Hegel, for two reasons: first, history is the history of real, actual human beings, not abstractions: second, although Hegel thought developments in art, philosophy, and so on had brought people freedom, as far as Marx could see it left them as impoverished and as enslaved as before. Marx could not accept that a philosophical theory, on its own, could so change the world as to set genuine people free. (1985: 63)

Anderson et al. make their readers aware that any position attributed to either Marx or Hegel cannot be simple – that various interpretations can always be made. They show that ideas can neither be presented as if they develop in a straightforward way nor can the theories of any theorist be classified without challenge to that classification. Classifying one theorist in a single word can lead to the subsequent oversimplification by other theorists following the same classification. The case made for Weber being an idealist originates in his interest in the role of ideas, especially in his study *The Protestant Ethic and the Spirit of Capitalism* (1965b).

> Weber did not dismiss the importance of ideas in shaping the course of history . . . *The Protestant Ethic and the Spirit of Capitalism*, argues not against Marx but against a certain kind of materialism which denied that ideas have any independent role whatsoever. . . . (1985: 63)

The fact that Weber did not dismiss ideas and their social role does not make him an idealist. In looking at the role of ideas Weber is also looking at the kinds of relationships people engage in together when they have some ideas in common. This is entirely consistent with Marx's view that history is created by real people and not metaphysical forces. Weber's argument is not, then, that religion or other ideas are a cause of material conditions as in this case, the development of capitalism. *The Protestant Ethic and the Spirit of Capitalism* is not a challenge to Marx's materialist view of history, nor is it a challenge to Marx's distinction between the base (material conditions) and superstructure (ideas and mental life). This is because neither Marx nor Weber suggest that there was a strict one-way causal relationship between the base and superstructure. Marx's contention that the most important influence on the institutions of society was the economic one does not mean that it is the only one. Hence, although Hegel thought that consciousness (ideas and thought) determined material being and Marx did not, Marx reformulated the argument to put the emphasis on the material rather than on consciousness. From this example we can see that the development of any social theory is not a matter of constructing diametrically opposed positions: in this instance, materialism is not the only alternative to idealism or idealism the only alternative to materialism. Anderson et al. reinforce this point when they say:

> So far as the development of religion is concerned, Weber attempts to give a thoroughly materialist account of how it is interwoven with political and economic interests, the structures of power and inequality in society, the development of states and so on, as well as depending on the interests and problems that arise from within religion itself. (1985: 64)

If Weber's account is a materialist account of the relationship between religion and material changes then how is it that he has been labelled idealist? The main reason for casting Weber in the role of an idealist is simply that he examined religion, and religion is seen as belonging to the realm of ideas. This shows the kinds of mistakes that can be made by making quick assumptions that lack a sufficient knowledge base about the history of ideas. The second reason often comes from not appreciating the purpose a theorist has when presenting an account. If Weber's thesis is seen as idealist, then his purpose might be read as that ideas alone can have the power to transform the world. However, if we follow Marx's argument that ideas can only have any effect if they are acted on by groups following their own interests, then Weber might be seen as being in general agreement with Marx. Hence, Weber's thesis was that ideas, if taken up by a certain historically significant group, could have a decisive influence on historical events. This is very different from saying that ideas determine history, which would mean arguing for an idealist conception of history.

In their analysis of Marx and Weber, Anderson et al. demonstrate a number of important issues about making comparisons. The main point is that many of the differences between Marx and Weber: 'are not located . . . in places where they are usually sought. The critical difference is not that one is a materialist, or economic determinist, and the other an idealist, for, in most respects, neither is more nor less materialist than the other' (1985: 68). Another point that Anderson et al. bring to the fore is the need to dig beneath common understandings about a theorist. That is, do not take secondary expositions at face value – they need critical evaluation in relation to the original work.

Now that you have read Example C, the message you should bring away with you is this. If someone has offered an interpretation of a theorist based on some form of comparison, that account is open to examination. You can do this by identifying the main places at which comparisons are normally thought to be located. These can then be examined in detail to see why such places have been located and what has been made of them by others and for what reasons. As Anderson et al. show, if this procedure is followed, you will usually find that things are not always what they seem.

PHILOSOPHICAL SCRUTINY

In this chapter we have examined ways in which ideas, interpretations and methodological assumptions can be presented to advocate acceptance of an argument; and conversely, how we can analyse such techniques and practices. Underpinning this chapter has been an implicit prompt to employ philosophical scrutiny when reviewing a literature. We need to think about and question the plausibility of what is being proposed as an interpretation of a state of affairs. What we are doing when we analyse the works of others is to dissect and reorganize all ideas and arguments, many of which are very complex and difficult to grasp.

It is often the case that what makes an argument difficult to understand is the way in which it has been constructed. The author of an argument may have committed, quite unknowingly, a number of methodological fallacies and mistakes in the use of language, and these create a confusing and misplaced position on a matter or question. Through philosophical scrutiny we can usually make visible these kinds of errors in logic and fallacies. There are two philosophers whose work is particularly relevant here: one is Gilbert Ryle (1900–76) and the other is Ludwig Wittgenstein (1889–1951).

Both Ryle and Wittgenstein had, amongst other concerns, reservations about the ways in which language and concepts were used to construct explanations and arguments about the nature of reality. In their separate ways each came to the conclusion that many problems in science were the result of a widespread and inappropriate use of concepts; and it was this that usually led to confusion. Ryle focused his attention upon the use of misleading expressions and mistakes made with inappropriate use of categories, while Wittgenstein had serious reservations about the attitude of science, in particular, the attitude towards generality and truth.

If we look first at Ryle we can see something of the nature of philosophical scrutiny. Ryle (1949) was interested in the details of how a conclusion was made. He was therefore interested in the routes by which an argument was put together. Through analysis he showed that the ways in which we tend to think about the world are based on long-standing mistakes. The first set of mistakes Ryle identified was what he called systematically misleading expressions. Here is an example: a robin is a bird; Stephen Hawking is a man. What is it, Ryle would ask, about these statements that makes them factual and able to be understood (i.e. meaningful)? Ryle was not interested in the particular facts in such statements; his interest is in what scientists and philosophers take to be the formal properties of such statements. That is, factual statements have syntactical similarities that can lead to confusions. One confusion is to treat facts as if alike: a bird is a thing just as a man is a thing, therefore both are objects. If this is the case then both can be studied in the same way.

This kind of logic might lead down a number of routes, all of which compound and continue the confusion. First, it might be assumed that birds and humankind are the same (a reductionist argument) which would be incorrect, if not meaningless. A similar assumption can be applied to some analogies. Defining society by comparing it to an organism might give it a quasi-ontological character leading us to believe that society is a real object rather than an abstract term, or, to take another analogy, defining the mind as if it were a computer might lead us to believe that the mind is a physical (i.e. material) object.

A similar misplacement can be seen in the use of words like beauty, justice, equality, intelligence, creativity, knowledge, wisdom and the like. The expression 'one is born beautiful' is a generalization; it assumes some universal understanding about the concept of beauty, as well as implicitly assuming some causal link based on the inheritance of physical features. It fails to ask a number of relevant questions, such as the following. What is meant by beauty? Who defined beauty? When was the definition given? What comparisons were made or what comparisons could we make to establish criteria? Beauty therefore is a concept not a fact: it is not an object in the world, and is not therefore something we could collect information on and thereby eventually arrive at some stipulate definition. Like the concepts of justice and equality, beauty is a characterization of actions and conventions in social relations that are relative and context dependent. As such, movement from the universal to the particular can, at best, be misleading and, at worst, meaningless.

Secondly, treating facts or interpretations as if alike might lead us to be confused about the alternative ways of thinking about the world. Take, for example, the statement that I might make: the chair I am sitting on is solid. My colleagues in the Department of Physics, however, tell me that my chair is nothing more than particles held together by forces I cannot see. How can my chair be two things at the same time? I cannot choose between the two seemingly alternative views on reality. This is because what seem to be contradictory positions are different positions; they cannot therefore be subjected to a comparative evaluation to assess relative accuracy and so determine which position is the more truthful or better.

What we have here, according to Ryle, is a muddling of the technical with the non-technical (i.e. commonsense) attitude. The muddle has its origins in trying to say that one kind of reality is superior to another, rather than saying it is different. The point here is that great care needs to be taken when attempting to compare things; judgements of relative worth cannot always be settled through a comparative exercise. The usefulness of one social theory cannot easily be compared with that of another, or one society shown to be superior to another, by subjecting each to a comparative evaluation. When such exercises are attempted they often have to leave out residual elements or make claims of a moral superiority in order to argue for one position over another. Recourse to morality or politics is, then, due to mistakenly attempting to compare things which are different and which cannot be judged in terms of universal logic.

We might go on to apply research methodologies and techniques that are incongruent with the phenomena we are studying. A classic example here comes from the body/mind debate. It is commonly assumed that the mind is different from the physical body, that it is resident somewhere in the brain of the body, and that it is the mind of a person which causes the person to act rather than merely respond. It is therefore assumed that the presence of a mind is what distinguishes humans from other forms of life. In particular, scientists have wanted to treat mental phenomena, such as attitudes, emotions and intellect, as if they were physical things. The motivation for this is the belief that events in the world can be explained in terms of causal relationships. Categorizing the mind as separate from the body is, according to Ryle, a major category mistake.

The nature of this category mistake resides in treating the mind as if it were a physical object rather than a process. For example, events in the physical world tend to be episodic: one thing happens and then another thing; such happenings occur in space and time. Mental events, however, do not have the same kind of episodic character as objects: they do not exist in a space nor as a distinct entity. Ryle suggests that in making assumptions about a mind/body dualism we can commit a number of misplaced descriptions due to the inappropriate use of the categories we use. He gives numerous examples of the category mistake, such as assuming that a university is something distinct from the buildings that we can see around it, or that team spirit is something that can be observed along with the activity of the sporting event itself.

Ryle is therefore drawing attention to the variety of ways in which categories (i.e. concepts we associate with the mind) are used to relate different things and thereby produce descriptions of those things. He is suggesting that we need to reflect on the categories we use, especially when using the appropriate 'mental' verbs to describe dispositions; that is, tendencies to act in certain ways. This is because many actions are not easily described using dispositional verbs. For example, we can describe the physical activity of someone mowing their lawn but find it more difficult to describe the process involved when someone is doing mental arithmetic. We cannot, according to Ryle, reduce the latter kind of activity to the former, because they are different. Added to this, Ryle observes, we do not need to reflect on the intricate rules or propositions of arithmetic in order to do arithmetic. The ways in which people do arithmetic can be very different; they might use a pen and paper, or employ objects to count with or do it in silent contemplation. Ryle therefore warns against assuming that such activities as arithmetic are somehow mysterious, as hidden away somewhere in an entity called the mind. What Ryle recommends is the use of thick description. He believed that it is only through a detailed, thick description that we can show the variety of processes people use to do what they do. This leads us to the work of Wittgenstein.

In his later work Wittgenstein (1953) had a great deal to say about the nature of making comparisons through the use of language and the benefits to be had from a thick description of phenomena. Although he did not deal with these as separate issues, for the sake of clarity we will consider them separately. The first point that needs to be made when looking at the work of Wittgenstein is that one of his main interests was with the attitude of science. Wittgenstein was not interested in saying anything about the findings of science but, like Ryle, was interested in, and had some serious reservations about, the ways in which scientific argument was constructed. Also like Ryle, Wittgenstein's ideas are difficult to translate into the social sciences, but we can get an idea of their usefulness with a simple example. When looking at something like witchcraft we might say that its outcomes are false. We might add, through a comparative assumption, that the deductions of science are true. But to some people the outcomes of witchcraft are true.

Therefore, as social researchers, we have a difficulty concerning the status of truth and falsity. Wittgenstein's interest was in such difficulties. He was not interested in establishing criteria for determining what is and what is not true. His interest was in what makes something either true or false and what kinds of statements are inappropriate for even trying to determine their truth or falsity.

Wittgenstein was therefore not assuming that everything that has syntactical similarities based on logical form is capable of being empirically proven to be true or false. His interest was in investigating the boundaries of factual discourse. The problem is, of course, that factual statements can look very similar to non-factual statements. It is easy to mistake a statement for a statement of truth. It is because people tend to think within certain institutional frameworks that some things are accepted as true and other things, that are outside that way of thinking, are regarded as false. Science, which dominates Westernized culture, and the witchcraft beliefs, which dominate life in Azande culture, are both institutionalized. Therefore, according to Wittgenstein, it only makes sense to talk about the truth of science within the theoretical basis of the institution of science, just as it only makes sense to talk about the use of witchcraft within the everyday life of Azande people.

Therefore Wittgenstein had reservations about the goal of generality in science. He was not critical of science or of the emphasis it placed on general explanatory frameworks. He was, however, concerned with the degree of emphasis placed on generality to the exclusion of other ways of understanding the world around us. His basic contention was that not all puzzles and problems require generality in order to be explainable. This, he thought, was especially the case with conceptual puzzles often associated with debates over methodology and theory: such things as clarification, analysis and even an understanding of how a phenomenon happens, cannot wholly be had from a generalizing approach. This is because, according to Wittgenstein, the ways in which a problem is stated can often lead to an inappropriate strategy for its investigation.

CONCLUSION

We stay with Wittgenstein to conclude this chapter. Wittgenstein makes a simple but useful distinction between puzzles which require information (i.e. more facts) and those that require clarification (i.e. sorting out). Many of the things we have said throughout this chapter are to do with clarification, about sorting out confusing and diverse ideas in order to recast them to make them clearer. Once we have collected sufficient literature we can begin to tackle our problem of understanding. But in collating the literature we are tackling the problem of information. Wittgenstein's distinction therefore informs much of what we have been advocating. He maintained that there are two main kinds of problem: problems of ignorance (there are things existing that we do not know enough about and therefore we require more information), and problems of confusion (we have the information but we do not understand what it amounts to). We therefore need to seek clarity in the information we have, rather than acquire more. The consequences of this distinction are many, but for us there is one that we specifically need to acknowledge. If we emphasize description, use core texts and subject them to careful analysis, we can be more assured that we will clarify our understanding and be saved from endlessly searching for more information and thereby compounding our confusion.

6

Mapping and analysing ideas

The information contained in the literature is often made up of specific theories based on certain choices people have made about the methodological assumptions they wish to employ in their work. As a researcher, the aim of your review is to extract, to an extent appropriate to your degree (master's, doctorate), those methodological assumptions. This means you need to elicit from the literature the ways in which core ideas, concepts and methodologies have been employed in argument and how they have been operationalized for empirical work. This process forms another part of the analysis element of the review and is essential if core ideas and concepts are to be properly identified from individual items and thereby used to produce a map of the knowledge on a phenomenon, topic or problem.

In this chapter we focus on some of the ways in which the literature of any topic can be mapped out. The main use of mapping a topic is to acquire sufficient knowledge of the subject to develop the necessary understanding of methodology and research techniques, to comprehend the history and diffusion of interest in the topic, and to undertake an analytical evaluation of the main arguments, concepts and theories relevant to the topic in order to synthesize from the analysis an approach or thesis that is unique, that is, your work. Mapping therefore enables analysis and synthesis to be undertaken; in mapping work on a topic, you undertake the task of construction, putting together the different strands and elements of work that make up the body of knowledge on the topic. The interesting thing is that different researchers coming from different subject backgrounds often map out a topic in different ways. This means that your map will never be definitive; it will always have the potential to be developed either by yourself or by another researcher at a later stage. This chapter will therefore look at the following questions.

1　What do we mean by mapping ideas?
2　What techniques can we use to map ideas on a topic or methodology?
3　How can analysis be used to map the use of tropes?
4　How can analysis help to construct the historic influences on a topic or development?
5　How can we use analysis of citations to reconstruct the history of a topic?

The point to note here is that the reviews produced by other researchers are essentially maps of a topic. It is these maps that you are expected to analyse in a way that is evaluative and critical. The first thing we will look at are some relatively simple techniques based on diagrammatic representation for producing a range of different maps on a topic.

MAPPING IDEAS

Given the amount of information usually found in a search of the relevant literature (the topic literature and literature on methods), some form of organization of that information is essential. Organizing the content of the literature into sections and subsections will enable you to make connections between ideas contained in different articles, books and work published over a given period of time. Classification is therefore a necessary part of the analytical stage of a review for two reasons. The first is that the analysis provides a descriptive foundation (i.e. map) for future evaluation and assessment of ideas on the topic. Without the use of classification, large amounts of information could not be processed in a way that is both systematic and progressive. Hence the second reason: mapping ideas from a literature can be done in different ways, to produce different maps. You need therefore to be methodical in spelling out how the map or maps were produced. This means being explicit on why you chose to highlight connections between authors that another researcher might not have done.

Classification

In everyday life we tend to classify things quite routinely as we encounter them without giving much thought to the process of how we typify things. There is nothing that we, as humans, do not place into some category or other. For example, we classify objects as types, such as cars, houses and offices. We do not give, unless required, the descriptive details of the object or process. We have, therefore, different levels of classification based on the needs of the situation and our particular purposes.

We can often give a simple gloss (overview) to an attitude or behaviour, and this will normally be adequate. However, even in everyday life, we are sometimes required to give descriptions that have increasing depth and/or breadth. This basic principle of a sliding scale of descriptive detail is also the basis for classifying and mapping ideas from the literature. However, when organizing ideas from the literature we are classifying it for a somewhat different purpose. Rather than taking a routine attitude to classification we are adopting a technical attitude.

This involves taking a reflexive approach to how we are classifying. It means seeking to evaluate the ways in which ideas on the topic have been conventionally organized. Classification, at its most basic, involves sorting and organizing things, such as ideas, into categories and labelling those categories; it is a way of reducing information into a manageable amount. This process of assigning ideas into categories requires you to make decisions about how an idea is to be classified and subsequently convincing others that the labels used to classify particulars are plausible. This gives classification its argumentational element.

There are two elements to the argumentational nature of classification in the social sciences. The first is that ideas are not subject to fixed categories. In botany, for example, plants are subject to relatively fixed categories: a species of plant cannot normally belong to more than one class. This does not mean that the classification scheme is fixed. The breeding of some plants can lead to them being placed in different classes – but plants, in general, are an example of things categorized according to a formal classification scheme. Ideas, theories, concepts and arguments, however, are not subject to such formal schemes of classification. This is because there is often considerable overlap between categories into which ideas can be placed. For example, where would you place the work of a theorist such as Harold Garfinkel? The problem here is that Garfinkel's work is based on a particular and distinct strategy and so is highly empirical. Placing his work into, say, the category 'qualitative' might be seen as too simplistic, if not naive. It is inevitable then, that categories in the social sciences tend to be informal and flexible.

Conventions do exist, many based on dichotomies, such as the positivist–phenomenological contrast. While the use of dichotomy can be effective as an introduction to some of the differences between ideas and methodologies, it can also be a cause of the types of category mistakes we looked at in Chapter 5 when we discussed the work of Gilbert Ryle. When classifying things in terms of contrasting labels, we need to avoid oversimplification and the absurd reductionism that obliterates the detail and complexity of a methodology. The detail and complexity of, say, a closely argued monograph can be lost if the category into which it is placed is too general or has too few sub-categories. We need to take a technical and reflexive attitude to classification, seeking to produce a symmetry between organizing ideas in the literature and thinking about how we have carried out that organizing.

Different types of maps

Mapping ideas is about setting out, on paper, the geography of research and thinking that has been done on a topic. At one level, it is about identifying what has been done, when it was done, what methods were used and who did what. At another level, it is about identifying links between what has been done, to show the thinking that has influenced what has been produced. You can use these methods to elicit knowledge about a topic and then prepare diagrams and tables to represent that knowledge in terms of the relationships between ideas and arguments that you have found. Mapping can therefore be an effective way of getting an overview of the topic.

A range of methods can used to classify the materials and ideas from the literature. These range from the relatively simple listing of features deemed important, to suggesting relationships between features.

If you employ a combination of these methods you can acquire two kinds of knowledge. Mapping the ideas in the literature necessitates that those ideas are organized into some kind of arrangement – a task that ensures you become familiar with the key concepts, theories and methods that have been used by other researchers in that field of study. You acquire what is called declarative knowledge about the topic; that is, what the topic is about. Thus, you would be able to describe the different methods of mapping the literature, but you may be unable to apply the different methods. This should be remedied when you are actually classifying and placing ideas into categories for yourself; it is the route by which you will acquire procedural knowledge – an understanding of how to apply declarative knowledge about classification (Jonassen et al., 1993). Added to this you will acquire procedural knowledge about the relationships between the elements that make up the knowledge on the topic. By looking for relationships between ideas you will be thinking analytically, learning how to see connections and how to create new and interesting schemes. By mapping you are structuring the knowledge on a topic and gaining an understanding of how it has been used; that is, you acquire knowledge of its content. The following are some descriptions and illustrations of common methods for mapping the knowledge on any topic.

Feature maps Feature maps are a method by which the content of many articles can be systematically analysed and recorded in a standardized format. The method entails recording the key features of a predetermined aspect of a study to:

- produce a summary schemata of the argument proposed by that study
- to locate any similarities and differences between other studies on the topic.

Note that an important part of keeping track of individual sheets of information you collect is to record some basic bibliographical details and even assign a code to each sheet (Figure 6.1, p. 146).

The procedure is self-evident. Design the sheet (a large sheet of A3 is recommended) according what information you need from the articles, books and other materials obtained. The individual sheets can be produced by hand and then, if required, stored on computer. There is no real advantage in using a computer if you have only a relatively small number of items. If, however, you have many items, say 30 or more, then some form of computer database can be useful. It will allow you to search the records using key words and to produce various combinations from all or part of the records. Many databases will also allow you to change the format, to add another category or to change an existing one. Table 6.1 (pp. 147–8) and Figure 6.2 (p. 149), taken from Hart (1994), show the use of a feature

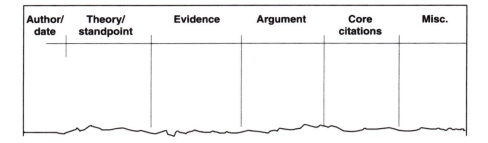

Author/ date	Theory/ standpoint	Evidence	Argument	Core citations	Misc.

Figure 6.1 *Summary record sheet*

map (or relationship map) to analyse some of the literature on advertising that has been produced from within a feminist standpoint.

This kind of analysis can also be recast into a format that makes visible the assumptions that have been found to have influenced research. The map, Figure 6.2, postulates the existence of a relationship between how the image of women is viewed and what Yanni (1990) and Shields (1990) suggested as a contributing factor causing it (advertising).

It shows in diagrammatic format the kind of argument Yanni and others are making about how women are objectified in society. The map shows this argument as a correspondence: that Yanni and others believe there to be a correspondence between the natural characteristics of manufactured goods and the artificial characteristics ascribed to women. Hence, they argue that women are reduced to the status of goods in a capitalist culture dominated by symbolism biased towards male views. The map, therefore, identifies the main abstractions in the argument to show how the idea of correspondence is used as an argument by Yanni and others. Many arguments depend implicitly or explicitly on relationships that are believed to exist, causing the presence of some phenomenon. While this example shows correspondence, Figure 6.4, also on advertising (discussed later), shows a stronger sense of the relationship between assumptions and argument.

You can also use feature maps to isolate and focus on specific aspects in the literature, such as the structure of argument that different authors have employed. Figure 6.3 (p. 150) is an example showing a worksheet that can be used for making comparisons between different authors working in the same topic field.

It is worth noting that we can use one map to construct another. In Figure 6.4 (p. 150) we can see a variant on the feature map. It shows the ways in which some authors have attempted to make a case for the existence of advertising. The basic argument is that advertising exists to sustain capitalist society. It does this by persuading people to purchase goods and services that are neither functional nor rational; that is, things such as electric toothbrushes, that people do not need in order to live. Notice in this

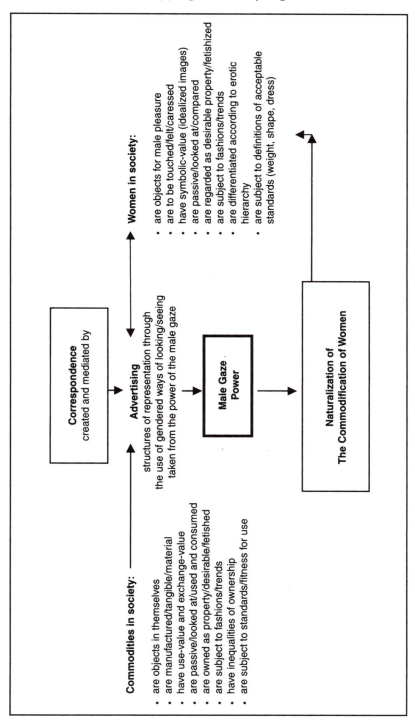

Figure 6.2 *A relationship map of an analysis of feminist analysis of advertisements for fragrance*

Table 6.1 *Extract from an analysis of feminist analysis of fragrance advertisements*

Author/date	Questions/concerns	Materials/evidence	Argument	Concepts/form of analysis	Main sources
Shields, 1990	How is meaning communicated through visual images, ads in particular? How do spectators of different sexes find pleasure in images constructed for the male gaze? What are the connections between ways of looking and ways of seeing? How can feminist analysis help in 'reading against the grain'?	Photocopy ads for cologne, Obsession ad, 2 illustrations, other studies.	Visual images communicate meaning through codes/messages which are produced within the dominant male ideology. Images reflect/reinforce/reproduce dominant cultural sexist, ageist discourse of attractiveness. Looking and seeing are gendered practices. Ads use gendered spectator and definitions of nudity (art) rather than nakedness (porn) to associate commodities with objectified male definitions of female attractiveness/sexuality. Codes/messages and referent systems can therefore be analysed using visual images to reveal the dominant ideology that specifies the pleasures of looking at, being looked at, and conforming to codes of attractiveness and presentational behaviour of the self.	Feminist/structural/semiotics. Male gaze and power of looking. Gendered spectator. Objectified/commodified female. Nudity and nakedness.	Williamson, 1978 Barthes, 1985 Nichols, 1981 Berger, 1973 Haug, 1987

Yanni, 1990	Other studies. No illustrations.	Ad images (visuals/text) continually devalue women while maintaining a priority/privilege to male experience and position of power to define convention codes.	Feminist critique. Addresses the nature and function of advertising through (1) the structure of representations (2) the process of commodification (3) the nature of fetishism (4) the power of ads.	Jhally, 1987 Berger, 1972 Williamson, 1978 Kappeler, 1986
How do women enter into the thing–people relationship differently from men?		Theories of commodities, representation and fetishism have failed to account for the unique position of women and their susceptibility to ad images.	Gendered ways of seeing: the male gaze.	
How can feminist analysis of ads provide evidence for the power of dominant ideological forms of constraint and suppression of women?		The material and symbolic meaning of women is misconceived by ads which misrepresent and objectify women for the sake of associating women's sexuality with commodities, as if their sexuality was a commodity.	Nudity and nakedness codes.	
		Women are therefore given material and symbolic value sharing the characteristics of commodity form represented in use value and exchange value.		
		Women are condensed physicality, displaced bodily and symbolized as objects and thereby it is made difficult for them to resist misrepresentations of the fetishized female image.		
		However, women can effect change through education, research and choice of images they view.		

	Author/date	Author/date	Author/date
(Key concept)			
Characterization/description			
Antecedents			
Evidence/data			
Consequences (therefore)			
Part of (major category)			

Figure 6.3   *Example of a worksheet*

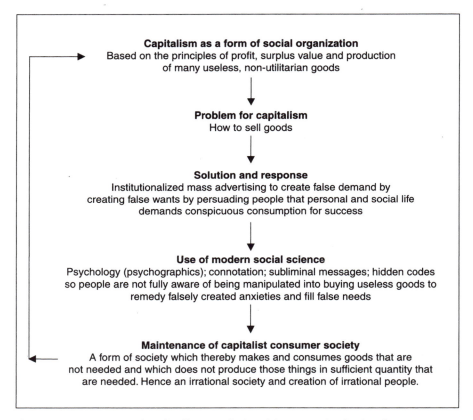

Capitalism as a form of social organization
Based on the principles of profit, surplus value and production
of many useless, non-utilitarian goods

Problem for capitalism
How to sell goods

Solution and response
Institutionalized mass advertising to create false demand by
creating false wants by persuading people that personal and social life
demands conspicuous consumption for success

Use of modern social science
Psychology (psychographics); connotation; subliminal messages; hidden codes
so people are not fully aware of being manipulated into buying useless goods to
remedy falsely created anxieties and fill false needs

Maintenance of capitalist consumer society
A form of society which thereby makes and consumes goods that are
not needed and which does not produce those things in sufficient quantity that
are needed. Hence an irrational society and creation of irrational people.

Figure 6.4   *An example of a linear relationship map: the logic of
assumptions about advertising*

figure the linear flow: the factors that have been identified as causal are arranged to explain several things rather than just one. You should also note the kinds of assumptions that give rise to such an explanation; for instance, the belief that advertising works through hidden structures that people are unaware of, and that create irrational people. The main assumption is, therefore, that most people cannot see that they are influenced by advertising to purchase goods and services that they do not really need. Maps are, of course, just representations of an argument that can be represented in other ways and any map is open to discussion. In the case illustrated in Figure 6.4 we might, for example, want to contend that people do know what the aims of advertising are, and that they are not duped.

Tree constructions In most literature you will find that some authors have dealt with general issues while others have looked at specific aspects of a problem or issue. In order to represent this you can construct different types of subject relevance trees. A subject tree aims to show the different ways in which the major topic has developed sub-themes and related questions. The tree shows how the topic has branched out. These kinds of trees can be what you want them to be, showing whatever level of detail you require. Figure 6.5 (p. 152) is an example: a subject relevance tree based on the general topic of advertising, showing some of the sub-topics within the general literature. In this example, only the topics are shown and not the specific authors who have produced work on these topics.

The order of a tree basically follows the kind of arrangement you will find used in libraries, such as the Dewey Decimal Classification scheme. It is based on the principle of general-to-particular. At the bottom of the tree are general ideas and concepts that are subdivided into further groupings of categories before finally ending in specific studies. It can therefore be an effective way to arrange the literature at the early stage of a review, because a subject tree can provide a summative picture of the topic area. This allows you to identify where, within the concerns of the topic, your research can be placed.

Tree constructions can also be used for further, more detailed, analysis. You can use them to identify the trends in the kinds of data-collection techniques that have been used and to make visible the kinds of methodological assumptions of any core paradigm-informing work on the topic. A tree can also be constructed to represent stages and trends associated with a phenomenon, for example, stages in the development of a concept (such as community) or stages in the development of a topic area (such as geographical information systems) or the structure of keywords in the vocabulary of a position within the social sciences (such as post-structuralism). When applied to such topics, these are usually called content maps.

Content maps All areas of knowledge are composed of a content that is structured according to some form of classification scheme, such as the Dewey Decimal Classification scheme. The content of a topic can therefore

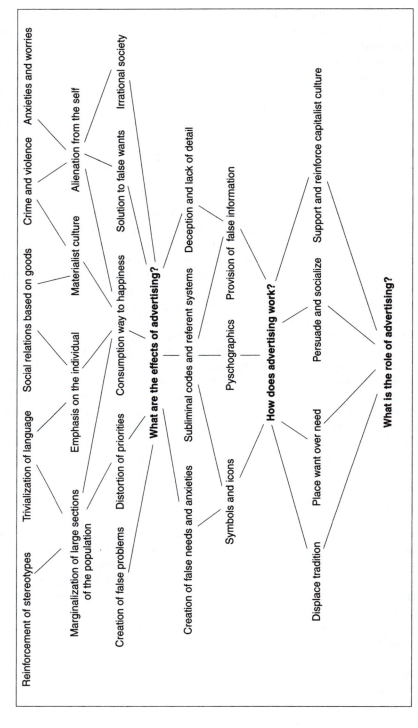

Figure 6.5 A subject relevance tree for the social science treatment of advertising

be organized in a hierarchical arrangement. A common arrangement is the top-to-bottom structure. Starting with the conceptual elements of a topic, you subdivide the topic into segments and the segments into levels; this creates a linear flow that can be represented in a diagram and can be the basis of a writing plan. It can be used to structure the important elements in the literature into sections for your written review. It also shows you what the researcher has selected as the important elements of a topic and the criteria they have used to organize their materials.

You also need to select attributes or characteristics from the literature and place these on the content map. Say, for example, that the topic is the range of methodologies and data-collection techniques that have been used to undertake qualitative research. Our strategy might be one of locating a sufficient number of studies categorized as qualitative and extracting from each the specific qualitative technique employed. We could then list these and begin to map them onto a content chart. Tesch (1990) identifies a number of approaches and techniques in qualitative research, which are shown partially classified in Figure 6.6 and listed overleaf (adapted from Tesch, 1990).

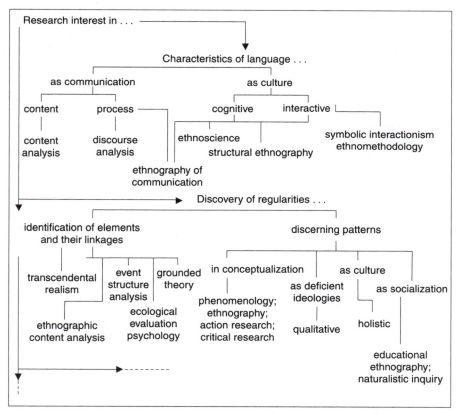

Figure 6.6   *Partial classification of qualitative research (adapted from Tesch, 1990)*

Different approaches to qualitative research

action research	ethnographic content	intensive evaluation
case study	analysis	interpretative interactionism
clinical research	ethnography	life history study
cognitive anthropology	ethnography of	naturalistic inquiry
collaborative inquiry	communication	oral history
content analysis	ethnomethodology	panel research
conversation analysis	ethnoscience	participant observation
delphi technique	experimental psychology	participative research
dialogical research	field study	phenomenology
direct research	focus group research	projective technique
discourse analysis	grounded theory	structural ethnography
document study	hermeneutics	symbolic interactionism
ecological psychology	heuristic research	transcendental realism
educational connoisseurship	holistic ethnography	transformative research
and criticism	illuminative evaluation	
educational ethnography	imaginational psychology	

Source: adapted from Tesch, 1990

Taxonomic maps   Closely related to content maps are taxonomic maps, sometimes called elaboration maps, that aim to show how a range of things can be placed into a general class. They also show differences between objects within the general class. Figure 6.7 shows a taxonomy for passenger cars, for example. The essential problem with any taxonomy is what is to count as an example of the general class or a subsection. For example, what distinguishes a luxury car from other cars? To be classified as a car does a vehicle have to have four wheels? What about vehicles with three or six wheels?

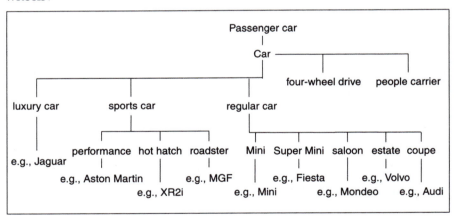

Figure 6.7   *A taxonomy of passenger cars*

This kind of taxonomy also shows another way information can be organized. This is through compotional tables or what are sometimes

	Expense		
	Purchase	Service	Fuel consumption
Jaguar	+	+	+
Aston Martin	++	++	++
Mini	-	-	- -
Mondeo	+	-	-

```
Key
+        = expensive
++       = very expensive
-        = inexpensive
- -      = relatively cheap
```

Figure 6.8   *Compotional characteristic map*

called semantic feature maps. An example is shown in Figure 6.8. The basic principle is of using a matrix structure to show particular characteristics of items from the taxonomy. There are numerous examples of this in the social sciences, such as Robert Merton's (1938) much used scheme of possible responses to the value set of a particular social system.

Semantic feature maps do not always have to be arranged in a table. Figure 6.9 (p. 156) shows a map of cultural criticism as represented in a book on popular culture (Berger, 1995).

Concept maps   In order to turn declarative knowledge into procedural knowledge you often need to know the linkages between concepts and processes. A concept map can be useful because it can be constructed to show the relationships between ideas and practice and include, if necessary, reference to relevant examples. Figure 6.10 (p. 157) shows some of the processes involved in undertaking an analysis of qualitative data. Note how different concepts can be linked in multiple ways and how emphasis can be given to some links. Also note the cause and effect or problem and solution structure that is an implicit assumption underlying all concept maps.

ANALYSIS AS A METHOD OF MAPPING

Analysis can be used to produce maps of the literature, and in the two examples at the end of this chapter we will look at the role of analysis in understanding the nature of ideas and perspectives in a literature. In the first of these examples, we look at how the particulars of language use can be analysed, through the technique of rhetorical analysis.

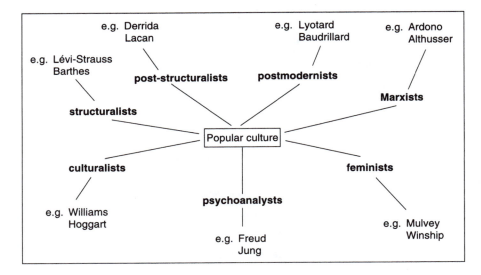

e.g. Derrida
Lacan

e.g. Lyotard
Baudrillard

e.g. Ardono
Althusser

e.g. Lévi-Strauss
Barthes

post-structuralists   **postmodernists**

Marxists

structuralists

Popular culture

culturalists   **feminists**

psychoanalysts

e.g. Williams
Hoggart

e.g. Mulvey
Winship

e.g. Freud
Jung

Figure 6.9   *Semantic map of critical approaches in cultural studies (based on Berger, 1995)*

Rhetorical analysis and mapping

So far we have made the assumption that much of what is found in a search of the literature will be academic articles and monographs. In many topic areas, however, the literature will be much more diverse than just articles and books. It will also be made up of non-academic materials, including such items as company reports, trade catalogues, parliamentary bills and other official documentation, popular magazines, advertisements, and other kinds of ephemera. There are various techniques, such as semiological analysis and content analysis that can be used to analyse these materials. We will not be looking at these techniques in any detail because they are more methodologically oriented and are not therefore particular to reviewing. Added to this is the abundance of instructional texts on how to do semiological analysis and content analysis. We will focus instead on rhetorical analysis, a technique more relevant to reading for reviewing.

Items such as advertisements or policy documents contain an element of persuasion. The degree of persuasion might vary from a moderate attempt to influence how you see something, to a tightly structured argument. Rhetoric, therefore, is the art of communicating to influence and to persuade; in particular, it is about the use of style in language – we are, of course, using the term 'language' in a very broad sense to include such things as written text, pictures, objects and diagrams. As such the use of rhetoric is a distinguishing feature of the sciences and the humanities. It is much in evidence in the fields of economics, social policy and political sciences; disciplines known for their argumentational character.

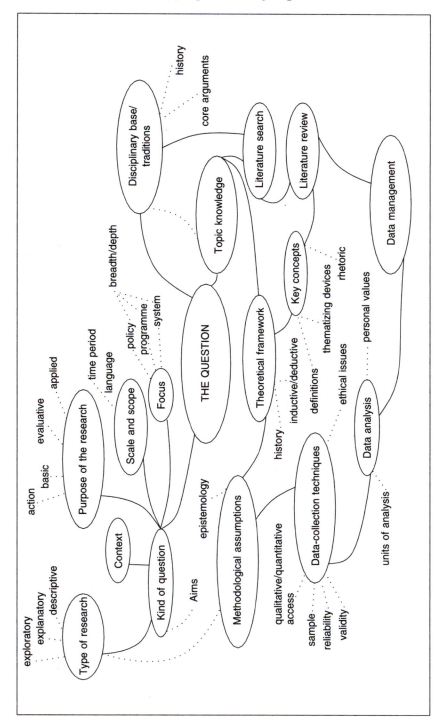

Figure 6.10 *Concept map (mind map): the context of research*

Rhetorical analysis is therefore the study of how language has been used to make an argument appear plausible. It involves analysing the elements authors have employed to construct their arguments. There are various sources you can consult on how to undertake an analysis of rhetoric: examples can be found across the literature of the social sciences. For example, in feminist studies Sara Mills (1995) provides a simple introduction to the analysis of 'text' to show the gendered use of words, phrases and images; in economics, the work of Henderson et al. (1993) contains some useful studies. In a moment we will look at an example of rhetorical analysis, but first we need to know more about what to look for when reading to analyse rhetoric.

List of rhetorical devices

In his chapter, 'How to do a rhetorical analysis, and why', Don McCloskey (Henderson et al., 1993) provides a list of rhetorical devices for students of economics. The basic ideas, however, are applicable to readers across the humanities and arts, and we look at each of these in turn now.

Ethos is the stance an author takes as a fictional character who has good reason to say what they are saying, that is, they can be trusted. To do this, an author has to establish their credentials by employing a range of techniques, such as referring to their experience, or their research, or making an appeal to morality or politics. The opening statement an author makes is important because first impressions count.

Point of view is a vantage point the author selects from which to make their argument or tell their story. This might involve using the first or third person style (passive style). The first person narrative is more personal and intimate while the third person style is more formal and impersonal. Some authors use both the first person 'I' or collective 'we' when they want to gain or express sympathy and the third person when they want to appear as an objective observer (see also note on style below).

Style is the way in which most researchers (who, generally speaking, attempt to be modest) express their ideas. They use phrases such as 'it often appears', 'is likely to be' and 'might be seen as'. These show the use of the passive voice to convey major clauses of an argument. Other authors attempt to appear more objective by using the passive voice in conjunction with evidence; they use phrases such as 'it is consistent with the data' and 'observed phenomena show'.

Gnomic present is a common technique to establish the legitimacy of a statement by connecting it to several other statements. McCloskey gives the following example from David Landes's book on economic history (1969: 562), 'large scale, mechanised manufacture requires not only machines and buildings . . . but . . . social capital . . . these are costly . . . the return on such investment is often long deferred . . . [the belief] that the burden has tended to grow . . . has become a myth' (cited in McCloskey, 1994: 326). In economic terms Landes makes a number of implicit assumptions about the knowledge his readers have. He is challenging the argument that the social costs of manufacture become more onerous with time – he makes a deductive conclusion that the latecomer to manufacturing can be at an advantage because they can reap the outcome of past investment without incurring equivalent cost to themselves. Landes's conclusion acquires its legitimacy and persuasiveness from common acceptance of the previous statements.

Story is the overall structure for the telling of an event. Academic stories, like everyday stories, have structure. A common structure is that of stating a past situation, stating what was done and then stating the outcome. The first two parts of the story are the plot line, while the ending is the conclusion. The conclusion is often an interpretation of events and is therefore argumentational. Conversely, you might be dealing with a state of affairs, say an interpretation, that is commonly accepted. You might therefore ask for an explanation for that interpretation. In doing so you would be asking for a story that provides a plausible account for assumptions implicitly made on a topic. The story itself can therefore be an object for inquiry.

Tropes are figurative phrases, such as 'the Prime Minister slipped on a banana skin today'. The main tropes are metaphor, synecdoche, metonymy and irony.

Metaphor is the use of something familiar to describe something more complex and not necessarily easily understood. Language is used metaphorically when using sayings such as 'fuelling the flames of racism'. There are numerous metaphors, such as 'body' metaphors when talking about the 'life-cycle' of a product, environmental metaphors when talking about the 'decay' of morality, and mechanical metaphors when talking about the 'cogs' of bureaucracy.

Synecdoche is figurative speech in which a part is substituted for the whole, or the whole for the part. For example, the Presidency, one person standing for a country, or 50 head of cattle meaning 50 cows.

Metonymy is similar to synecdoche in that the name of one thing is substituted for that of another related to it, as in the 'crown' for the monarch or 'the bottle' meaning alcohol.

Irony is when you say one thing but mean the opposite, as in 'don't worry about me, I'm fine'. Irony is often used to draw attention to some stance or point of view an author has taken. It allows an author to talk about the incongruity of a theory or piece of research in a humorous or mildly sarcastic way. Irony is a common methodological trope in the social sciences. It is often used to compare everyday activities with theoretical accounts to show the incongruity between what is rationally expected according to the theory and what actually happens.

Rhetorical analysis in use

Policy documents can be a major source of material, providing a subject for a thesis, as well as a technique of analysis. The toolbox of rhetorical terms outlined by McCloskey (1994), along with advice on reading plans (Mandelbaum, 1990) and policy analysis (Throgmorton, 1994; Fischer and Forester, 1993) can be useful in identifying the argument authors and organizations propose as policy. Example A is taken from a document produced by a major metropolitan city council in pursuit of government funding for a project. The document was part of a competitive bid for substantial funding intended to stimulate the regeneration of areas in economic decline. The objective of the example is to look at the rhetoric used in the bid document to see how the argument for funding was made for a deprived city area in the UK. Two major sections of the document are examined: the vision statement, which briefly states what the programme, if successful, aims to achieve within the five years of its tenure; and the area profile, which identifies the needs and opportunities for the area. **Turn now to Example A at the end of this chapter (p. 162).**

Having read Example A, you will have seen how a range of rhetorical devices can be identified and shown to be integral to an argument. Although we have not looked at all the kinds of rhetoric present in the document nor at the whole document itself, you should be able to appreciate the usefulness of rhetorical analysis. There are several areas that could be expanded relatively easily from our initial analysis. For example, the use of metaphor is a major device in the bid. The ideas and notions that are the basis of these metaphors have long and interesting histories. In methodological and theoretical terms, the use of community-based metaphors could be a starting point for extended discussion and evaluation. The point is, look to map, as well as to analyse, the origins of rhetorical devices that are used to present a case. In this way you will be able to make connections between ideas in terms of their history and contemporary use. This will provide the materials and knowledge by which those ideas that have been mapped out can be described and, significantly, subjected to assessment and evaluation.

CITATION MAPPING AND ANALYSIS

When an author of, say, an article refers to the work of another author they have cited a source and the reference to it might be included in the main text of the article or it might be part of the general bibliography. Either way it has been a practice for some years now to collate the citations from across the different disciplines into citation indexes which indicate subject relationships between the current article and previous publications. Sources can include, for example, articles, papers, theses, books, reviews, correspondence and, perhaps, information from visits to electronic sites. Regardless of the length of the bibliography, the following bibliographic details are generally recorded: the title, author, and when and where the item was published. This information can be very useful for investigating the linkages between authors in order to map out the development of an idea, technique or theory.

Most citation indexes are published by the Institute for Scientific Information in Philadelphia and are available in many academic and some public libraries. Many indexes of journal articles are now being combined with citation indexes of works cited by those articles indexed. The latest versions such as Social Sci Search are available on-line from DataStar, Dialog and through BIDS (Bath Information and Data Services). BIDS provides access to citation indexes and to some full text articles. The main citation index relevant to the social sciences is: *Social Sciences Citation Index*; ISI. This is currently produced three times each year and covers over 1,400 multi-disciplinary journals. Two of the main on-line databases that include citations are Social Sci Search (DataStar/ISI) and Arts & Humanities Search (Dialog/ISI).

Uses of citation searching and mapping

In order to build up a knowledge of a subject area, information on the relationships that exist between different authors, at different times and across different disciplines, is useful. Analysis of the citations on a topic can help towards meeting this aim by allowing a researcher to map the intellectual relationships that exist in the literature on a given topic and thus to reveal the otherwise implicit linkages between the origins of an idea, its development and its implementation. Example B is an applied use of citation indexes. It is just one of many forms of analysis that can be undertaken using citation indexes. The example aims to show the main uses of citation analysis for mapping the development of a topic. It belongs to the history of science and deals with a comparison between what someone remembered as having happened and what the citations of the literature recorded as having happened. **Look now at Example B starting on p. 167.**

General comments

Garfield's analysis of Asminov's account of the development and proving of DNA theory is a good illustration of the use of citation analysis. It shows how the work of an author like Asminov can be verified. In this case some 72 per cent of the events for which Asminov gave full details were verified by Garfield. This is more than simply duplicating the work in the history of science. Garfield's analysis identified new connections and authors not mentioned by Asminov. Four of the authors identified by Garfield and not mentioned by Asminov played a significant role in the development of DNA theory. This shows that even a scientist who had a remarkable memory, such as Asminov, can forget to mention some things.

So, in Example B, we have seen that citation analysis can add to the accounts that scientists give about the development of a theory or technique; it can show new connections, as well events that appear to have been significant but have no identifiable connection to earlier work. Locating work outside the chronological line is one way of identifying work that might be at the very edges of the paradigm, that can reveal something about the nature of originality. Analysis of citations is also a method that can augment traditional historical research into the history of a topic, because the compilation of the citation indexes is so thorough that a permanent record is available. Added to these points is the nature of constructing citation networks. The diagram, although difficult to construct, can be far superior to a narrative account of the development of a topic. You are able to see the connections between events much more easily than with a textual narrative. By mapping connections in a diagram the structure of the knowledge is made visible, with the core and the boundaries of work in the field shown – perhaps exposing gaps and making possible the selection of a space for your own research.

CONCLUSION

Mapping the ideas, arguments and concepts from a body of literature is an important part of the review of the literature. You can use many different methods in whatever way you deem appropriate to your analysis. Their use will enable you to find your way around the literature, to identify the key landmark studies and concepts and at the same time build a picture of the relationships that exist between individual pieces of work.

EXAMPLE A   A BID DOCUMENT

Analysis of a bid document relating to Newtown South Aston, Birmingham, adapted from 'A vision of Newtown South Aston', Birmingham City Council.

A VISION FOR NEWTOWN SOUTH ASTON

Only 30 years ago there were 35,000 people living in Newtown South Aston where only 12,000 live today. Conditions then were far from ideal but clearance and depopulation have been followed by deprivation, crime, poverty, ill-health and lack of employment which will not be put right simply by improving the physical fabric of the area (important though that is).

> If I was in charge of millions of pounds for the development of Newtown, I'd put some more radical thinking to the problem than just throwing more good money after bad.

Newtown South Aston is a vital part of the Birmingham inner city. It plays a role providing both a living and working environment, but our vision is to help it do better and to transform it – people, businesses, land and property – into a success story. By taking advantage of the economic opportunities the area offers and by harnessing the potential of its people we can tackle the issues of social deprivation and environmental blight that have come to characterize the area. This bid has been prepared with the willing support of local business organizations, potential developers, the public and voluntary sectors, and the community itself. These will also be the partners in the Company Limited by Guarantee which we propose as the delivery mechanism.

We aim to achieve determined and creative progress towards a self-sustaining community. This is the ambition of the people and the businesses of Newtown and with the help of the whole community it is achievable. We must create a climate in which the cycle of poverty, ill-health, crime and unemployment is broken. Getting people into work by improving education and creating job training opportunities is the most important thing we shall do.

So this bid proposes a new deal for Education and Training via a Training Education Zone. Newtown South Aston people will get a first-rate education and training to help them get good jobs in the area, resulting from business growth and relocation, and in the wider Birmingham labour market. Local employers have stated their intention to employ local people who have the right sorts of skills. Overall the bid will result in 2,800 new jobs in the area.

Over the lifetime of City Challenge, the face of Newtown South Aston will be changed. As well as training, education and employment, the following changes will take place:

Over 100 acres of land will be developed for business and industry, housing and community use, serving Newtown South Aston and frequently the wider City. Three key sites, Lucas, King Edward's Trust and Newtown Shopping Centre, will be brought back into productive use.

Existing businesses will be enabled to relocate and expand in the area; prime sites will be provided for new industries within a mile of the City Centre, practically on the national motorway network; and office development will come to Newtown.

New private houses and changes in some current management arrangements will help to diversify the housing tenure and increase choice, encouraging people who work in the area to live there too.

A network of community development activities will enable the wider community to play a full part in developing and managing the area. Community enterprise will be supported, particularly to deliver some local services and to tackle problems of tipping rubbish and the fear of crime.

Eight innovative and creative ideas will be independently monitored and evaluated, in conjunction with the community, using the City's Higher Academic Institutions where appropriate to assess their success and potential for working elsewhere in the City and nationally.

The bid builds on the unique value of Birmingham Settlement, the South Aston Community project and the work of the Aston Commission. It also recognizes the remoteness of the Council's services and proposes the innovative step of devolving the Council's local functions in parallel with the City Challenge structure.

People who don't live here say it's a deprived area – that annoys me, Newtown has got a hell of a lot going for it, swimming baths, community centre and a far better nursery provision than, shall we say the upper-class areas.

Five years from now Newtown South Aston will be on the way to being busier, cleaner, safer, more prosperous, healthier and more firmly linked to the rest of the City Centre. Its education and training services will be a model for inner city areas to follow and its ugly and blighted vacant sites will have disappeared. Increasingly the local community, including its business and voluntary sector, will be organizing and running itself.

It will be an inner city village, in the best sense of the word, in which people want to live or work or both. That ambition is at the heart of all regeneration and we make no apology for giving it priority.

Lastly it must be said that the commitment of all parties is so strong that it will be unrealistic to imagine that the work will stop on the 22 April 1992 – the date for the bid submission. We shall carry on putting the machinery in place and developing the proposals in this bid over the coming months so that by the same time we are invited to present those proposals to Ministers, the proposals will have been further developed and their framework is likely to be in place. Both of these demonstrate our absolute commitment to improve Newtown South Aston, making the most of the considerable opportunity City Challenge brings.

The bid document opens with the following vision statement:

> Only 30 years ago there were 35,000 people living in Newtown South Aston where only 12,000 live today. Conditions then were far from ideal but clearance and depopulation have been followed by deprivation, crime, poverty, ill-health and a lack of employment which will not be put right simply by improving the physical fabric of the area (important though that is).

In the next section the McCloskey classification is applied to the vision statement.

Ethos

The author notes the changing situation of the area, in a way that is reminiscent of the past. The phrase 'only 30 years ago . . .' signifies that the area has undergone change that is relatively recent and therefore dramatic. The impact of change is emphasized as wholly negative with the string of terms 'deprivation, crime, poverty, ill-health and lack of employment . . .'. As listed these terms characterized the area, putting words into the reader's mouth. There is the implicit assumption here that if readers of the document were to visit the area they would also use such terms as *deprived* to characterize what they see. There is also in the statement the notion that the cultural environment is connected to the physical environment. The problems of the area will not, it is claimed, be put right simply by attending to the physical environment. Therefore an initial argument is being made for emphasis to be placed on the culture (or community ethos) of the area. This is reinforced by the reference to earlier attempts at improving the area. The word *clearance* in particular refers to the physical environment while also conjuring up common images of the conditions created by the high-rise system of buildings of the 1960s and early 1970s. Therefore this bid is signifying that it will look at the social as well as the physical environment; it is different from what has gone before and therefore more likely to be successful. The general ethos of the document is one that might be expected from a committed and informed agency.

The next thing to note is how the second paragraph answers a number of reader's questions. For example, why should public money be spent on this area? The importance of the area is emphasized; it is a 'vital part of the . . .

inner city . . .'. Along with the role of the area the potential and opportunities of the area are emphasized. Given the importance placed on the area, a problem is defined which needs a solution. If left unattended the problem might have serious consequences for the city. Regeneration will need co-operation and support from local business as well as from residents, but does this support exist? Again, references are made to a range of general organizations including developers and charities. The word *partners* in association with *company* provides an economic orientation to the bid: it gives the impression of a business-driven approach. Hence we see the implied reader: a government keen to have a business management approach to the running of public funded programmes. We can also begin to appreciate how the rhetoric is intended to mimic the style that the author attributes to the reader. Terms and phrases common to a government department, for example, *economic opportunities*, *land and property*, *success* and *delivery mechanism*, all set the ethos for the argument in terms that will be understood by the organization that will evaluate the bids.

If so many organizations are involved or are interested in the area (i.e. local business organizations, developers and voluntary organizations) why is it that they cannot regenerate the area without extra funding? The document acknowledges the support of local organizations, but makes the point that the problems of the area are too great in scope for local solutions to be effective. The irony is that local organizations need to be involved, but to be effective they need to be co-ordinated by an external agency; the one which will be established if funding is forthcoming. Added to this is the implicit criticism of initiatives taken in the past which attempted regeneration but which not only failed but were very costly. Hence the significance of the anonymous quote. Acknowledgment is given to images of wastage of public finance. Not only the quote but also the actual author of the bid document remains anonymous. The extensive use of *we* and reference to the document as *this bid* engenders sympathetic reading. It does this by conveying the impression that the organizations mentioned, along with the people of the area and the local authority, are the *we*, as if all were acting as a collective with the shared goals.

Gnomic character

The City Council, as the principal stakeholder and partner in the project, and implicit author of the bid document, must justify why they should be trusted with the programme if the bid is successful. In other words, what makes the local authority an expert capable of managing a major inner-city regeneration scheme? The bid document must therefore make a case for the combine, headed by the local council, to be seen as the only one able to manage the regeneration despite the failure of previous attempts. An appeal to a knowledge and understanding of the area is used as part of the argument; it provides a story worthy of belief. This is done in various places through this extract. But the main device in use is to supply some general images and then to suggest a solution that is both critical and different from what has gone before and which distances the local authority from previous programmes. Among the general assumptions are that the area is very deprived and that no one would choose to live there. Those who could, moved out of the area when it was previously rebuilt. However, regeneration will attract people back to the area. This is because the old sense of community will be re-established. The story of the once imperfect but populated community and of how it was destroyed is the basis of the argument: the purposes of the bid talked about self-evaluation along with the willingness to embrace different ideas and practices, especially working with local business.

Metaphor

There are a number of interesting metaphors in this document. The body metaphor is used in phrases such as the *lifetime* of the project and in the argument that the project will be the *heart of all regeneration*. The use of the organic metaphor provides the impression of an area that can be revived, as it were, from a critical state. It also provides arguments for seeing the agency as the *vital* organ for the resuscitation of the area. The document acts as the diagnosis of the problem – describing the symptoms of the disease (blight) which needs to be treated if it is not to spread or kill the area. The diagnosis is provided along with the prognosis if the treatment is not forthcoming. Hence, the problem and its solution can be more easily viewed. A second metaphor used is the environmental metaphor. This is used to describe the processes that will be used to regenerate the area. References to *climate*, *cycle* and *self-sustaining* create an argument for the environmental health needed in the area. This is equated with cleansing not only the physical fabric of the area but also its social problems. There is also an organizational metaphor, which is used to convey how the regeneration scheme will be managed and what some outcomes will be. The agency will be the *delivery mechanism* that by putting the *machinery in place*, will enable the local community to be *organizing and running itself*. Underlying these metaphors there is another; a theoretical metaphor about community. The notion of an *inner city village* is very symbolic. It trades on notions about the area as it was and how it might be again – as an area characterized by the quality of social interaction. This notion links firmly with a large literature on community, using the traditional paradigm of the rural/urban divide: life in a rural setting is an idealized construct in which people are somehow happier and more contented than their urban counterparts.

The author of the bid document is using the analogy of community to link various ideas that are current in social policy. One is the idea that if the traditional community can be re-established it will provide a panacea to many social problems, such as crime. It includes people taking responsibility for themselves and for the area in which they live. This implies that people should not always look to the state to provide help and support; they are the best judges of what needs to be done and therefore should initiate actions to solve problems at the local level. This comes out in the bid document in references to local consultation and partnership with all sections of the local community. The argument of the bid is that it is possible to re-establish community by giving back to local people a sense of responsibility. One of the aims of the project will be just this; to create a self-sustaining community.

EXAMPLE B   THE HISTORY OF DNA THEORY

Based on Garfield (1979).

In his book *Citation Indexing, its Theory and Application in Science, Technology and Humanities* (1979) Eugene Garfield shows how citation analysis can be used to map structural relationships of a topic and how it can be employed to verify the history of a discovery. Using Isaac Asminov's account of the discovery and verification of the DNA theory of genetic coding, Garfield undertakes an interesting exercise in citation analysis. He had two main aims. The first was to undertake a comparative evaluation of the account given by Asminov of the development of DNA (which Asminov based on his memory of events) with references from the citation index that also reported developments. The second was to see if Asminov had missed anything from his account that might be important for further developments. Garfield shows in the schemata in Figure 6.11 (p. 168) the basic stages in the strategy.

According to Asminov (1963) the development and verification of DNA theory spanned the period 1820 to 1962. It involved 40 events and in descriptions of 36 of them the names of the investigators were given. Asminov also identified some 43 key connections (relationships) between investigators and events which are reproduced in Figure 6.12 (p. 169) as a network diagram. Each node is numbered to identify the investigator credited with the research at that stage, the time the research was under-taken and the type of research. The nodes are grouped by general type along three columns to show the development of the three oldest research areas: protein chemistry, genetics and nucleic acid chemistry. The separate lines of research evident in the early nineteenth century began to show signs of merging by the mid-1950s, combining to form molecular biology.

Having constructed a network diagram from Asminov's account, Garfield then turned to analyse the citation indexes and relevant abstracts. His aim was to see if Asminov's account was correct and find out if he had missed anything. This involved searching the literature based on the names and subjects given in Asminov's book. The main problem Garfield encountered was how to select relevant papers from the literature. After 1945 it became

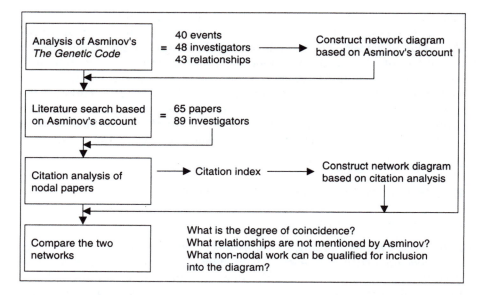

Figure 6.11 *Garfield's strategy for mapping the development of DNA-code theory and verification*

the custom to publish a finding in several journals and in series, each stage of a development warranting a paper. Therefore some developments have produced many papers.

Garfield decided to select papers on the basis of those identified by Asminov. This tactic had a major benefit. It is often the case that first announcements do not contain extensive bibliographies. They are usually brief reports followed at a later stage with a comprehensive account and long bibliography. Garfield's search located 65 papers which reported the nodal events with 89 researchers being credited with authorship. These papers were then subjected to a citation analysis using the citation indexes.

Using the references to the 65 papers as primary sources the indexes were searched. This identified connections between the papers and enabled another network diagram to be constructed. This is shown in Figure 6.13. The numbering of the nodes are Asminov's, but the arrows connecting the nodes are from Garfield's analysis of citations.

The connections in Figure 6.13 represent only a small part of the total literature on the nodal events concerning the development of DNA theory. The selection made by Garfield shows the need for criteria to be set and strictly followed when selecting papers to represent the core knowledge on a topic. What we have in Figure 6.13 (p. 170) is the minimum network for representing the connections between papers. Nevertheless 59 relationships (shown by the number of arrows) are identified. By extending the scope of papers the diagram could be expanded, possibly showing other connections.

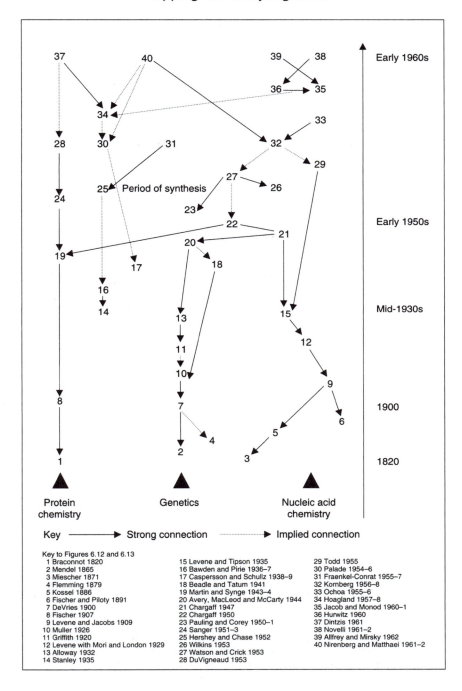

Figure 6.12   *Network diagram of DNA development and verification according to Asminov (adapted from Garfield, 1979: 84)*

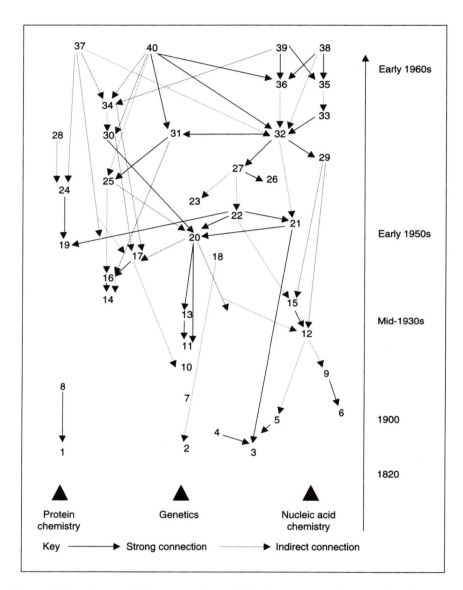

Figure 6.13   *Network diagram of how DNA theory was developed and verified according to citation analysis of connection among nodal papers (adapted from Garfield, 1979: 88)*

Comparative analysis

If you compare the map produced by Asminov with that constructed by Garfield then a useful comparison can be made, using a range of criteria such as: the basis of those citations duplicated; the judgements on the relative importance of individual citations; and the identification of the single most important development. If we apply these criteria we can see a large degree of corroboration between the two accounts. Garfield's analysis shows that Asminov's account is a reliable source on the development of DNA theory. Garfield shows that Asminov did identify many of the significant events and had ranked them in an order of importance that is very similar to the citation indexes. The differences, however, are also interesting. Garfield's analysis of citation reveals 31 references not identified by Asminov. As Garfield's analysis shows, some of these were important to the development of DNA theory.

7

Writing the review

The literature review as a piece of academic writing must be clear, have a logical structure and show that you have acquired a sufficient range of skills and capabilities at an appropriate level. The written thesis or dissertation needs to be viewed as the evidence of your capabilities as a researcher. When you are ready to write up your work, you have one major task: how do you adequately, appropriately and interestingly describe, explain and justify what you have done and found out? The main vehicle for this is the thesis or dissertation, so we begin this closing chapter by reformulating the many comments we have made into the following definition.

***Definition*: Thesis**

It is a document divided into parts that expresses, not necessarily in linear form, a coherent argument or investigation. A thesis should therefore be a holistic demonstration of the skills, intellectual capabilities and scholarship of the research student. It must show thought and the structures of reasoning on which the research is based; it is not just a record of research done. Hence it must say something that is based on existing knowledge, developing that knowledge using reasoned argument, sound evidence and a critical and reflexive stance.

Added to these functions of the thesis or dissertation as a whole, the literature review should show that all relevant documents, both published and unpublished, have been identified and analysed. This means demonstrating that all the main concepts, theories, theorists and methodological approaches relevant to the topic have been identified, understood and critically evaluated. For these reasons the review is not a continuous piece of writing: it might well have several sections dealing with different concerns and different levels at different locations in its structure. The main challenge is to ensure that all of these demands are met in a review that flows, leading the reader from one set of ideas to the next, and that provides systematic reasoning for the topic you have identified for your own research project. The purpose of this chapter is to provide some guidance on thinking about and preparing to write the review; to do this it addresses these questions:

1 How can the literature review be used to justify the topic?
2 What formats are useful for arranging the review of the literature?
3 What is meant by criticism and how can you be fair in your critical analysis?
4 How do you start to write a literature review?

What we will look at in this chapter are the elements that can be used to construct your review, by showing the role of the review as a proposal for your research and as the means for identifying and justifying your topic.

THE REVIEW AND ITS USE

Through the preceding chapters we have taken a journey that has shown the reasons for reviewing a literature, the methods that can be used to extract and organize information, and how different ideas can be mapped out so that connections between them can be made. The literature review has no single purpose. Its purpose will be largely dependent upon the type of research that you intend to do. Some of the kinds of research that you can undertake were outlined in Chapter 3. However, the key objective that all reviews share is to provide a clear and balanced picture of current leading concepts, theories and data relevant to the topic or matter that is the subject of study. This basic requirement is not an end in itself but a starting point for thinking about and planning the review. The first thing we will look at, therefore, is the argumentational function of the review, before moving on to look at some technical aspects of the writing process.

The review and the research proposal

One of the main reasons for writing the review is to make a proposal for the research you intend to do. This means that your review of the literature must provide a methodological rationalization for your research. You need, then, to demonstrate that you understand the history of your topic. The history is the assumptions and definitions other researchers have employed to study the topic. It is your responsibility to investigate this history in order to provide the story of how the topic was defined, established and developed. We noted in the previous chapter that chronological narrative is the most common arrangement for presenting the methodological story because it is the easiest to use; it follows the kinds of story structure with which many of us are familiar: this happened, then this, then this and so on. However, the story structure needs to be adapted for academic writing, and later in this chapter we will look at some ways in which this can be done.

In each part of your methodological story you are aiming to make a recommendation for your research. As a recommendation, your review needs to be a structured argument that in its simplest format achieves the following.

Knowledge-based elements:

1 a description of previous work on the topic, identifying leading concepts, definitions and theories;
2 consideration of the ways in which definitions were developed and operationalized as solutions to problems seen in previous work;
3 identification and description of matters other researchers have considered important.

Argumentational elements:

1 a description of what you find wrong in previous work on the topic;
2 a proposal for action that might solve the problem – your research;
3 an explanation of the benefits that might result from adopting the proposal;
4 a refutation of possible objections to the proposal.

How and where in your review you place emphasis on each of these is a matter for you to decide. However, you should have sufficient material for the task. The analysis that you will have done when reading the literature should provide sufficient material, and understanding of that material, to make a proposal for your own research. From your notes, three kinds of resources you should employ are:

1 the relevant vocabulary with alternative definitions of words and concepts;
2 summaries of the methodological arguments found in key texts;
3 your assessments of how key definitions and methodological assumptions have been operationalized.

The results of your analysis might also provide you with ideas for the structure of your review. When undertaking argumentational analysis of key texts you will probably have recognized that most authors adopt a generic structure to present their case. This often has the arrangement we have just noted for the argumentational elements. This structure can be used at the end of your review to summarize the analysis that you have made. You can also employ elements of it at different places in your review to provide formulations of what you have said, providing summative signposts of where your argument is leading. As a result, when you provide your conclusions and bring each of your formulations together it is more likely that your argument will be cohesive.

What you are required to do, therefore, is to make a compelling case for your research, that your research will in some way make a contribution to our understanding of some phenomenon. This can mean a range of things depending on what kind of research you intend to undertake. For example, you might be arguing for the use of a methodological approach that has been used in another discipline. Hence you will be proposing to undertake a methodologically based piece of research; this might involve providing an illustration of the usefulness of a methodological approach. Alternatively, you might be interested in looking at prior attempts at solving a practical problem. Your interest here might be in identifying factors that have been critical to the success and failure of such prior work. Hence you will be aiming to do a piece of research based on evaluation. There are many other types of research that you might want to do. The main point at this stage is that all research has a history. It is this history that provides the precedent for further work; it is what forms the starting point for your proposal. **In Example A at the end of this chapter we look at the process of research from the point of using the literature review to identify and justify a topic. You should read the example now.** As you do so, you will see illustrated the non-linear way in which a research topic is often identified and how it goes through a process of redefinition as further information is found in the literature.

Having read the example, you should note the following points which provide a brief summary of Atkinson's justification:

- Atkinson's preface and review of the literature is a clear justification for his topic;
- he employs the basic but very readable narrative approach to his justification;
- he provides an introduction in which the interest in the topic is explained;
- he begins to let the reader know about the problems and doubts he had had about the topic and how it had been defined and studied by other researchers;
- his analysis of the literature is used to find fault with previous works;
- this is then used to make the suggestion that an alternative approach is needed and, most important, that he knows what that alternative might look like.

As Atkinson's study shows, with many pieces of research, where you start and where you end up can be two very different things. He started with an idea for a positivist piece of research, but ended up with a qualitative study inspired by ethnomethodological concerns. This was due partly to the contingent nature of research and partly to his own scholarly work. As a researcher you must expect opportunities to arise; you must therefore be prepared for the unexpected. This means not giving up when you hit a problem. It also means being prepared to follow leads that initially seem obscure and even dissident, that is, not the usual way of doing things. Atkinson in his account of how this work took direction gave an account of all of these happenings.

THE STRUCTURE OF SCHOLARSHIP

We have already indicated that there are a number of functions for a literature review and in Chapter 1 we looked at scholarship in some detail. In this section we will look at some aspects of scholarship which tend to characterize a good review. This discussion is governed by considerations of what is an appropriate academic style. In the example provided by Atkinson we were able to show the argumentational nature of some literature reviews along with his stylistic stance on requesting open-mindedness. In this section we can follow up what we mean by this attitude when we look at the practice of criticism.

What is criticism?

A major theme of the preceding chapters has been the practice of criticism; it was advocated when we talked about analysis, mapping ideas and understanding arguments. In terms of your research, whether it is applied or theoretical, the application of a critical attitude should be demonstrated in the thesis. The main points which characterize effective criticism are:

- agreeing with, or defending a position, or confirming its usefulness through an evaluation of its strengths and weaknesses;
- conceding that an existing approach or point of view has some merits which can be useful, but that others need to be rejected;
- focusing on ideas, theories and arguments and not on the author of those arguments, so as to produce careful, considered and justified evaluation;
- being aware of your own critical stance; identifying your reasons for selecting the work you have criticized and recognizing the weakness in your critique;
- selecting elements from existing arguments and reformulating them to form a synthesis: a new point of view on some subject matter;
- finding fault in an argument by identifying fallacies, inadequacies, lack of evidence or lack of plausibility;
- identifying errors in a criticism made by another to provide correction and balanced criticism thereby advocating the usefulness of the original work and reasons for rejecting the criticism made of it.

You may remember that fallacies in argument were discussed in Chapter 4, where we saw how some positions can be shown to rely on mistaken beliefs about what is the case or what counts as evidence. When critiquing an argument it is easy to commit a number of fallacies that will damage the force of your argument and should therefore be avoided. For example, you may strongly disagree with what someone else has said or how they have said it, but attacking them personally will not refute what they have to say

– attack their ideas and their argument, do not make a personal attack on them. Related to this is the fallacy of believing you have criticized an argument by attacking the motive of its author. You may wish to point out what the motivation was for someone when they made a claim, but this will not refute what they said. It may even provide added weight to your opponent's position. Finally, if you believe that an argument is bad, it is not sufficient to produce a counter-argument that is equally bad; one poorly constructed argument does not refute another equally fallacious argument.

Criticize fairly and openly

When it comes to writing up your critical evaluation or critical appraisal of the work of others there is a convention that requires you to treat the work of others with due respect – as you would expect others to treat your work. You may feel that this attitude is not always evident in academic work, but it is good practice, a good starting point for acquiring good academic standards. Some basic pointers about what makes fair treatment when dealing with the work of others are set out below.

A main requirement is that you summarize the views and arguments that others have made in a way that is fair. This means not assuming that a reader is familiar with the work with which you are dealing. It also involves acknowledging, where appropriate, what points you agree with in an advocate's work. This is not just about showing how reasonable you can be by projecting a scholarly image for yourself. It may be that you will find some intellectual worth, some pointers, for your own work. Such good practice also demonstrates that you are able to extract what might be useful and possibly that you are able to create a new synthesis. Also avoid a stance that is heavy with statements. Although you need to state what you have found deficient in an argument, it is not enough simply to provide a list; an explanation is also required. In order for your criticism to be legitimate you need to provide a structured explanation showing what you have found wrong in an argument. This means focusing attention onto the major points of the argument and not on minor details. This might mean, as we will see shortly, that you work your way systematically through the main elements of the argument. This will show that you are able to pick out the major elements of the argument. In doing this you must avoid unsubstantiated criticisms or using hypothetical examples; if you do, it will only trivialize your analysis.

Structure of criticism

Refuting an argument or series of arguments is therefore not something that can be done lightly; it demands structured thought based on analytical evaluation. In Chapter 4 we discussed some of the ways in which you can begin to think systematically about analysing and evaluating arguments. In this section we want to discuss what it means to be systematic when producing a refutation of an argument. The list below gives the structure of an argument developed by Toulmin (1958) which is explained in Chapter 4; for each element, criteria are given for the reader to assess the adequacy of its application for the writer. The point to note is that we can work our way systematically through the different elements of an argument that employs this kind of structure. Toulmin's structure can act as our guide and at the same time provide us with a structure for our writing.

- *Claim*   clarity, plausibility, cogency, consequences, practicality.
- *Evidence*   amount, relevance, reliability, reproducibility, credibility.
- *Information* details, sources, contacts, time periods.
- *Warrant*   robustness, degrees of connection, assumptions, rhetoric.
- *Backing*   problem awareness, admissibility, strength, validity.
- *Conclusion* logic, substantiation, consequences, plausibility.

We take as our starting point that we have the following aims: first, to show the structure of reasoning that someone has employed; secondly, to find fault with some or all of that reasoning; and thirdly, to show the possibilities of our position. This seemingly simple story structure can be very effective. It will allow you to move in a systematic way through an argument and, if sufficient attention is paid to detail, allow a coherent position to be established at the end. One way of thinking about this is that you have the task of taking your reader from one position, that your advocate has stated in their argument, to another position, which you are advocating. Working through an argument we might think about writing our analysis by framing the argument itself, that is, saying what the argument is about and how it is made up. In doing this we will be framing the position of the argument; and showing what stance the advocate has taken on a matter. This might mean: working through the claim that is made and the evidence that has been provided; then examining any warrants that are made, either implicitly or explicitly and then describing the scope of restrictions, if any, that have been imposed. After this you move on to your critique.

Taking the claim first, you can apply a critical assessment by approaching it from a number of different standpoints. Writers make a number of mistakes when stating a claim, which you can look for and then point out any you find. For example, they tend to be vague about what it is they are claiming. This might be due to a lack of clear definition or mistaken use of a concept. Whatever the reason you can pick out extracts from the argument and show its vague character. Another example allied to vagueness, is over-statement – a trick some advocates use to convince others of the plausibility of their argument. The belief is that if you say something enough times then others will believe it. Show in your critique the number of times the claim has been made in the argument. If a claim is made many times, select extracts to show any differences between the claims, especially if the same evidence is being used for all claims. Point out any moral or political claims. These are often the most vague because they are the most difficult to define. Claims based on policy recommendation, value or interpretation can often be shown to be logically absurd (*reductio ad absurdum*), that is, if taken to their logical conclusions would result in a nonsense. Here is one example: crime is a manifestation of genetic make-up, therefore people who commit crime cannot help doing so and should not be punished, therefore the only action that can be taken is. . . .

Once you have dealt with the claims, move on to look at the evidence used to substantiate the claims. Your aim here is to show that the evidence is lacking in some way, that it is insufficient, biased or irrelevant. The following list illustrates the types of evidence under different categories that many people use in an argument. You need to scrutinize all the evidence, summarize what has been used, then look at each category and type in detail. The objectives are to show that you understand the nature of the evidence and how to produce a critique of how others have acquired and employed it.

- *Statistics*   primary, secondary, descriptive, analytical.
- *Testimony*   personal, expert, primary, secondary, historic.
- *Examples*   first hand, general, detailed.
- *Hypothetical examples* impossible, abstracted, plausible.
- *Hypothetical scenarios* cause and effect, process oriented.
- *Personal experience*   anecdotal, narrative, recent, historic.

If statistics are employed, inquire into their source; find out where they came from and ask for what reasons they were selected. If you find no adequate reasons then focus on the data and analyse them systematically for their relevance to the argument. Look for reasons in the techniques used to collect the statistics and in the specific assumptions of the methodology. Show a willingness to question even those statistics that are generally accepted as true; especially those statistics used to support a definition of a situation. The point to remember is that statistics are an outcome of categorization and decision making; they are created, and are not natural or universally true. The same point applies to the use of interpretation. All data requires an interpretation; no data – especially statistics – speak for themselves. Discuss the interpretation your advocate has given of their evidence: how have they used it to support their claim? Also try to assess the appropriateness of any statistical tests that they have used.

In some cases you might find that you have little argument with the data, but disagree on their meaning. Point out any data that are either inconsistent or trivial, yet which have been used as a central support for the argument. If you can use the same evidence as your advocate and show a different – even opposite – conclusion, you will have produced a strong refutation. This is because you will have pointed out errors made by your advocate in their reasoning. This does not have to be long and elaborate. In the example on Marx (Example A, Chapter 4) we saw how, in a few hundred words, Marx turned the tables on a traditional and long-established belief. You will be better able to challenge an advocate's reasoning if you have thoroughly examined what assumptions underlie their argument. Having shown what political, moral or value judgements an author has relied on, you will be able to show how evidence has been used in support of a re-defined position, in other words, how your advocate has actively sought the kinds of evidence that will corroborate a preconceived position. This might also mean looking at the kinds of quotes and extracts your advocate has used in the work. The use of evidence will have been a matter of careful discrimination for your advocate. You can therefore discuss what has been selected and show contradictions and opposing views that exist between the experts in the field. This also extends to how others have used the same testimony for different purposes. You can therefore bring in other studies that have used the same experts to show that there is no definitive way to use a concept or study.

Your final element at this stage might be to summarize the strengths of what you have been critiquing. This might be necessary as you may want to use some of the components in the literature to develop your own position. The final stage then consists of showing the problems in the argument with which you have been dealing. This might mean showing what the gaps are in the reasoning, use of evidence, the source of evidence, the influence of assumptions, or the logic of what interpretations have been made and the logical consequences of the conclusions. The kind of material and structure to use at this stage is a matter for you to decide. But remember to follow the basic maxims set out by Toulmin and use the components that he suggests are useful for the analysis of an argument. Here is a summary of some of the main points for sound argument.

- *Structure*   use a reliable structure that is explicit.
- *Definition*   define the terms you will use carefully using clear examples.
- *Reasons*   provide the reason for anything you have included as support.
- *Assumptions*   substantiate your assumptions; do not leave them as implicit. Use only reliable assumptions that are free from value judgements or are based on valid reasoning.
- *Fallacies*   avoid fallacies, such as generalization, abstraction and misplaced concreteness.
- *Evidence*   use only reliable documented evidence in the public domain that is legitimate and relevant not trivial.
- *Authority*   avoid appeals to authority, convention and tradition.

Legitimacy and academic style

By using the literature on a topic you are using the ideas, concepts and theories of other people. It is therefore your responsibility to use the work of other people in a way that is balanced, fair and legal. This involves ensuring that you are citing sources correctly and, where necessary, not infringing copyright or even the Data Protection Act. In this section we will discuss briefly two areas listed below which can help you to comply with academic conventions and the law.

1 *Legitimacy*   what it means to produce legitimate work.
2 *Style*   what it means to use conventions in academic writing.

To avoid criticism of your review you must use your sources properly. You will be expected not to violate the standards and values of academic work. There are a range of actions you might take that could throw your work into question. Here are some of them.

- *falsification*   misrepresenting the work of others.
- *fabrication*   presenting speculations as if they were facts.
- *sloppiness*   not providing correct citations.
- *nepotism*   citing references of colleagues that are not directly related to your work.
- *plagiarism*   the act of knowingly using another person's work and passing it off as your own.

All of these can easily be avoided by paying attention to detail. This means being scrupulous in your record keeping and ensuring all details of works used are fully and correctly cited. All of this brings into play the need to be aware of the copyright laws that govern published work and any laws being prepared for work in electronic media such as the internet.

Although the law on copyright is constantly developing and changing, we can summarize the current position as follows. Copyright gives legal protection to the creators of certain kinds of work so that they can control the ways in which their work is used. Copyright protection is automatic; once a work has been produced it has copyright. There is no need to formally register the work. It is sufficient only to mark a work with the © symbol to remind people that copyright does exist on a work. Therefore copyright can apply to anything that is presented in such things as books, journals, newspapers, music, photographs, illustrations, diagrams, videos and television broadcasts. Copyright protection for data on the internet is very much in a state of flux, but at the present time try to think of this data as subject to the principles applying elsewhere. These are the things that researchers are most likely to want to use. This places special responsibilities on libraries, archives and information providers in general. Libraries place restrictions on the amount of material that can be copied by a researcher or supplied from a reproduction or copy. Libraries and researchers, however, are allowed certain privileges under copyright. These privileges are called 'fair dealing' which allows a researcher to copy limited amounts from journals, newspapers, books and the like, but only if the copy is for research purposes. Fair dealing is not defined in the Copyright Act 1988 but is accepted practice. It is taken to mean copying for the sake of personal use is acceptable as long as it does not infringe the economic rights of the copyright owner (e.g., copying instead of purchasing the item). Added to this you can sometimes copy an item in its entirety. For example, articles from newspapers and periodicals published say, 20 years ago, can normally be copied by a researcher for their work. However, it is always advisable (and courteous) to get permission in writing from the copyright holder before you copy. This is especially important if you intend to include more than 10 per cent of an article in your thesis or you want to reproduce the whole of something, such as a map or diagram.

In terms of the evidence you use to support your argument the careful selection of appropriate sources is also important. The kind of works you cite will influence the credibility of your work. For example, if you want to source some current application on genetics, an article cited from the *British Medical Journal* will have more credibility than an article from a tabloid newspaper like the *News of the World*. The reverse may be true of course if you are working on, say, a topic in popular culture. There exists therefore a continuum of credibility in materials.

In addidition to copyright and legitimacy, another important issue is academic style. By style we are referring to such things as use of tense, voice, and grammatical structure. Although some elements of style tend to be characteristic of a particular discipline, there are certain conventions to which most academics attempt to conform, and the thesis has conventions of its own, which are outlined below.

In terms of tense, the first chapter of most theses is usually written in the present tense with references to literature in the past tense. Those chapters that deal with the literature review, methodology and data collection tend to be written in the past tense as they are about research that has already been done. The chapters on findings, interpretations and conclusions often use a combination of past and present tense. Past tense is used when referring to your research and present tense to your ideas when discussing what your findings mean.

In terms of using either the active or passive voice, it often helps to have variety in the thesis. It is usually acceptable to use the active voice (me, I, we) when describing such things as how you came to choose your topic. The active voice can provide a more personal dimension for the reader, aiding understanding of your research and placing the reader in your shoes, as it were. However, there are times when the (impersonal) passive voice ('the research was done', rather than 'I did my research') can be useful. The passive voice can provide not only variety in a long document, but also ensure anonymity for respondents, because you are not referring to them by name, for example, 'It was unclear that . . .' or 'I was informed that . . .'.

Finally, some words and phrases that are common in everyday language are inappropriate for use in a dissertation. For example, 'it is obvious', 'it is welcome', 'it is a fact' and 'everyone can see' are value judgements and should not be used. Also words such as 'very', 'fantastic', 'crucial', 'unique' and 'etc.' should be avoided. This is because words and phrases such as these are unnecessary and imprecise. Remember, too, to use words such as 'normally' very carefully, or perhaps avoid them altogether. Bear in mind that you are not writing an opinion column for a popular magazine but a piece of research, a logical convincing argument. Hence, there is no place in such writing for you to use discriminatory language (e.g., sexist) except for the purposes of illustration. Most professional associations such as the *British Sociological Association* have published guidelines on the use of language which you are advised to refer to. Here are some examples of discriminatory language followed by suggested alternatives.

Workman   Worker
Ladies   Women, females
Man-hours   Workhours
Laymen   Lay people, general public

WRITING YOUR REVIEW

There are many books on general writing techniques that can be of help to the researcher when writing up their work. What we will do here is to give some basic ideas on the process of thinking about the writing of the review. One way of thinking about the task is to see it as an opportunity to display what you have done and what you have learned. Think of it as providing information for your readers and your tutor. The benefits that readers will get from your writing will be many. They will see how you have extracted the main points from the literature by undertaking analysis, and how you have reconstructed the main idea in your own words by producing a critical synthesis. Your reader will thereby learn more about the topic than they may have known previously. From your point of view, writing your thesis will place you at the postgraduate level and success will give you your ticket into the academic community. The satisfaction derived from writing up your research into a coherent piece of text will, hopefully, outweigh some of the difficulties that you will naturally experience during the process. Therefore, it is important to emphasize that all writing has difficulties and it is not something that only other people can do. Writing is something that most of us can do if we persevere.

Problems and solutions

Not many people find writing easy. If this is true for you, you might find it helps if you write a little at a time. Most people find writing a coherent piece of text something that demands time and effort. For some people the time and effort required can be an excuse to do nothing or very little. As often happens, you will find that the more you write the better you get at it and, believe it or not, the more you enjoy writing, the more you will want to write. Nevertheless, most of us, however experienced, still have problems putting our ideas down for others to read. Table 7.1 includes three common problems with some suggestions on the causes and possible solutions. There are a number of helpful guides already available for students on writing and managing your work and time, so for the remainder of this chapter we will focus our attention on the processes and stages of organizing yourself for writing.

Table 7.1 *Writing: some problems, causes and solutions*

Problem	Possible cause	Solutions
Lack of time.	Especially for part-time study, life makes many demands.	Time management. Make writing a part of your personal leisure time. 'Socialize' family and friends to recognize that your work is important.
Unfamiliar with different styles, especially academic.	Familiar only with style used in the workplace. Lack of academic background.	Reading different styles. Work at understanding different conventions for different situations.
Not used to writing at length.	Used to face-to-face communication. Rarely use writing for argument and persuasion, hence not familiar with tenses, the possessive and grammatical conventions.	Reading and learning. Writing short pieces. Subdivide work into manageable sections.

The review is a piece of structured writing. It is intended to be read as a formal statement of the results of your analysis. It is therefore a description of current work and issues on the topic. The primary objective is therefore to furnish necessary but sufficient information to demonstrate that you have thought carefully about the knowledge on the topic that is contained in the literature. This objective can be achieved in a range of formats, employing a range of techniques to present information and analysis. For example, text, tables, diagrams and schematics can all be used to convey the results of your analysis and provide an official record of research. It is therefore a public document and as such is a record of the history of research on the topic. It is therefore probably going to be the only record of your research. One implication of this is that your thesis might be the only public place in which you are acknowledged as the person who carried out the research. Added to this is the possibility that your thesis might form the basis of further research by another person. It is for such reasons that it is worthwhile investing the time and effort in planning the writing of the thesis. For the review chapter as with all the other chapters of your thesis you will therefore need to plan carefully in advance.

Have a plan

It is important in the early stages of your work that you develop a pattern to guide your efforts. This pattern begins with your general plan of work – the plan for the research as a whole. This is usually a part of the research proposal. Keep to the plan as far as possible, but expect, and be prepared, to take an opportunity if it arises. Things will inevitably happen to delay you and these need to be overcome. Sometimes, however, a discovery is made, often in a completely serendipitous way, which will give you an opportunity to change the research. It might be the availability of some data that you did not know about or expect to be available. Or it might be a sudden appreciation of the worth of an approach not hitherto considered in the area in which you have been looking. You will therefore need to make a decision on what to do – whether to ignore your discovery or use it. In most cases such discoveries are seen as problems that are thought to be a threat to the original plan, causing you to experience a minor crisis that disrupts the flow of your work. Try to see such things not as problems but as a challenge. Ask yourself what the advantages are of following this unexpected opportunity. Try to think through where this opportunity might lead and what it might bring to your understanding of the topic. In this way you will continue to be working on your research. More important, you will be evaluating what you have already read in the light of your discovery. Hence, your knowledge and analytical abilities will be moving on even if the writing process has been temporarily delayed.

The thing is, of course, to get your discovery down on paper (or computer). This needs to be done as soon as you think that you have grasped the significance of the discovery, and you can continue to do so as you think about the topic. Notes in the form of rough jottings can be an invaluable way to think and write at the same time and they will also provide you with an indicative structure for writing up your ideas. The point to grasp, therefore, is that taking time to play around with ideas can be very beneficial and a great aid to the analytical process of systematically identifying relationships between ideas. It is at this stage, when you are writing up your ideas, that a pattern can be useful: if you approach the writing up in much the same way each time you will soon become familiar

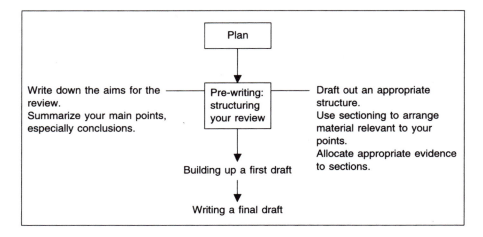

Figure 7.1 *Thinking about starting to write*

with the process and thereby know what to expect. Usually, the writing process has some basic stages (see Figure 7.1), which we look at in turn now.

Pre-writing: structuring your review

Having compiled your plan, you will need to consider how to structure your review in readiness for writing your first draft. This is the stage at which you define your purpose and choose an appropriate structure for your argument.

Define your purpose This is when you clarify your purpose in terms of what you are aiming to achieve. This needs to be a clear statement that is expressed in no more than a few short sentences. It can help if you write down the aims of the review and include them in the introduction to the review chapter. The aims are therefore the main reference point for the review. The content of the review should realize those aims in a way that is clear, systematic and direct. To do this, you need to think about the arrangement of the chapter, and in a moment we look at three possible arrangements. At this stage, however, remember that your notes need to be organized in a way that addresses your aims. Try to arrange your materials into three basic blocks (each with as many subsections as you feel are necessary):

- *Summary of existing work on the topic* This includes the different ways in which the topic has been studied (methods and methodology) and the issues different authors have highlighted as a result of their work.

Identify the different ways key terms and concepts have been defined or used.

- *Critical evaluation of previous work* Assess the methodologies and methods that have been employed previously to study the topic and evaluate the relative strengths and weaknesses of the literature. The key thing in this block is to make visible the map of methodological assumptions in the literature.

- *Some general and specific conclusions about work done to date on the topic* General conclusions can be about the overall direction of work on the topic in relation to earlier more foundational work. Specific conclusions are about identifying gaps, fallacies and failures in previous work in order to show the legitimacy of your own approach.

One thing to remember is that you will not have the space to write down everything you have found in the search and review of the literature. So, when arranging your materials for the chapter think carefully about what is strictly necessary to meet your aims. Anything that falls outside this criterion ought to be placed to one side and not included in the review. It might, however, be placed into the general bibliography of works consulted but not cited in the main body of the text.

Choose an appropriate structure for your argument If you have a structure that you can work with, then you have a starting point to begin writing. There are a number of possible structures that you can use. Table 7.2 (overleaf) shows three of them.

Elements can be taken from each of these patterns. However, if you are making recommendations then in all cases you need to explain the benefits of those recommendations. This is the most popular arrangement for writing a recommendation:

- describe what is wrong; what the problem is;
- make a proposal to solve the problem;
- examine the benefits that would result if the proposal were adopted;
- acknowledge and refute any possible objections to the proposal.

A recommendation therefore needs to be clear and systematic and using this kind of structure will help you to achieve this, as well as helping you to be clear about the potential benefits of the recommendations that you are proposing. This means using evidence from the literature to show the positive aspects of failures that you have identified. There is a degree of irony in critical evaluation for when showing the shortcomings of previous research you are also saying that these failures are good for your own. This is because they will enable you to make a case for your approach to the topic. A major element in this is the use of evidence, which takes the form of extracts selected from other studies or data. Whichever is the case, your

Table 7.2   *Possible structures for your argument*

Problem-awareness pattern (summative evaluation)	Cause and effect pattern (analytical evaluation)	Possible solution pattern (formative evaluation)
• Describe the nature of the problem: give examples of the problem showing its extent; offer evidence that the problem exists; develop a definition of the problem. • Show the relevance of the problem to the reader: provide specific evidence/argument of negative effects. • Explain the consequences if nothing is done or if current state continues: provide evidence of effects/current practice; summarize the problem situation. • Outline the parameters of the problem (definitional argument). • Outline an approach (recommendations) for tackling the problem situation.	• Establish the existence of the problem (problem awareness): propose possible causes of the problem; show the main factors underpinning the proposed causes. • Clarify any confusing areas: eliminate any improbable, irrelevant causes/definitions; provide evidence for causes/definitions eliminated. • Focus attention on proposed cause/ definition: provide evidence for proposed cause/ definition; summarize the argument. • Suggest course (recommendations) of action to deal with the problem.	• Consider definitions and solutions already tried: give relevant examples of solutions tried; show why they failed or were inadequate; show factors causing failure; provide evidence of factors. • Consider possible alternatives: distinguish between alternatives; provide summary of possible effects of alternatives; make a choice from alternatives by elimination; provide evidence for elimination and choice. • Summarize the problem, solutions tried and why they failed and give recommendations for alternative approaches.

proposal will rely heavily on other sources, so is important to use them correctly.

Looking more closely at these three possible structures (in Table 7.2) remember that they are not prescriptive, but merely suggestions to help you to think about what you want to say. The point is to use them as a resource, exploiting them in any way you think is appropriate to your purpose. Before we leave this section we look at an example that shows one of these structures working in practice.

In Chapter 5 we looked at definitions, in particular, at the work of Émile Durkheim on the topic of suicide. We showed that Durkheim wanted to define the subject-matter for sociology and show how the discipline could be scientific – Durkheim had an argument to make. Using the analytical pattern, we can summarize the main elements in Durkheim's literature review (see Table 7.3, p. 190).

Using structure to present your reasoning We have emphasized previously (in Chapter 1) that good academic writing needs to be coherent, systematic and clear. For it to be coherent means that it works as a whole, that the author's style is consistent, and that it does not wander from the topic. Different sections might have cohesion, but these sections need to have sufficient relationships built into them in order that the whole is coherent. The different sections should therefore be seen as the different parts making up an argument; each has sufficient and necessary information, when combined in an appropriate structure, to make an argument. We have seen this in different examples used throughout this book, including examples taken from the work of Atkinson and Durkheim. Both looked at suicide, but each of them had to make a case for their particular definition of the topic and to give adequate reason for that definition. They did this, as most authors do, through the structure and arrangement of their texts.

In the example by Atkinson we saw how he communicated his ideas and argument using structured text. This emphasis on the structure and arrangement of text is important, because when we are making an argument the act of writing forces us to think much more carefully about what it is we are proposing. To some extent writing down an argument avoids the circumvention often found in spoken language. It also encourages us to pay careful attention to the linear arrangement of our argument, helping us to clarify our meaning and intention. If we have a structure to guide the presentation of our argument, then we will be better able to look at what we are proposing and to see where the significant points are, what relationships need to be emphasized and where reiterations would help the reader to follow our argument, and to help us position this piece of writing within the research as a whole. The three examples of structures (problem-awareness, cause and effect, possible solution) show us how we can begin to think about arranging our ideas in a systematic way. However, we may also benefit from thinking about the logical arrangement that we might want to use in our writing.

Table 7.3 *The analytical pattern applied to* Suicide

Elements from the pattern	Elements in *Suicide*
Propose possible cause of the problem.	Durkheim characterized suicide as a social rather than an individual act thereby challenging conventional perspectives and positions. He argued that it is influenced by the degree of attachment a person has to their community. Hence, a starting point for his argument (his hypothesis) is that the more strongly a person is attached to their community the less likely they are to commit suicide and vice versa. This is the beginning of his gradual development of a definition.
Describe the nature of the problem.	Durkheim introduces statistical data to show the extent and patterns of suicide in some European countries. He further develops his definition through a series of minor formulations of his hypothesis. He does this through a dialogue with himself, so odd examples could be accounted for within his definition.
Show factors underpinning the proposed cause.	From the patterns in his data Durkheim begins to identify a number of variables that are connected to his main thesis. He identifies variables such as religious faith, marriage and economic conditions as significant factors in understanding (explaining) patterns in the data.
Clarify any confusing areas.	Durkheim constantly summarizes his definition throughout the first part of his argument. This reinforces his position and is often used to strengthen the significance of his evidence and weaken opposing positions.
Eliminate any alternative proposals for cause.	Durkheim systematically eliminates alternative explanations and definitions. He does this by showing that there are no substantial connections between suicide, as recorded, and current explanations.
Focus attention on proposed cause/ definition.	The radical nature of what Durkheim proposed ensured his ideas would get attention. But he constantly keeps his thesis at the forefront of his argument by reiteration and reformulation, using evidence throughout his work to eliminate alternatives. Hence, his deductive approach – stating his thesis at the beginning of his work, then developing it through use of evidence – helps him to make a strong case for the existence of social facts as the subject-matter for sociology.

There are a number of arrangements that we could use. For example, if we want to show the historical development of work on a topic we would be interested in using a chronological arrangement. In the section 'Constructing meanings' in Chapter 5 chronological structure was applied to the concept of community as a part of the argument. The different definitions of community were presented in order of the dates of the publication for different studies. The point to note is that chronology was used as part of the argument; it was not the argument itself. It was used as a method for organizing the materials that, to a particular audience, would have had some familiarity. The writer could have expected the audience to be familiar with most if not all works on the list. This leads on to another method that can be used, called familiar-to-unfamiliar ordering.

The reader of the study on community was presented with familiar material, the stock of knowledge on the topic and concept. This can be an effective method, especially when introducing a controversial proposal or argument that you think the reader will find difficult to understand. Beginning with something already known, then introducing analysis and observations that might be new to the reader, it is often an effective way of furthering the reader's understanding. They may, of course, not agree with the kinds of observations made about the common methodological policies of community studies, but they will have been given something to think about. You might also have noticed that this example used an inductive structure. That is, it went from the particular to the general.

Both chronological and familiar-to-unfamiliar arrangements can be incorporated into either an inductive or deductive structure. The example we gave of Durkheim's *Suicide* shows the use of a deductive structure. His argument proceeded from the general statement (thesis) to the particular details and illustrations. It is deductive reasoning that characterized the work of the classical Greek logicians, such as Aristotle and Plato. The classic example of this form of reasoning is this:

1 All humans are mortal (major premise).
2 Jane is human (minor premise).
3 *Therefore* Jane is mortal (conclusion).

In terms of methodology we can often see a relationship between the way in which an argument has been written and the methodology used by authors in their work. Figures 7.2 and 7.3 (overleaf) show this relationship.

Writing a first draft

Whatever else you do during the time you allocate for writing, you must actually do some! It is very easy to get distracted by even the most trivial events – almost anything can be more attractive than writing, so you need to develop the habit of writing. This may mean doing the obvious, such as setting aside a regular time of the day or evening. Even if you only scribble

Deductive procedure for research	Deductive structure for writing
The researcher tests a theory	Introduction: theory and thesis statement.
Hypothesis or research questions are derived from the theory	Key questions from the theory and thesis. Particular illustrations and examples given to show the reason for the questions.
Concepts and variables are operationalized	Definition of key concepts: discussion. Elimination of possible alternatives: discussion.
An instrument is used to measure the variables in the theory	Data-collection technique employed. Specifics of data: discussion.
Verification of the hypothesis	Findings related to hypothesis and theory: discussion

Figure 7.2   *Deductive writing structure*

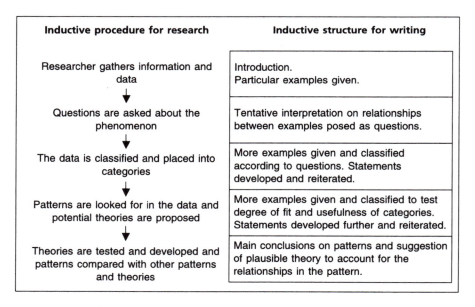

Inductive procedure for research	Inductive structure for writing
Researcher gathers information and data	Introduction. Particular examples given.
Questions are asked about the phenomenon	Tentative interpretation on relationships between examples posed as questions.
The data is classified and placed into categories	More examples given and classified according to questions. Statements developed and reiterated.
Patterns are looked for in the data and potential theories are proposed	More examples given and classified to test degree of fit and usefulness of categories. Statements developed further and reiterated.
Theories are tested and developed and patterns compared with other patterns and theories	Main conclusions on patterns and suggestion of plausible theory to account for the relationships in the pattern.

Figure 7.3   *Inductive writing structure*

notes and fiddle about with diagrams you will soon become habituated to the task. Such self-discipline soon leads to the need to spend time writing or thinking about and planning to write. Many research students only realize this once they have completed a piece of work. They miss the need to do work; often finding that they do not know what to do with their time. However, during the writing stage some output is necessary. There are a number of ways to think systematically about the content of your writing including the following.

- Think about the needs of the reader: what will they be looking for and expect to read?
- Think about the parts of each chapter: how can sectioning be used?
- Think about the introduction: how can you announce your purpose and topic?

Think about the needs of the reader This does not mean producing a structure for the entire thesis. It means taking each part of the thesis, say a chapter, and selecting the kind of structure that is best suited to the material you have decided to put in that chapter. Therefore even at this stage you will be editing your material and at the same time thinking about content. A useful technique is to pose a number of questions, called the writer's questions. The idea is that if you are aware of who will read your work and what they will need to know then you can work towards producing work that is suited to your reader. The kinds of questions to think about are:

1 How much knowledge can we assume the reader will have?
2 What will the reader want to know?
3 How will they read my dissertation?
4 What kinds of answers to possible questions will I need to provide?

In the first instance your tutors will read your work. You can assume that they will have some knowledge of your topic and the methodology you employ in your research. However, other tutors might also read your work and you cannot assume that they will be familiar with you or your research. Therefore, ensure that everything is clearly explained and that all concepts are defined. You must also ensure that all your references are correct and that you have cited all those works that you have used.

What will they expect to find in the chapter? Your tutors will expect to find a piece of academic writing that meets certain criteria. It will need to be clear, systematic and coherent. The ways in which the work of others was used must be described. The techniques used to analyse ideas need to be explained and justified. Comments and critique need to be balanced and substantiated with argument and evidence. The reader will therefore be assessing your work, looking for evidence based on the following criteria:

1 you have worked on the project;
2 you have reviewed the literature relevant to the topic with thoroughness and open-mindedness;
3 you have identified the key ideas, concepts and methodologies from the literature;
4 you have taken a cross-disciplinary approach;
5 you have recorded your sources accurately and consistently;
6 your analysis is systematic, comprehensive and relevant.

Think about the parts of each chapter   It can be useful to break up a chapter into sections using subheadings. Once you have a general idea of what needs to go into the chapter as a whole, think about how you will take the reader from one piece of information and analysis to another in a way that is logical. You might have descriptive information at the beginning of the chapter, followed by analysis, and finally have as a conclusion some form of positive or evaluative critique. Thus, you will have three broad parts, each of which could be further subsectioned. You will, of course, also need an introduction (we will look at introductions later). Once you have an indicative structure begin filling in the subsections with your materials. There is no need to do this sequentially unless this suits your particular way of working. Most writers work on different sections at different times. There are a couple of reasons for this. First, it provides a way of managing what often seems a large task. Rather than trying to work though the task from beginning to end, breaking it up and working on different sections in a random way can make the task seem less daunting. Secondly, some writers find that this way of working helps them to make an ongoing review of the content; this method encourages them to move backwards and forwards over what they have written and thereby redrafting becomes a part of the process. Finally, once you have written something do not go over it in an endless way trying to make it perfect. Some reworking and corrections are nearly always necessary. Proof-reading is therefore an essential stage. If someone else does this for you, take their criticisms in a positive way. The objective is, to put it crudely, to get your work down on paper and not to try to write a classic.

Writing an introduction   Trying to write an introduction is by far the most common problem most writers have when it comes to communicating their ideas. Many people tend to leave the introduction until the main body of their text has already been drafted. In this way they have a better idea of what it is they want to say to their readers about what they will be reading. However, before you begin to write you need to know the purpose of what you will be writing. For this reason a draft introduction can be a useful guide for the main body of text. A good place to start is with the objectives of your review. Write down what it is you want to achieve with your review and why. Throughout this book we have provided lists and explanations of the kinds of objectives that a review should fulfill; use these in whatever way you deem appropriate to your own work.

When planning the introduction think about the review as a whole. In operational terms your review has two dimensions. One is to provide information; the other is to persuade your reader that you have a case that you have identified a gap in existing research which you can fill through your own research. The introduction should also employ these two aims. There are certain things you can do to achieve both of these. To persuade others that your have a case worth considering and have chosen an argumentational structure that is appropriate for your purpose and materials. Different structures were discussed in an earlier part of this chapter. To meet the information needs of your reader think about the following questions.

1   How much information does the reader need?
2   How much do they already have?
3   How do I want them to use the information?

Consideration of these questions will help you to select the amount and kind of information that will be sufficient and necessary for the task of writing the introduction. Remember it is not necessary to include reference to every piece of material that you have located; selection and editing are as much a part of the process as reviewing. Your reader will have more respect for you if you present only relevant information. Therefore, it is often more effective to plan the main body of the text first, breaking it up into subsections with appropriate subheadings before writing the introduction. This means that the introduction will be one of the last things to be written.

As you sort your material into sections, begin to think about the support that will be adequate for the information. There are two kinds of support you can provide to help your reader understand what it is you are saying: information support and interest support. Information support is the pieces of information that you are providing, while interest support helps keep the attention of your reader. This does not mean that your writing has to be entertaining; a review aims to be scholarly. Table 7.4 (overleaf) summarizes elements of both types of support.

You can employ both informative and interest devices in your introduction as you might in the main body. Your introduction needs to be concise. This makes an introduction a difficult section to write because you have to include the five main components shown in Table 7.5 (overleaf).

Added to these is another job for your introduction. You may be looking at a topic that has a long history and you might assume that your reader will think nothing new could possibly written on it. In your introduction you therefore need to show this is not the case by grabbing the attention of your reader from the very beginning. This can be done in a number of ways. For example, you might make a bold statement that contradicts

Table 7.4   *Information and interest support*

Information	Interest
Facts – statements and statistics.	Anecdotes – stories and personal experience.
Expert testimony – quotes and extracts.	
Examples: cases – instances and illustrations.	Visual aids – diagrams and charts.
	Lists of points.
Explanation – discussion.	Rhetorical questions – prompts to make the reader consider.

Table 7.5   *Five main components of an introduction*

Aim	Means
1 To announce the topic of your review.	A clear and concise statement.
2 To state the purpose of your review.	A careful explanation of what you aim to achieve.
3 To explain the relevance of the topic.	An indication of its importance in the literature.
4 To establish your credibility.	Information on why you should be seen as competent to write about this topic.
5 To preview the main points that you will make in the main body of the text.	Advance notice of the structure of your text, possibly including your thesis statement.

preconceived expectations about the topic or you might give a startling statistic. Whatever device you use, it needs to be highly relevant to the topic and needs to focus attention onto the information that follows.

Re-working the draft   The first draft should be just that: a first, tentative outline of what you want to say based on a planned structure. Never attempt to do it all in one go. Every writer goes through a series of drafts, gradually working towards something with which they can be satisfied. Therefore, once you have something that has content and some structure, begin to reflect on it. At this stage you need to analyse it in terms of its clarity, structure and coherence. Look for disjunctions between the main ideas. Ask yourself if the argument is logical and is expressed in a way that is clear and easy to follow. Be aware that clarity can vary throughout a piece of writing. Ascertain which parts are clearer than others, rewriting those parts that need more explanation. Check your use of evidence and rhetoric. Have you made any claims not backed up with appropriate evidence?

The following will help you to do some editing – a necessary task that will improve what you have written, helping to make it clear, simple and consistent.

1   Identify unclear or excessively long sentences and rewrite into shorter ones.

2   Examine each paragraph to ensure it covers only one topic.
3   See if any important paragraphs can be rewritten to be more effective.
4   List the topics for each paragraph to ensure that you have links between them that are sequential.
5   Replace jargon with either an everyday word or explain the meaning of the jargon.
6   Check that the verbs are active and not passive.
7   Look for unnecessary adjectives and delete vague qualifications such as 'very'.
8   Look at the analogies and metaphors you have used and check that they are appropriate.
9   Look for pompous and unnecessarily long words and replace them with simpler, more sensible words.

Some of these points we have looked at earlier under writer's style. In terms of coherence see if the introduction is sufficiently linked to the conclusion and main body of the text. This demands that you reflect on the overall structure. You can do this by summarizing the points made in each paragraph. Check whether each point has a logical link, developing on the previous point in some way. This is an effective way of editing out anything that is not strictly needed for the argument. You are looking at the arrangement and sequence of sub-clauses in your work and at what kind of evidence you have to support those clauses. There are a number of presentational devices that may help and some which you should avoid, in order to give more coherence to your work; examples are shown in the list below.

Sentences	Express one idea in a sentence. Ensure that all your sentences have a subject, verb and object.
Paragraphs	Group sentences that express and develop one aspect of your topic. When another aspect of the topic or another topic is introduced use a new paragraph.
Consistent grammar	Use sentences and paragraphs with appropriate use of commas, colons and semi-colons. This is sometimes difficult to achieve, but look out for incorrect uses of punctuation that affect the meaning.
Transition words	Use words that link paragraphs and which show contrast and development in your argument, such as, 'hence', 'therefore', 'as a result', 'but' and 'thus'.

Analysing your own work is not easy, but it is necessary. Using what we have looked at in this section should help you to be reflexive and analytical, leading to the improvement of your writing. Remember that one of the most effective ways of understanding how to write is to read as widely as possible. Look for examples of good and bad writing. Try to identify ways in which other authors have structured their arguments and used various methods and techniques to express ideas. Things like the use of structure and style have no copyright on them, so you can borrow and adopt ideas for your own work just as other people will borrow and adopt your ideas.

CONCLUSION

This chapter has provided advice and some guidance on how to write a review of the literature. In many ways it has been linked to the themes and argument in the book as a whole. You should be aware that all types of research benefit from a systematic review of the literature. Many different techniques for analysing ideas and arguments have been shown. In themselves these techniques, such as mapping ideas, do not constitute a review of the literature. They are some of the means for understanding what the literature is about and what different authors intended to produce in their research. Hence, there has been an emphasis on the role of thinking about ideas, reflecting on the purposes an author had when undertaking their research, and how this activity requires a particular attitude. We have considered the importance of tolerance, understanding and open-mindedness when interpreting and evaluating the research of others. In short, when you come to do your literature review you need to check that the review:

1 shows a clear understanding of the topic;
2 all key landmark studies have been cited and most discussed;
3 develops, through gradual refinement, a clear research problem;
4 states clear conclusions about previous research using appropriate evidence;
5 shows the variety of definitions and approaches to the topic area;
6 reaches sound recommendations using coherent argument that is based on evidence;
7 shows a gap in existing knowledge.

Above all, you should feel confident that you can prepare a literature review that will comply with the above criteria – and I hope that this book has gone some way towards giving you the confidence, guidance and ideas to do so.

EXAMPLE A   JUSTIFYING YOUR TOPIC

Based on Atkinson (1982).

Atkinson and his collaborators had been researching suicide for several years and in *Discovering Suicide* he justifies his work. This may not seem particularly noteworthy, but given that by 1927 there were over 4,000 works on suicide and by 1961 another 2,000 further studies (Atkinson, 1982: 189), anyone studying the topic would need to provide clear justification for looking once again at what so many had already researched. We want to look in some detail at Atkinson's rationale for studying suicide. This is because he provides a coherent explanation of how he came to choose the topic and how he developed a way of researching it that was different from what had gone before. It might help if the structure of *Discovering Suicide* were outlined before looking at specific sections of it. The full title of the work is *Discovering Suicide: Studies in the Social Organization of Sudden Death* and we can gain an understanding of its structure from the list of contents at the front of the book:

PART I: SUICIDE AND SOCIOLOGY
1. Background and Introduction to the Research
2. The Suicide Problem in Sociology
3. Suicide Research and Data Derived from Official Sources
4. Alternative Sociological Approaches to Suicide Research

PART II: SUICIDE AND THE SOCIAL ORGANIZATION OF SUDDEN DEATH
5. Registering Sudden Deaths: Official Definitions and Procedures
6. Some Relevant Factors in Imputing Suicide
7. Common-Sense Theorizing about Suicide
8. Ethnomethodology and the Problem of Categorization

As we can see, the monograph is divided into two parts. The first part provides the justification for this research into suicide, while the second is mostly the research itself. In giving over nearly half of the 225 pages to justification, Atkinson shows that he is keenly aware of the need to explain the choice of a familiar topic. We are going to look at:

• how he came to choose suicide as a topic for research;
• his attitude to criticizing works in the literature;
• how he justifies research into what appears to be an over-researched topic, that is, finds a gap for his research.

We can begin with the section 'Conclusions' at the end of Chapter 2. The sociological interest in suicide can, Atkinson argues, 'best be characterized as "fascination from a distance" . . . For it was the *issues* posed by Durkheim in a book which just happened to be on suicide itself, rather than the *phenomenon of suicide* itself which has stimulated most of the socio-logical interest' (1982: 31).

Atkinson makes part of his claim at the start of Chapter 2. He says that Durkheim chose to study suicide as a topic in order to develop his socio-logical theories. We can therefore impute that Atkinson is interested in studying suicide as a topic in its own right and this is one thing that makes his work different from that of Durkheim. Atkinson adds to his claim that, although there has been extensive sociological interest in suicide, little research has addressed the problems inherent in empirical research of suicide. He claims that methodological difficulties, which he will deal with, have never been faced because very few people have undertaken an empirical study of suicide. Thus Atkinson is saying that his work is different from that of Durkheim and the several thousand other studies. Working from these claims and the surrounding text, we can extract the reasoning Atkinson employed to construct his argument. We begin with the preface, where Atkinson gives his reader a global summary of his reasons for the topic and its treatment.

An open-minded approach

Very few researchers tell their readers how their topic was chosen. In the preface to his book (which he expands in Chapter 1) Atkinson reflects how he came to study suicide in the way he did. He possibly felt the need to use this preface to justify the topic and also to justify the way he approached and studied suicide. His study is strongly ethnomethodological, a relatively recent development in social science that has been misunderstood by many social scientists. In the UK there are only a dozen or so ethnomethodological researchers. While this is not the place to examine the status of the approach, we need to recognize that it has a bearing on the status of Atkinson's work. First, Atkinson shows he is aware that ethnomethodology is unpopular among social scientists. Secondly, he is claiming to have looked at suicide in a way very different from other studies. Finally, Atkinson asks his reader to come to the work without prejudice: although his study was inspired by ethnomethodology, he wants the research to be read on its own merits and not with preconceived opinions about ethnomethodology.

Atkinson tells us how he came to employ the 'ethnomethodological turn' in research and why he chose suicide as the topic. The study began life as doctoral research in the 1960s. This was a time of expansion for sociology and the social sciences in the UK. Expansion was accompanied by debates over ways of thinking about the social world and social reality. As an empirically oriented researcher, Atkinson tells us that debates over method and methodology posed difficult challenges for empirical research: debate over, for example, the verification and reliability of data, the relationship between data and hypotheses, and competing interpretations and explanations of data. In the spirit of scholarship he explored these debates, mainly through reading but also through personal contact with some of the main theorists and researchers engaged in the debates. Through reading and talks with others, Atkinson embarked on a journey which took him through most of the major paradigms in the social sciences, exposing him to the main debates and issues concerning the relationship between theory and empirical research. As an empirical researcher, Atkinson says that he reacted against the traditional approaches, finding these to be too far removed from the description of real-world activities.

The structure of his book shows that Atkinson intended to undertake two projects – a review of the literature about suicide and an empirical study of how a death becomes defined as a suicide. Atkinson tells us that the literature review showed that the two projects could not easily be separated in this way. Having delineated the role of suicide in the methodological debates within sociology, Atkinson says;

> Having got that far . . . I found I could no longer distinguish satisfactorily between the two enterprises, as my views on the suicide literature were so closely bound up with a very particular empirical problem which underpinned so much of the research on suicide by sociologists . . . namely the status of the data used in testing hypotheses. (1982: xiii)

His review therefore provided clarity and intelligibility to the main methodological debates within sociology, for example, disputes between psychology and sociology, and between positivists and non-positivists. The use made of studies like Durkheim's *Suicide* led Atkinson to his particular approach to the topic. This came out of the literature review. It was through the review that he was able to reassess conventional paradigms to find that these debated suicide rather than studied it. He wanted an approach that enabled him to describe the details of how society, through such agencies as the coroner's court, define (i.e. accomplish) a death as suicide. None of the existing approaches would give a sufficient purchase on this aim. By being in the right place at the right time (and through reading) Atkinson encountered ethnomethodology. The rigorous detail and descriptive analysis of finely recorded activities in real settings is a major characteristic of ethnomethodology. This was different from conventional theoretical approaches. It stood outside, and to a large degree still stands outside, conventional social science research. Ethnomethodologists' concern with describing empirical activities from within rather from without gave Atkinson the approach he needed – it was different, distinct and with the attraction of being seen as dissenting.

How the topic was chosen

Atkinson came to his topic – as many researchers do – through a course of undergraduate teaching. He was asked to prepare a paper on the question: 'How much deviance is there?' Having looked at the statistics and definitions about deviance, he began to question them.

> On turning to the recommended sources, it struck me as obvious that, to varying degrees, they only told part of the story. It was also obvious that . . . sociologists seemed singularly unconcerned by the problematic nature of the figures and

were not inhibited about making far-reaching generalizations on the basis of crime rates, suicide rates. . . . (1982: 3)

Atkinson attempted to make a case for why the question set could not be answered using the numerical data or definitions available. His paper was received, he tells us, with 'considerable displeasure'. He was accused of focusing on mundane problems that were already known about and which were of no concern to sociologists. This response led Atkinson to pursue his concerns. Although text books advocated caution about generalizations and stressed the need for rigour, in practice, sociologists did things differently. They seemed to have little concern for the integrity of data and were too willing to make generalizations in spite of methodological difficulties (1982: 4). Atkinson therefore saw this inconsistency between formal theory and subject attitude as a 'discovery'.

At about the same time, he applied for a research post. As his topic he used what interested him: difficulties with numerical representation of deviance (1982: 4). He thought crime statistics had special difficulties and would be too complicated. Suicide rates seemed more 'clear cut' and attractive for the proposal. He thought suicide had been written about less and someone he knew had attempted suicide. Added to this, suicide was a central interest in sociology and Durkheim's study had relied heavily on statistics. Thus, Atkinson's initial interest was to work within existing approaches. He aimed at calculating rates more accurately so that better data could be collected for more reliable testing of hypotheses. His main concerns at this stage were therefore with a positivistic research project. But his research turned out to be very different.

Developing the topic by changing the focus

Atkinson tells us that he began by reading the sociology of deviance. His aim was to focus on the problems of rates associated with the data used for talking about suicide as a social phenomenon. However, the literature was far more extensive than he had assumed. He also realized it covered many disciplines and there were many debates between disciplines and within them about suicide rates. His positivist approach was soon dropped in favour of an interactionist approach. After reading works from the symbolic interactionist approach, Atkinson took up pursuit of the labelling approach to deviance. Work of interactionists like Becker (1963) and Lemert (1951) seemed to be more empirically oriented than positivistic studies. His plan now was to undertake an interactionist study of suicide. However, in his journey through the literature he came across a thesis that had done just this. Douglas (1966) had produced a detailed critique of Durkheim's *Suicide* from an interactionist approach, and examined the social construction of suicide statistics. Atkinson's initial reaction was to discontinue with this topic, but realizing that someone else was thinking in similar ways to himself encouraged Atkinson to continue.

Taking Douglas's work, Atkinson attempted to model the suicide process. Using materials that he had gathered, he played around with a range of research strategies in his attempt to extend the work done by Douglas. Atkinson realized, however, that there were errors in Douglas's work. These centred on Douglas's treatment of how definitions of suicide were treated by officials (e.g., coroners). Douglas had focused on the meaning of suicide to see how rates were socially constructed. He had not looked at how coroners and other officials do defining work to arrive at a category to assign to the corpse. Added to this, Douglas had made no concrete recommendations on how a study of defining work might be done. This led to a thorough critical analysis of Douglas's work, which Atkinson reports in Chapter 4 of his book. From this we can see how the general review of the literature can lead to specific reviews that show and debate the main issues and highlight the main problems of previous research.

Atkinson's critical evaluation of Douglas's work did not indicate what he should do next. Nobody had, it seemed, gone beyond an interactionist treatment of the topic. Atkinson was therefore breaking new ground. What had begun as a study within an existing paradigm was turning out to be something new, possibly using a very different paradigm. Most of the research was complete by this stage: Atkinson had already done the major parts of the project. The search and review of the literature were done and a large amount of empirical data had been collected (from newspaper cuttings, observations in coroners' courts and the like). His problem was what to do next. This is where opportunity came into play, although Atkinson, in part, made his own opportunity. When looking at labelling theory, he remembered encountering work by a group known as ethno-methodologists. He had assumed that ethnomethodology was a variation of symbolic interactionism, because many authoritative scholars in sociology had wrongly interpreted ethnomethodological studies as interactionist. The opportunity to rethink this assumption arose through a visit made by Harold Garfinkel to the University of Manchester at the time that Atkinson was there. Garfinkel, as the founder of ethnomethodology, together with other ethnomethodologists, demonstrated to Atkinson that: 'ethnomethodology was not just another type of "labelling theory", but had apparently irreconcilable differences with symbolic interactionism as well as with other sociology of which interactionists were also critical' (1982: 5).

Atkinson was therefore faced with a common problem in research. He had to re-evaluate the work he had done so far. This meant criticizing some of his earlier writing on the topic. He had to learn how to be self-evaluative and to acknowledge his own mistakes in interpretation and understanding. But, just as significantly, he had to rewrite his thesis – it was now something very different from what he had originally conceived it to be.

Atkinson's experiences show the non-sequential structure of research. Very few research projects proceed on what might be the recommended structure of reading–research–writing up. Atkinson's went something like this: 'reading–writing–research–writing–research–writing–reading–research–writing' (1982: 6). This structure is more characteristic of most research projects. It indicates something of the processes we actually encounter as researchers, because of thinking things through and not taking things for granted or unquestioningly accepting interpretations other researchers have made. This developmental nature of a topic and self-reflective attitude is shown in the arrangement of Atkinson's book. Atkinson describes this in the following way:

> Thus the topic originally chosen turned out to be one which had been already examined at some length from an interactionist perspective. In examining the various responses to the problem, those of Kitsuse and Cicourel (1963), Cicourel (1968) and Sudnow (1965) had seemed the most useful from the point of view of designing empirical research (see Chapter 3) and these writers, it emerged later, were ethnomethodologists and not the simple interactionists they are often presented as being. There were also serious empirical difficulties in the way of doing research along the lines suggested by those who advocated the use of a 'sequential model' (e.g. Becker, 1963) or an exclusive focus on social meanings (see Chapter 4). The initial search for an official definition of suicide, coupled with problems which arose out of earlier encounters with coroners', subsequently suggested that the question, 'How do deaths get categorized as suicides?' was the most appropriate way of formulating the research question (see Chapter 5) And that question, it was to emerge later, was not unlike the kind of question an ethnomethodologist might have asked (see Chapter 8). Perhaps not surprisingly in view of that, the kinds of results obtained in trying to find an answer (Chapters 6–7) were later found to be consistent with some of the more important contentions of ethnomethodology. (1982: 7)

Justifying the research

Chapter 2 of the study, 'The suicide problem in sociology', is subdivided into the following parts: 2.1 Introduction; 2.2 Deference to Durkheim; 2.3 Positivism; 2.4 Sociologism; 2.5 Functionalism; and 2.6 Conclusions. It is in these sections of his book that Atkinson attempts to justify his research into suicide. We have already indicated the reason for this; but how does he do it? The first thing to notice is the use of the convention of subheadings. He breaks the task down into logical and consistent categories. These may not be the categories everyone would choose but they do fulfill Atkinson's aim: to provide adequate scholarly warrant for his claim. As you might expect, Atkinson covers the major aspects of the conventional approach to suicide: Durkheim's work, positivism, the functionalist perspective, and the difference between sociology and psychology. However, the main thrust and structure of Atkinson's approach can be seen in how he makes clear that his work is very different from that of Durkheim. So, we will focus our attention on this section.

If Atkinson wants to claim that his study is an original contribution to our knowledge of suicide then he would be expected to show how this is so. This would usually be taken as involving a clear explanation of how his work differs from Durkheim's. One of the things Atkinson therefore attends to is the place and role attributed to Durkheim's *Suicide*. In Kuhnian terms, Atkinson points out that Durkheim's study of suicide was a paradigm innovation, in that it created a new way of looking at something. Using a range of authoritative sources, Atkinson argues that Durkheim's study provided a clear example of the distinctive possibilities of sociology. It gave proof that sociology was capable of producing law-like studies, which are comparable to the natural sciences. Durkheim showed how sociology could be done. As a consequence his work has been used by successive generations of social scientists to demonstrate the scientific basis of sociology (and the social sciences in general). It has also been used to illustrate the place of social explanation in contrast to psychological explanation: that even the most seemingly individualistic (or psychological) act has social rather than psychological causes.

Pointing out the place and status conferred on *Suicide*, Atkinson attempts to show how all subsequent sociological works on suicide have been conducted within the original Durkheimian framework, that subsequent studies have not come up with anything different. They have used the same kinds of numerical data (suicide rates) and have therefore produced confirming evidence. Anyone following Durkheim's example will, Atkinson points out, produce no surprises. They may produce a replicative study, claims Atkinson, but 'may be put off by the prospect of having to compete with someone as eminent as Durkheim, and the internal structural pressures within sociology against embarking on suicide research come to look fairly substantial' (1982: 12–13).

Atkinson, however, focuses the justification for his research on methodological grounds. Having shown the fascination with Durkheim's study, Atkinson looks for reasons for this fascination. Some of these we have just mentioned: the examples it provides and the arguments it makes. But *Suicide* is also a methodological study, in that it established a distinctive sociological explanation, based on a range of methodological assumptions. These assumptions included holism and structuralism, which focused attention on the explanation of behaviour by reference to processes occurring in larger social structures. As a consequence, the enduring interest in *Suicide* has been methodological and theoretical. Subsequent studies have been about refining Durkheim's original research or about debating its strengths and weaknesses. They have not, according to Atkinson (1982: 10) 'been of the phenomenon which members of a society call "suicide"'. Therefore, Durkheim was not so much interested in suicide as a topic, but as a resource to demonstrate a methodological and theoretical argument. He used suicide rates to argue for the existence of social facts and that these were to be regarded as concrete things. Properties of social groups, such as cohesiveness, could be measured using numerical indices. Durkheim was thus able to argue that social science, like the natural sciences, looked at facts not in a personal, but in an objective way.

Atkinson does not dispute Durkheim's intentions or criticize what he achieved. He does, however, reinforce his main point:

> the extensiveness of [the general sociological interest in suicide] is of little help to the would-be researcher into suicide. For from whatever stance one approaches the research, one is faced with fundamental and unsolved methodological problems which appear so obvious that it initially seems strange that they have been given so little attention in the past. That is, whether one's interest is in the relationship between sociological and psychological modes of explanation or in anomie theory, and whether or not one considers oneself a positivist, functionalist, conflict theorist or whatever, important decisions have to be made about the status and adequacy of the data chosen for analysis. . . . Not only is the widespread interest of sociologists in suicide of little help in solving the methodological problems faced by the empirically oriented researcher, but that the character of that interest probably accounts for how it is that such fundamental and obvious problems were ignored for so long. For the difficulties . . . are only likely to emerge as obvious at the point of designing or attempting to do empirical research, and hence to remain hidden from the view of the philosophers, theorists and teachers who use suicide as nothing more than a 'substantive' example in debates about ideas. (1982: 32)

Appendix 1: the proposal

Many universities require higher degrees applicants to write a research proposal before they start their research. The following notes provide a guide to the structure and content of the generic research proposal.

Section	Indicative contents
Working title	Describe the breadth and depth of the topic and indicate the methodology to be used. If necessary use a title and a subtitle.
Introduction (abstract)	Summary of the research topic, describing the major problem or issue and where the gap lies for your research together with an indication of what your research will achieve.
Scope	State the limitations for the research, for example, time period, language, subject areas, regions and sample along, with unit of analysis, for example, policy, programmes, behaviours – to emphasize that no claims for generalizability beyond these limits will be made.
Aims	General statements on the intent or direction for the research – where you intend to go; include reference to the methodological, practical and theoretical aims.
Objectives	Specific, clear and succinct statements of intended outcomes from your research, for example, search and review of the literature and assessment of a debate.
Justification	The rationale for doing the research on the topic; why the research needs to be done on this topic or problem. Make reference to the literature, gaps in knowledge, potential usefulness of a methodology and possible benefits of outcomes for understanding, practice and policy. Provide key references in support of your case.
Review of the literature (indicative)	Describe briefly the history of the topic identifying key landmark studies which indicate the methodologies used and arguments made; show the major issues or practical problems to identify the gap you intend to look at in your research, and then indicate what will be some likely research questions (for qualitative research) or hypothesis (for quantitative research). If necessary, show how key terms have been defined and used. Aim to show what contribution your research will make to the literature.
Methodology (indicative)	A concise justification for the methodological approach you intend to employ and what data-collection and analytical techniques you will use. No need to describe the methodology, but justify the following: use of qualitative or quantitative

approaches; use of an existing approach within an existing paradigm; explanation of why alternative methodologies were rejected or not; the use of techniques for data/evidence-collection techniques and anticipation of problems and issues, for example, ethics and access to data; indication of how the data will be analysed; and include agreements from corroborating organizations. Any variables to be operationalized should be defined. Provide references in support of your case.

Provisional work schedule | A general indication of the timetable for completing the research; usually broken down into manageable segments, indicating the tasks necessary to complete each assuming that there are no problems. Often divided according to the sections in the dissertation. Include slippage time.

Resource requirements | Identify any equipment that you will need for your research, for example, computing, access to special libraries or cost for field visits; if using postal questionnaires estimate printing and postage costs.

References cited and indicative bibliography | This is the bibliography of all works cited in your proposal; often includes works not cited that will be followed up in the main research.

Related materials | Any materials that can support your justification or indicate your argument for collecting or using a particular kind of data, for example, computer game and video. Include in this section letters from corroborating institutions that give you access to necessary data or people.

Appendix 2: how to cite references

It is important to cite correctly all the sources that you use in your review of the literature. This appendix gives you guidance on how to cite the most commonly used materials in academic work. It is based on the British Standard BS 1629: 1989 and BS 5605: 1990. There are three basic criteria for citing references.

- Clear – citations must give full details of the item.
- Consistent – always cite in the same way.
- Correct – use the proper structure.

CITING REFERENCES IN THE TEXT

When you use another person's work in your text you always need to make an appropriate acknowledgement. There are two straightforward methods which you can use to reference the work of other people:

Number system
Author–date system

The number system

This is based on numbering text references. The text reference is just the relevant number and follows in the order to which it is referred in the text. Here is an example from Goffman (1959: 79). The text reads:

> And when we come to be able properly to manage a real routine we are able to do this in part because of 'anticipatory socialization',[82] having already been schooled in the reality that is just coming to be real for us . . . the individual may even be able to play out the part of a hypnotic subject[83] or commit a 'compulsive' crime[84] on the basis of models for these activities that he is already familiar with.

At the foot of the page, these are the notes:

82 See R.K. Merton, *Social Theory and Social Structure* (Glencoe: Free Press, revised and enlarged edition, 1957), page 265 ff.
83 This view of hypnosis is neatly presented by T.R. Sarbin, 'Contributions to Role-Taking Theory. I: Hypnotic Behaviour', *Psychological Review*, 57, pages 255–70.
84 See D.R. Cressey, 'The Differential Association Theory and Compulsive Crimes', *Journal of Criminal Law, Criminology and Police Science*, 45, pages 29–40.

The numbers in the text correspond to individual bibliographical items that are placed at the bottom of the page, end of the chapter or the end of the work. There is no rule on where you place the citations. The advantage of placing them at the bottom of the page is that it allows the reader to see them as they read; they have no need to turn to the end of the chapter or work. The advantage of placing them at the end of the chapter is that all citations for each chapter are kept together and you will have a limited number as each chapter will start from 1.

The advantage of placing them all together at the end of the work is that you will have a continuation running from 1 with each having a unique number. No separate reference list or bibliography is required. Initials are given before the surname.

Advantages of this system are:

- It allows comments and observations to be made that could not be included in the main body of the text.
- If you have many references in one paragraph it can help you to provide text that is less cluttered.
- References on a particular debate or idea can be bundled up into one number.

The author–date system

This is the system used in this book; it is based on inserting brief details of the citation into the text and is known as the Harvard system. Here is an example from Heritage (1984: 21–2):

> Thus, rather than opening up the question of the actors' understandings of their practical circumstances, the properties of their judgements, the conditions under which courses of action might be initiated or abandoned, the scope and occasions under which actors might revise some view of the situation and so forth (Garfinkel, 1952), Parson's interest in the *subjective* was narrowed to describing the *psychological* processes, through which the internalised values were sustained in the face of frustration, the actor's thoughts and feelings were viewed as simply *intervening variables*. (Parsons et al., 1951: 64; emphasis added)

This extract shows how Heritage indicates the sources of what he is talking about. There are other ways of employing the system; for example:

> Parsons's *voluntaristic metaphysic* (Scott, 1963; Proctor, 1978), lies at the heart of the Parsonian conception of action. . . . (ibid.: 11; emphasis added)

Again in this extract is a phrase developed by others – Scott and Proctor – is used to categorize Parsons's conception of action. In a more direct form you can also use the method to attribute argument in this: 'Parsons (1937: 733) argues that'. All claims about what another person has said and argued therefore need to be sourced and referenced and it is important to give page numbers as well as author and date. In the last example this is given in the number 733. You can also use the format p. 733; with the p. standing for page. However, to be consistent use one way or the other.

All items referenced in the text can now be placed in the bibliography. This needs to be arranged alphabetically. For example:

Parsons, T. (1937) *The Structure of Social Action*. New York: McGraw-Hill.
Proctor, I. (1978) 'Parsons' early voluntarism', *Sociological Enquiry*, 48: 37–48.

Advantages of the author–date system are:

- the reader can see whose work you have used and when it was published,
- making revisions to the bibliography or inserting other references is relatively easy, you do not have to re-number all the citations,
- you will normally have one bibliography at the end of the dissertation.

You may, of course, find authors using a combination of the systems, but you should find one or the other system will suffice for your needs and it is easier to be consistent if you stick to just one.

Citing material in the list of references

There is a very wide range of material that you might use in your review and other writing. Here is a list of the main types of materials requiring citation.

Books	Journal articles	Government publications	Electronic information
single author, multiple author, edited, corporate author, reference work, multi-volume work.	learned, professional, house magazines, newspapers.	parliamentary, departmental, public bodies, local authorities, statistics.	journals, software, web pages, newsletters, CD-ROM, commercial databases.

Books

A reference to any book should cite the following key bibliographic details, for example:

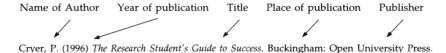

Cryer, P. (1996) *The Research Student's Guide to Success*. Buckingham: Open University Press.

For a chapter or paper in an edited collection use the following format:

Smith, J. (1991) 'What are examiners looking for?', in G. Allan and C. Skinner (eds), *Handbook for Research Students in the Social Sciences*. Brighton: Falmer Press.

Journal articles

These should follow the format in this example:

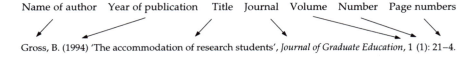

Gross, B. (1994) 'The accommodation of research students', *Journal of Graduate Education*, 1 (1): 21–4.

Government publications

Use the templates for government publications and reports in the following example:

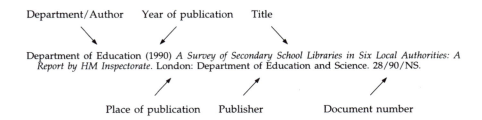

Department of Education (1990) *A Survey of Secondary School Libraries in Six Local Authorities: A Report by HM Inspectorate*. London: Department of Education and Science. 28/90/NS.

Electronic information

Increasingly there are many electronic sources of information that can be used in research. Use the following templates to cite materials located on electronic databases and software employed in research. Because of the ephemeral nature of much material on the web, which is constantly being updated and replaced, record the date on which the site was 'visited' if no other indication of date is given.

Web pages, for example:

Retrieval method   Host and domain name   Path and file name   Date of visit

http://www.bulb.Bath.ac.uk/BULB/home.html (1 May 1998).

Electronic journal articles, for example:

Sloan, B. (1995) 'Crime statistics: how valid?', *Social Work Review Online*, 2 (3): March. email: swr@howard.gov.uk

Appendix 3: presentation of a dissertation

It is important to present your thesis according to the standards laid down by the British Standard BS 4821: *Presentation of Theses and Dissertations*. The following is a summary of the standards required for the presentation of a master's dissertation.

Length   10,000–15,000 words

Copies   2+ copies to be submitted to the university

Main elements (indicative)

Overview Technicalities	1	Title page
	2	Abstract
	3	List of contents
	4	List of illustrations and tables
	5	Acknowledgements
	6	Definitions and/or abbreviations

Argument Knowledge Research	7	Main body of the text
		    Introduction and aims of the research
		    Review of the literature
		    Methodology and data-collection techniques
		    Results
		    Discussion
		    Conclusion/recommendations (including strengths and weakness of your research and further research to be done)

	8	Appendices (optional)
	9	Glossary (optional)
Literature search	10	Bibliography of items cited in the text
	11	Bibliography of items read but not cited in the text

Title page

Full title including subtitle
Your full name
Qualifications for which the thesis is being submitted
Name of organization to which the dissertation is being submitted
Relevant department or faculty
Month and year of submission

Layout and presentation

A4 paper $70g/m^2$–$100g/m^2$ white
Word processed or printed using clear typeface (i.e. not italic or fancy typeface)
Twelve point for main text
Double spacing of lines; quotes and footnotes single space
Margins: left-hand = 30mm, right-hand = 20mm
Paragraphs flush left
Quotes longer than five lines indent by five characters
Number all pages – normally centred bottom of page
Chapters to start on new page

Appendix 4: managing information and keeping records

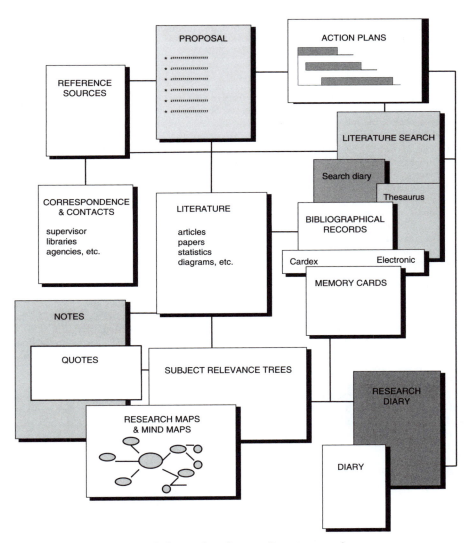

Figure A4.1 *Managing information from a literature review*

Information	Suggested format	Information	Suggested format
proposal	ring binder	notes	ring binders
action plans	wall chart	quotes	cardex
search diary	note book	relevance trees	wall charts
thesaurus	cardex	mind maps	ring binders
literature	magazine boxes	research diary	note book
correspondence	ring binder	contacts	cardex and diary
diary	desk diary		

An essential part of searching and reviewing a literature is record keeping. It cannot be overemphasized that strict management of the search is an important task for the researcher (Orna and Stevens, 1995). Keeping accurate, consistent and correct records are the basis of good project management. We will therefore focus attention on the following elements needed for sound project management: the research dairy; maintaining bibliographic records; and using abstracts.

The research diary

Keeping a diary of the research can be an effective way to keep control of the information the research generates. A diary, or research log, can be a simple ring binder in which you should keep a note of the following:

1 Records on the literature search. These should include: every hardcopy and electronic database searched, the times they were searched, and what vocabulary was used for the search.
2 Notes on what items have been obtained and which have been ordered, say, through inter-library loan. This will help to keep track of the literature; it provides a reminder of what items have been obtained and which need to be followed up.
3 A place to keep a copy of the research proposal and, very important, plan of work and plan for searching the literature. These plans are an important reference source and if referred to regularly will help to draw attention to what needs to be done when.
4 Serendipitous finds in the library or references in texts, together with possible new contacts, can be noted. These notes can then be used as a reminder for updating action plans.
5 Weekly to monthly plans of what needs to be done can be written into the diary. This includes what needs to be read and what notes and other tasks need to be done. As they are done they can be ticked off showing that the work is progressing.
6 Instructions on how to use the technology that is encountered can be recorded in the diary. For example, make notes on instructions for searching CD-ROMs, along with the addresses of useful web sites.

The research diary is therefore a useful tool. It is also a record of what has been done and what has not been done. It can be used to construct notes for the methodology section of the dissertation and provide notes on any evaluation that may be provided on the success of the research.

Maintaining bibliographic records

Keeping track of items you find in your search and research is very important. If you do not keep detailed records of everything you find it will be impossible to provide accurate citations in your work. There are a number of methods to construct and maintain a bibliography. The manual method amounts to establishing a card-index. Each item is indexed onto one or more cards. The cards are then arranged in some logical order, say alphabetically.

The massive amount of literature available means that many researchers now use electronic means to store, organize and retrieve citations. There are a number of ways a personal computer can be used to create a personal bibliography. In practice, it is becoming easier to record bibliographic items first in the diary and then to transfer these onto a personal computer.

A range of software for constructing bibliographies is commonly available. Some people adapt word-processing packages, such as Word, while others invest in dedicated software, such as ProCite. Even the simplest of word-processing packages can be used. They can provide a means to produce lists of items and can be regularly updated. However, they lack some important functions. One of these is the ability to search the bibliography for a key term. Another is the ability to retrieve only a selection of items. The more sophisticated packages enable the researcher to print selections of records in a variety of formats for different document types. The key advantages of electronic databases are:

1   retrieve bibliographical records in a variety of predetermined formats to suit different needs, for example, the different styles demanded by different journals;
2   search the bibliography using key words;
3   automatic arrangement of items according to different criteria, for example, date of publication, by author or by key word;
4   spell check;
5   annotate the record;
6   download data from CD-ROM and on-line databases into the bibliography;
7   automatic changes of typography to meet needs of different journal styles;
8   edit records easily and transfer to other parts of the database. Copies of parts or the whole of the database can be made, thereby providing bibliographical lists.

Using abstracts

The large number of books, articles and other documents that are usually found in a literature search necessitates some method for summarizing what they contain. A range of abstracting services exist that provide, in printed and electronic formats, abstracts of materials published.

There are two main types of abstract: an informative and an indicative. An informative abstract provides a summary of the principle arguments and data of the original document. An indicative abstract provides a short summary of the intention of the author while allowing the reader to decide whether the full article is worth obtaining to read. Abstracting services, such as those found on many CD-ROM databases, provide either or both informative or indicative abstracts of the items it contains. Using the abstracts can be an efficient use of time when deciding which items should be read and which need only to be noted.

Reading abstracts often gives a good idea of how to write them. The informative abstract usually has the same structure as the original document:

- Purpose   The purpose of the research; what the author was attempting to achieve (aims). The abstract will normally use words and phrases from the original document.
- Method   The method(s) used to do the research will be listed. Only brief details will be provided because it is assumed that the reader will know about methods and methodology.
- Results   A key phrase or sentence is used to provide brief information on the results of the research. These will be the result of the research and will contain no assessment of those results that the reader of the abstract can use to judge the relevance of the original document.

The indicative abstract does not always follow the structure of the original document. It attempts to provide some guidance on the value of the document to our understanding of the topic. The indicative abstract usually attempts to provide a summary of the contents in a sentence or two and what follows is a brief assessment of the document. This can be an outline of the argument its author makes or the contribution that has been made to understanding an issue or topic. It might also mention the usefulness of references or material that has been appended. Figure A4.2 shows a typical abstract.

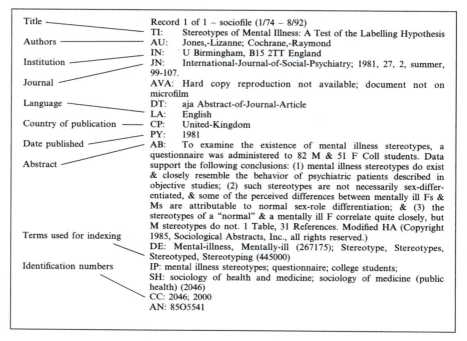

Figure A4.2 *An abstract (adapted from Sociofile SilverPlatter CD-ROM)*

Appendix 5: checklist of dos and don'ts for reviewing

There are some basic 'dos and don'ts' when writing a literature review. Here are some of the major rules for good literature reviewers.

Do . . .

- identify and discuss the relevant key landmark studies on the topic;
- include as much up-to-date material as possible;
- check the details, such as how names are spelled;
- try to be reflexive; examine your own bias and make it clear;
- critically evaluate the material and show your analyses;
- use extracts, illustrations and examples to justify your analyses and argument;
- be analytical, evaluative and critical and show this in your review;
- manage the information that your review produces: have a system for records management;
- make your review worth reading by making yourself clear, systematic and coherent; explain why the topic is interesting.

Don't . . .

- omit classic works and landmarks or discuss core ideas without proper reference;
- discuss outdated or only old materials;
- misspell names or get date of publications wrong;
- use concepts to impress or without definition;
- use jargon and discriminatory language to justify a parochial standpoint;
- produce a list of items, even if annotated; a list is not a review;
- accept any position at face value or believe everything that is written;
- only produce a description of the content of what you have read;
- drown in information by not keeping control and an accurate record of materials;
- make silly mistakes, for example, orgasm in place of organism;
- be boring by using hackneyed jargon, pretentious language and only description.

References

Anderson, R.J., Hughes, J.A. and Sharrock, W.W. (1985) *The Sociology Game: An Introduction to Sociological Reasoning*. London: Longman.

Asminov, I. (1963) *The Genetic Code*. New York: New American Library.

Atkinson, J.M. (1982) *Discovering Suicide: Studies in the Social Organization of Sudden Death*. London: Macmillan Press.

Ayer, A.J. (1946 [1936]) *Language, Truth and Logic*. London: Victor Gollancz.

Barthes, R. (1967) *Elements of Semiology*. London: Jonathan Cape.

Becker, H. (1963) *Outsiders: Studies in the Sociology of Deviance*. New York: Free Press.

Beloff, H. (ed.) (1980) 'A balance sheet on Burt', supplement to *The British Psychological Society*, 33.

Berger, A.A. (1995) *Cultural Criticism: A Primer of Key Concepts*. London: Sage.

Bolton, D. (1997) 'A retrospective case study of convergence within a higher education institution'. MA dissertation, School of Information Studies, University of Central England in Birmingham (unpublished).

Button, G. (ed.) (1991) *Ethnomethodology and the Human Sciences*. Cambridge: Cambridge University Press.

Carnap, R. (1929) 'The scientific conception of the world: the Vienna Circle', in M. Neurath and R. Cohen (eds), *The Scientific Conception of the World: The Vienna Circle*. Dordrecht: Reidel.

Cohen, L.J. (1986) *The Claims of Reason*. Oxford: Oxford University Press.

Coleman, J.C. (1968) 'Studies in ethnomethodology', in J.C. Coleman, G.E. Swanson and A.F.C. Wallace, 'Review symposium: Harold Garfinkel', *American Sociological Review*, 122–30.

Cosser, L. (1975) 'Presidential address: two methods in search of a substance', *American Sociological Review*, 40 (6): 691–700.

Cuff, E.C. and Payne, G.C.F. (1984) *Perspectives in Sociology*, 2nd edn. London: Allen & Unwin.

Douglas, J. (1966) 'The sociological analysis of the social meaning of suicide', *European Journal of Sociology*, 7: 249–98.

Durkheim, É. (1970 [1897]) *Suicide: A Study in Sociology*. London: Routledge.

Durkheim, É. (1984 [1893]) *The Division of Labour in Society*. London: Macmillan.

Erikson, K.T. (1966) *Wayward Puritans*. New York: Wiley.

Evans-Pritchard, E. (1937) *Witchcraft and Oracles among the Azande*. Oxford: Oxford University Press.

Fischer, F. and Forester, J. (eds) (1993) *The Argumentative Turn in Policy Analysis and Planning*. Durham, NC: Duke University Press.

Fisher, A. (1993) *The Logic of Real Arguments*. Cambridge: Cambridge University Press.

Flint, K. (1993) *The Woman Reader 1837–1914*. Oxford: Oxford University Press.

Francis, D. (1986) 'Advertising and structuralism: the myth of formality', *International Journal of Advertising*, 5: 197–214.

Francis, D. (1987) 'The great transformation', in R.J. Anderson, and W.W. Sharrock (eds), *Great Debates in Sociology*. London: Allen & Unwin. pp. 1–36.

Garfield, E. (1979) *Citation Indexing, its Theory and Application in Science, Technology and Humanities*. Philadelphia, PA: ISI Press.

Garfinkel, H. (1967) *Studies in Ethnomethodology*. Englewood Cliffs, NJ: Prentice-Hall.

Garfinkel, H. (1991) 'Respecification: evidence for locally produced, naturally accountable phenomena of order, logic, reason, meaning, method, etc. in and as of the essential haecceity of immortal ordinary society (I) – an announcement of studies', in G. Button (ed.), *Ethnomethodology and the Human Sciences*. Cambridge: Cambridge University Press.

Geertz, C. (1980) 'Blurred genres: refiguration of social thought', *The American Scholar* (Spring).

Gerth, H.H. and Wright Mills, C. (eds) (1948) *From Max Weber*. London: Routledge.

Giltrow, J. (1995) *Academic Writing*. Cardiff: Broadway Press.

Goffman, E. (1959) *The Presentation of the Self in Everyday Life*. London: Penguin.

Goffman, E. (1968) *Stigma*. London: Penguin.

Goldman, L. (1964) *The Hidden God*. London: Routledge & Kegan Paul.

Goldman, R. (1987) *Reading Ads Socially*. London: Routledge.

Hanfling, O. 'Body and mind'. *Arts: Philosophical Problems*, Units 1–2, A313. Buckingham: The Open University.

Hart, C. (1993a) 'The social production of an advertisement'. PhD thesis, Manchester Metropolitan University (unpublished).

Hart, C. (1993b) 'Where are the advertisements in research on advertising?', British Sociological Association Annual Conference: Research Imaginations. University of Essex, April.

Hart, C. (1994) 'By gum pet you smell gorgeous: representations of sexuality in perfume advertisements', British Sociological Association Annual Conference: Sexualities in Social Context. University of Central Lancashire, 28–31 March.

Hempel, C.G. (1965) *Aspects of Explanation*. New York: Free Press.

Henderson, W., Dudley-Evans, T. and Blackhouse, R. (eds) (1993) *Economics and Language*. London: Routledge.

Heritage, J. (1984) *Garfinkel and Ethnomethodology*. Oxford: Polity Press.

Hinderer, D.E. (1992) *Building Arguments*. Belmont, CA: Wadsworth.

Hospers, J. (1988) *An Introduction to Philosophical Analysis*. London: Routledge.

Jhally, S. (1987) *Codes of Advertising*. London: Francis Pinter.

Jonassen, D.H., Beissner, K. and Yacci, M. (1993) *Structural Knowledge: Techniques for Representing, Conveying, and Acquiring Structural Knowledge*. Hillsdale, NJ: Lawrence Erlbaum.

Jones, K. (1997) 'Community as a documentary reality'. PhD thesis, University of Central England.

Kahneman, D. (ed.) (1982) *Judgements under Uncertainty, Heuristics and Biases*. Cambridge: Cambridge University Press.

Kuhn, T. (1970) *The Structure of Scientific Revolutions*. Chicago, IL: University of Chicago Press.

Landes, D. (1969) *The Unbound Prometheus: Technological Change and Industrial Development in Western Europe from 1750 to the Present*. Cambridge: Cambridge University Press.

Law, J. and Lodge, P. (1984) *Science for Social Scientists*. London: Macmillan Press.

Lemert, E.M. (1951) *Social Psychology*. New York: McGraw-Hill.

Lévi-Strauss, C. (1963 [1958]) *Structural Anthropology*. New York: Basic Books.

Lévi-Strauss, C. (1964–72) *Mythologies*. 3 vols. Paris: Pion.

Lipmann, W. (1922) *Public Opinion*. New York: Harcourt Brace.

McCloskey, D.N. (1994) 'How to do a rhetorical analysis, and why', in Roger E. Blackhouse (ed.), *New Directions in Economic Methodology*. London: Routledge. pp. 319–43.

McFarlane, A. (1979) *The Origins of Modern English Individualism*. Cambridge: Cambridge University Press.

Mandelbaum, S.J. (1990) 'Reading plans', *APA Journal*, Summer: 350–8.

Marx, K. (1950) 'Value, prices and profit', in K. Marx and F. Engels, *Selected Works in Two Volumes*. London: Lawrence & Wishart.

Mayo, E. (1933) *The Human Problems of Industrial Civilisation*. New York: Macmillan.

Merton, R.K. (1938) 'Social structure and anomie', *American Sociological Review*, 8: 672–82.

Mills, S. (1995) *Feminist Stylistics*. London: Routledge.

Moorbath, P. (1993) 'A study of journals needed to support the project 2000 nursing course with an evaluation of citation counting as a method of journal selection', *ASLIB Proceedings*, 45 (2): 39–46.

Nichols, W. (1981) *Ideology and the Image*. Bloomington: Indiana University Press.

Oakes, P.J., Haslam, S.A. and Turner, J.C. (1994) *Stereotyping and Social Reality*. London: Blackwell.

Orna, E. and Stevens, G. (1995) *Managing Information for Research*. Buckingham: Open University Press.

Parsons, T. (1951) *The Social System*. London: Routledge.

Pattern, M. (1990) *Qualitative Evaluation Methods*. London: Sage.

Payne, G. (1993) 'The community revisited: some reflections on the community study as a method', British Sociological Association Annual Conference, Essex, 5–8 April.

Phillips, E.M. and Pugh, D. (1994) *How to Get a PhD: A Handbook for Students and Supervisors*, 2nd edn. Buckingham: Open University.

Piaget, J. and Inhelder, B. (1955) *The Growth of Logical Thinking from Childhood to Adolescence*. London: Routledge & Kegan Paul.

Popper, K. (1959 [1934]) *The Logic of Scientific Discovery*. London: Hutchinson.

Radcliffe-Brown, A.R. (1952) *Structure and Function in Primitive Society*. London: Cohen & West.

Russell, C.A. (1983) *Science and Social Change: 1700–1900*. London: Macmillan.

Ryle, G. (1949) *The Concept of Mind*. Harmondsworth: Penguin.

Saussure F., de (1966) *Course in General Linguistics*. New York: McGraw-Hill.

Schlick, M. (1949 [1936]) 'Meaning and verification', in M. Feigl and W. Sellars (eds), *Readings in Philosophical Analysis*. Vienna: Springer.

Schütz, A. (1967) *Collected Papers: Vol 1 – The Problem of Social Reality*. The Hague: Martinus Nijhoff.

Shapin, S. and Schaffer, S. (1985) *Leviathan and the Air Pump: Hobbes, Boyle and the Experimental Life*. Princeton, NJ: Princeton University Press.

Shields, V.R. (1990) 'Advertising visual images: gendered ways of seeing and looking', *Journal of Communication Inquiry*, 14 (2): 25–39.

Simon, H.A. (1957) *Models of Man*. New York: Wiley.

Spencer, H. (1969 [1884]) *The Man Versus the State*. London: Penguin.

Tesch, R. (1990) *Qualitative Research: Analysis, Types and Software Tools*. London: Falmer Press.

Thomas, S. (1986) *Practical Reasoning in Natural Language*, 3rd edn. Englewood Cliffs, NJ: Prentice-Hall.

Thouless, R.H. and Thouless, C.R. (1990) *Straight and Crooked Thinking*, 4th edn. Sevenoaks: Hodder & Stoughton.

Throgmorton, J.A. (1994) 'The rhetoric of policy analysis', *Policy Science*, 24: 153–79.

Tönnies, F. (1955 [1887]) *Community and Association*. London: Routledge & Kegan Paul/East Lancing, MI: University Press.

Toulmin, S. (1958) *The Uses of Argument*. Cambridge: Cambridge University Press.

Trigg, R. (1993) *Rationality and Science*. London: Blackwell.

Turnbull, C. (1971) *The Mountain People*. London: Jonathan Cape.

Turner, B.S. (1984) 'Orientalism and the problem of civil society', in A. Hussain (ed.), *Orientalism, Islam and Islamists*. Brattleboro, VT: Amana Press.

Weber, M. (1965a [1930]) *The Theory of Social and Economic Organisation*. Oxford: Oxford University Press.

Weber, M. (1965b [1930]) *The Protestant Ethic and the Spirit of Capitalism*. London: Allen & Unwin.

Williams, R. (1980) 'Advertising: the magic system', in R. Williams (ed.), *Problems in Materialism and Culture*. London: Verso. pp. 170–95.

Williamson, J. (1979) *Decoding Advertisements*. London: Marion Boyars.

Wright Mills, C. (1978 [1959]) *The Sociological Imagination*. Oxford: Oxford University Press. pp. 195–226.

Wittgenstein, L. (1972 [1921]) *Tractatus Logico-philosophicus*. London: Routledge.

Wittgenstein, L. (1953) *Philosophical Investigations*. Oxford: Blackwell.

Yanni, D.A. (1990) 'The social construction of women as mediated by advertising', *Journal of Communication Inquiry*, 14 (1): 71–81.

Index